MW01119698

Branding and Designing Disability

Over the past fifty years, design and branding have become omnipotent in the market and have made their way to other domains as well. Given their potential to divide humans into categories and label their worth and value, design and branding can wield immense but currently unharnessed powers of social change. Groups designed as devalued can be undesigned, redesigned and rebranded to seamlessly and equivalently participate in community, work and civic life. This innovative book argues that disability as a concept and category is created, reified, and segregated through current design and branding that begs for creative change.

Transcending models of disability that locate it either as an embodied medical condition or as a socially constructed entity, this book challenges the very existence and usefulness of the category itself. Proposing and illustrating creative and responsible design, DePoy and Gilson include thinking and action strategies that are useful and potent for "undesigning," redesigning, and rebranding to meet the full range of human needs and to enhance full participation in local through global communities. Divided into two parts, the first section presents a critical examination of disability as a designed and branded phenomenon, exploring what exactly is being designed and branded and how. The second part investigates the redesign of disability and provides principles for redesign and rebranding illustrated with examples from high-tech to place-based sustainable strategies.

The book provides a unique and contemporary framework for thinking about disability as well as providing relevant design and branding guidance to social scientists, designers, engineers, and others interested in embodiment issues.

Elizabeth DePoy is Professor of Interdisciplinary Disability Studies at the University of Maine, USA.

Stephen Gilson is Professor of Interdisciplinary Disability Studies at the University of Maine, USA.

This book completely rethinks the idea of disability in new and innovative ways by starting with the concept of disability as design. The authors ask us not how to critique "normal" but how we could redesign it. A groundbreaking analysis that makes it impossible to think about disability as we have in the past.

Lennard J. Davis, University of Illinois, US.

Branding and Designing Disability

Reconceptualising Disability Studies

Elizabeth DePoy and Stephen Gilson

Routledge
Taylor & Francis Group

LONDON AND NEW YORK

First published 2014
by Routledge
2 Park Square, Milton Park, Abingdon, Oxon, OX14 4RN

and by Routledge
270 Madison Avenue, New York, NY 10016

Routledge is an imprint of the Taylor and Francis Group, an informa business

© 2014 Elizabeth DePoy and Stephen Gilson

British Library Cataloguing in Publication Data
A catalogue record for this book is available from the British Library

Library of Congress Cataloging-in-Publication Data
DePoy, Elizabeth, author.
Branding and designing disability : reconceptualising disability studies /
Elizabeth DePoy and Stephen Gilson.
pages cm. – (Routledge advances in disability studies)
Includes bibliographical references.
1. Disability studies 2. Sociology of disability. 3. People with disabilities.
I. Gilson, Stephen French, author. II. Title. III. Series: Routledge
advances in disability studies.
[DNLM: 1. Disabled Persons–psychology. 2. Disabled Persons–
rehabilitation. 3. Disability Evaluation. 4. Evaluation Studies as Topic.
5. Social Isolation. 6. Social Values. HV 1568.2]
HV1568.2.D456 2014
362.4–dc23
2013034622

ISBN 13: 978-0-415-63538-7 (hbk)
ISBN 13: 978-0-203-09354-2 (ebk)

Typeset in Baskerville
by FiSH Books Ltd, Enfield

Printed and bound in the United States of America by Publishers Graphics,
LLC on sustainably sourced paper.

Contents

PART 2
Undesigning and redesigning   221

Illustrations

Figures

Tables

Boxes

Foreword

Lighting the blue touch-paper and the blue badge

Branding and Designing Disability: Reconceptualising Disability Studies is an incendiary book. Its title lays out its ambition to disrupt the very notion of disability.

To date, where disability and design are written about in the context of each other, a prevalent theme has been the need for design to become more "universal." Or, more ambiguously, to become more "inclusive," used to mean two rather different things: when applied to design outcomes, inclusive in the sense of not excluding people on the basis of impairment; when applied to the design process, inclusive in the sense of involving disabled people throughout. In the spirit of "Nothing about us without us," the latter is as political as it is practical. It involves not just impairment, but also identity, culture, diversity and other concerns of disability studies.

I have argued that disability studies just as pressingly needs a more sophisticated understanding of design – in all *its* diversity. This time, this is tactical, rather than ethical (although who is to say that designers would not warm to deeper engagement with them, about design?). If we demand more appropriate design, then I believe that we should include more radical designers in the mix, designers not chosen so much for their disability-related expertise as for the sensibilities that they could contribute.

In this book, Elizabeth DePoy and Stephen Gilson do something remarkable: having begun by considering disability, design and by association, branding, they return to disability anew. If *Design Meets Disability* has been said to view design through the lens of disability, then *Branding and Designing Disability* turns its lens on disability. The authors suggest that design and branding create disability in the first place and argue against the existence of ("the myth of") disability culture.

Their ambition is nothing less than the redefining, redesigning and rebranding of disability itself. A core concept is that of the "disability park," a collective term given by the authors to institutions, interventions and anything else "designed to define, attract and contain" disabled people: "persons branded as disabled," as the authors put it. Having built up this model, the manifesto culminates in a call for "using design and branding to *dismantle* [my italics] the disability park." This aspiration feels more subversive than the common espousal of universal design.

A universal book about disability would be a contradiction in terms, because disability implies uncontainable diversity. Ditto design. So how refreshing that the authors build such a strong thesis, yet at the same time the book contains many other voices. The inherent contradictions, as much as the resonances, should enliven and deepen a wider debate for years to come. How provocative and thought-provoking.

Boom...hmmm.

Graham Pullin
University of Dundee, UK
September 16, 2013

Part 1
Scope and craft

1 Branding, designing and marketing humanity

> An ideology that cannot withstand intense challenge is invariably anti-progressive. Through questioning, ideas grow to be more robust and compelling.
>
> (Randy Schutt, 2010)

Over the past thirty years, disability scholarship has joined hands with multiple dialogic fora, giving dynamic substance, multi-dimensionality, and complexity to its shape and scope. Disability has been invited into the humanities and the sciences for analysis and response, ascribing increasingly colorful hues to its scrutiny. Yet, the tug of war between disability as an "undesirable that individuals have" versus disability portrayed as impedance of human flourishing resulting from complex hostile or neglecting contexts continues to occupy much of the disability studies scholarship and discourse of the twenty-first century. We would suggest that this theoretical tension, while useful in the conceptual adolescence of disability studies, must grow into adulthood if profound, sustained, and broadened social change is to be realized within an increasingly advancing globalized, corporatized, market context.

Because of the contemporary hegemonic place and role of design in a market-driven environment situated within the visual and material cultures of the twenty-first century, we devote our work in this book to a careful examination of designing humans as category members within mythic divisions that are blockaded with vague and movable boundaries and contain unquestioned institutionalized beliefs. We argue that despite the existence of the word and the perception of disability as a real and stable entity, disability is an artifact of design and branding, with the current relativistic motifs and labels no longer useful in the twenty-first-century global market economic context. Hovering under the cultural radar of well-intentioned citizens and genuine helpers, be they laypersons or professionals, contemporary disability design is manipulative, employing diverse and surreptitious crafts and containment mechanisms that impose negative valuation, truncated rights, limited opportunity, and even poverty, on those branded with this title. But contrary to negative critique with no point beyond conceptual sparring, we follow the sage words of Randy Schutt which opened this chapter. Within questioning, we find opportunity guiding contemporary redesign and rebranding necessary to hasten and direct vital and timely social change.

In the introductory chapter, the context, analytic framework, and scope of the book are laid out. We begin with a short essay on how we arrived at this conceptual point and then commence the work of specifying definitions of design and branding and other constructs seminal to our thinking in this work. Equipped with clarity of lexical tools we then enter the world of design, in which concretes and ideas coalesce to create identity and signify value. We finish the chapter with examples and the "so what" of the book.

How we arrived at this point

Our formal but initially narrow entry into the designer house of human categories and thus disability began with personal queries about why equipment such as crutches and walkers were not widely diverse in design and material. Given the permanence of these accouterments and to some extent their adoption as body parts (Shannon, 2011), our initial curiosity focused on why has there been a failure to recognize these devices as part of one's outfitted, visible identity (Wolfendale and Kennett, 2011), particularly now that walking supports, canes, reading glasses, and now even bifocals, are available in commercial venues and allow choice of styles and prices.

However, once design thinking (Fast Company, 2006) entered our consciousness, we began to notice it more expansively in public, private, and subtle forms, inciting broader and more complex questions about proportions, spaces, places, objects, and subjects. Sleuthing through design scholarship and praxis specifically to answer questions about the origin of and evidence supporting contemporary design standards for accessible architectures, we came face to face with Vitruvian Man, DaVinci's masterpiece, depicting ideal man as eight heads tall with his genitalia located at "body central" (Gilson and DePoy, 2007; Lester, 2012). In essence, positioning Vitruvian Man as the human symbol of ideal proportions and thus the fundamental foundation for built environment dimensions, designs even the typical body as underwhelming, incorrect, and ill-fitting (Gilson and DePoy, 2007; 2011). Moreover, mass-produced items for negotiating and functioning within built environments, for example chairs (de Dampierre, 2006), operationalized the Vitruvian body as desirable, keeping the male imagery and mythic proportions omnipotent in design of public spaces, building standards and product design, even in a world which ostensibly celebrates diversity. Moreover, norming proportionality on a design which today would be diagnosed as acromegaly or gigantism seemed so very ironic to us, given the disdain for and ill fit of the atypical body within contemporary environments.

At least for us, a short dip into design was not possible, once its power had revealed itself in crafting valuation, meaning, opportunity, and more profoundly, the boundaries beyond which humanness is extracted from a living corpus. As process, product, and attribute, design, and its conceptual and crafted associates not only have a profound historical presence, but are omnipresent in contemporary times and thus beg for interrogation and analysis in constructing current conceptualizations and retooling the future of disability. Design is conceptually, functionally, and visibly activated as an intellectual and action agenda for understanding and praxis in the global context in which it is entrenched and used to benefit multiple agendas. We see design throughout the palpable and abstract awaiting full engagement.

Before moving to substance, we take on anticipated skepticism about the central tenets of this work. In this book, we situate social change within context, not in opposition to it. In a screen-mediated world, we would suggest that strategies such as sit-ins, protests, and occupations are useful in raising awareness but not sufficient, by themselves, to produce fundamental change. While we agree with indictments of the market economy as in part causal of disparity and inequity, those issues are not the substance of this book as they are much broader and longitudinally enduring than the change that we are advocating and believe can start to occur now. Because our universe is an expanding playground for marketing, branding, and design with capitalism seen as the "bad boy" of many narratives, we would suggest the stories need to change. Marrying market strategies to art, science, and philosophy provides the intellectual material for innovation that does not throw the proverbial bad boy baby out with the bathwater. Nor do we believe that the market will move over and contract so that others can move in. So, given the permanency of market thinking, along with its successful actors and strategies, this book argues for the use of what will remain constant, but reframed within fairness, thoughtfulness, choice, and respect for humanness.

A second point that we emphasize and introduced at the beginning of this chapter, building on disability as constructed, is the challenge to understanding disability as a stable or useful category. Undesigning the fiction of disability and the beliefs that surround its fabled constancy is the essential prerequisite to diverting energy away from inaction and channeling it into eliminating designed inequality.

So let us begin with the precision of lexical clarification.

Defining design

Looking back to the fifteenth and sixteenth centuries, the term design was used to describe a scheme, mark, or designation. Perhaps because of its origin as scheme, Terzidis (2007) distinguishes the process of planning, which he refers to as scheming, from designing, a creative, imaginative act.

According to Terzidis (2007), the word design emerged in part from classical Greek, in which it designated incompleteness, "the strive to capture the elusive" (p. 1). Over the years, design has taken on expansive and vague proportions, denoting a range of properties of an entity, of thinking and creative process, of deliberate intentionality, and beyond. The quotation below illustrates this scope.

> Design: Design is the planning that lays the basis for the making of every object or system. It can be used both as a noun and as a verb and, in a broader way, it means applied arts and engineering. As a verb, "to design" refers to the process of originating and developing a plan for a product, structure, system, or component with intention. As a noun, "a design" is used for either the final (solution) plan (e.g. proposal, drawing, model, description) or the result of implementing that plan in the form of the final product of a design process. This classification aside, in its broadest sense no other limitations exist and the final product can be anything from socks and jewelry to graphical user interfaces and charts. Even virtual concepts such as corporate identity and cultural traditions such as celebration of certain holidays are sometimes designed. More recently, processes (in general) have also been treated as products of design, giving new meaning to the term "process design."
>
> (http://en.wikademia.org/About_design)

The definition above begins to reveal the immense reach of design, not only as multiple entities, but in diverse contexts, some crisply delimited and visible and others ethereal.

Ascription of the term "hybrid thinking" to design adds yet another dimension to the construct, characteristic of post-postmodern disciplinary marriages. In this vernacular, design thinking refers to a well-informed problem solving process with intentionality of outcome always held in the spotlight (Lockwood, 2009). Yet, the elements of visual décor, recognition of planfulness, usability (Fukasawa and Morrison, 2007), and/or style inhere in the process, distinguishing it from other methods of problem solving and its reliance on multiple fields of knowledge differentiating design from hybrid thinking. In hybrid approaches, problems are both defined and resolved by an orchestra rather than a soloist or even a quartet. As such, design became one of the most significant and powerful influences both in reflecting and shaping social and political phenomena, and as asserted by Fry, is now compulsory as the agent for political change.

> A future worth having requires political transformation of social and economic life, underpinned by a praxis more capable of enabling directing and maintaining affirmative change than existing institutions of democracy (for they lack the appropriate nous and techne) ... The

kinds of changes that are so vital require another kind of politics united with dynamic transformative agency...A task of such magnitude requires many thinkers, a great deal of rethinking, new thinking, and a large amount of focused conversation within and between the fields of politics and design.

(Fry, 2011: 4)

To further sharpen the boundaries of design, we distinguish it from similar and overlapping constructs, style, and fashion. All three terms have great relevance to identifying and marking categories of humans as we discuss throughout the book. Style is a recognizable and patterned "look." The word "style" can be traced back to the 1300s, where it was used to denote a form of expression primarily in writing (stylus) and then expanded to a recognizable appearance of one's clothes. However, fashion took its primary place in the world of attire while style continued to be applied to more expansive domains.

For our work, we would suggest that design is defined as substantive, multifaceted, planful, powerful, useful, political, and intentional, whereas style is a design patina. That is not to say that style is less potent than design in transmitting identity and recognition. To the contrary, style is a visible public layer of design, imbued with judgment (The Rawness, 2008). Visibility provides an excellent segue into the observable of branding. We now move to that discussion.

Branding

Once again, history illuminates our thinking. In the 1400s, the term "brand" was a physical mark, often cauterized into the flesh. A brand not only bespoke ownership, but by the 1600s, if sported by a person, stigmatized him/her as criminal. In today's market context, branding has taken on epic proportions, using images, logos, and even abstracts to broadcast identity and its value. Contemporary branding has moved away from product attributes to direct what people think about product meaning.

Building on previous work (DePoy and Gilson, 2011), we define branding as the purposive crafting and ascription of concrete through conceptual marker including but not limited to logos, images, concepts, ideas, and policies, to an entity for diverse intentions. Within the market economy, branding serves to create product recognition, public relations, and value to promote consumption and maximize profit.

Interestingly, recent marketing literature suggests that given the intention of branding to create identity, branding has moved internal to reveal "corporate personalities." This move creates a persona for the purpose of manipulating an alliance not only between a consumer and purchase object but more fundamentally between consumer and what he/she is led to believe the producing company embodies. Thus in essence, the public becomes private and personal only through the mediator of a signifier. This strategy is powerful, given the potential of a single idea, sound, abstract, or visual to create and animate presence, intention and perceived trustworthiness of an entity that is itself in existence to profit from those who are manipulated into the grand narrative of a relationship with an unknown corporation (Layman, 2012).

As we discuss in subsequent chapters, the continued denial of the importance of marketing talk from helping service sector members therefore mediates against intentionally harnessing the power of branding for social change, as service providers while not in the directors seat, cannot remove themselves from design and branding, particularly as the helping sector increasingly incorporates into multiple market entities.

Branding is so omnipotent that scholars such as Holt (2002), building on the work of Horkheimer and Adorono (2002) and McLuhan and Fiore (2008), have elevated this practice to cultural iconography. The process of branding gives rise to self-definition and group valuation (Einstein, 2012).

Closing the lexical circle between branding, design, and its partners, the most successful brands are usually created by individuals with strong design background. Branding is, in effect, the act of designing. The act of branding is one of emotion and the most emotional connection you can have is through visual stimulation (Layman, 2014).

As noted above, we see branding as more expansive than visual logo. However, the observable is centrally embedded in the twenty-first century as technology has made screens and visual interfaces omnipresent, creating a visual culture of herculean proportions. "Beyond catalyzing changes in what we do, technology affects how we think" (Turkle, 2003). Moreover, as noted by Turkle (2011), despite the reluctance to admit the human connection to objects, we are mesmerized by them, engaged in their meaning, "companionship" (p. 9), and connection to our identities and thoughts. And while design expands its outcome beyond the visual, in essence, the design process itself is a vision concretized or abstracted for human intention.

Designed disability

In our 2011 work, we introduced our perspective on the critical role of design and branding in understanding and explaining disability. That discussion formed the foundation upon which we build our current argument asserting disability and the narratives that surround it as artifacts crafted by design and branding.

In a recent presentation entitled "Designer Disability" that we gave at the Society for Disability Studies, Guzman, (personal communication), remarked that marketing theory did not do explanatory justice to understanding disability as a cultural group that experiences social discrimination and exclusion. In concert with Riley (2006), we disagreed, suggesting that in the twenty-first century and consistent with post-post-modern thinking, disability is no longer exempt from the market economy, business, contemporary cultural market trends, and its design and branding processes (Adair, 2002; Pullin, 2009; Riley, 2006). Rather, this synthetic lens is seminal to explaining disability as created, marked, circumscribed, and commodified by designated products, spaces, fables, economic arrangements, and abstracts that not only design and brand its amorphous and erratic membership, but also positions it as a target market segment ripe for commodification and economic exploitation (Claiborne and Aidala, 1983; Seldon, Bartholomew, and Myddelton, 2007). However, although sounding ominous, this complex analysis makes lucid the methods through which a market construction of disability creates new actionable pathways to elegant social change.

While we begin with the claim and supportive evidence that design and branding simultaneously shape and reflect value and devalue regarding bodies (Mullins, 2009; Owens, 2010), we emphasize the "how" and the "so what" in this book once the initial argument has been presented. That is to say, what can the analysis of disability as function of design and branding bring to crafting and implementing innovative methods for its "undesign and redesign" to advance equivalence of opportunity, citizenship, and choice? How do we accomplish this aim without casting blame or disparaging remarks against any sector or group, and then what thinking and action methods do we use for constructive criticism, undesign and redesign? How do we challenge the institutionalized and unquestioned beliefs that the atypical embodied is in need of extraordinary help as it is currently designed and branded? What language do we use when we void its truth value but still acknowledge its design? How do we become heard as optimists despite critical questioning?

The successes of design and branding in so many other domains, render them compelling for understanding disability as story, for venturing to rupture cultural memes and practices, and thus for precipitating change. As affirmed in a recent TED Talk by Hockenberry (2012) "design is facing the given with intent." We would not only agree but assert that with well-informed, innovative intent, design and its branding relative can meet socially responsible aims necessary for undesign of the stigma, segregation, constructed beliefs, and negative valuation of disability to one of redesign as a given element of humanness (Prestero, 2012).

The disability park

Because the disability park is a major construct in this work, it makes its first brief appearance in this chapter and then is discussed more expansively throughout the book. Building on previous work (DePoy and Gilson, 2011), the park is identified as the primary target of social change. As a pervasive market phenomenon doing its job well, the park serves to contain a diverse swath of individuals branded as disabled in systems of separated and stigmatized services, language, products, and knowledge (Gilson and DePoy, 2012). Reiterated throughout and a major point to be made here is that we do not view the park developers, administrators, and employees as intentionally exploitive or even cognizant of the negative consequences of park outcomes. To the contrary, success in dismantling abstract and place-based containment and disadvantage in the park is in large part dependent on employee reflection, negotiation and informed collaborative activity.

Artful guidance

Because of the focus on design and branding as the means of change, we have turned to art for guidance (Goodwin, 2007). Art criticism provides a sound and fruitful framework for discussion and analysis in our classes and thus we share the principles here. Viewing social change as a work of art in progress maintains scrutiny without eviscerating the beauty of the process. Three steps guide this work and the design of Part 1 of the book:

1   Describing the work (the scope).
2   Interpreting the work (what does it mean?).
3   Evaluating the work (is it what it claims to be? is it interesting? does it "work"?) (Goodwin).

Chapters two through eleven provide detailed discussions of the current design and branding of disability as well as an interpretation and evaluation according to Goodwin's guidelines. Within these chapters description and interpretation of each domain of design and branding are proffered. Chapters nine through eleven evaluate disability design and branding through identifying and unpacking specific crafts that have been used in each arena to create and maintain this large and still growing mythical population category. Before leaving this chapter, however, we provide definitions and exemplars of two more major constructs that guide our thinking, undesign and redesign, the focus of Section 2. As stated by Goodwin:

> The most important thing to remember is that, although we may each be in this ... [reading] for different reasons, we are all (presumably) striving to make more and better works of art. Your [redesign] is to be a rigorous and rich process of taking your work apart and putting it back together – better than before – with the help of this lively critical forum.
>
> (Goodwin, 2007)

Goodwin's vision for art is our model for undesign and redesign of disability. Undesign refers to the postmodernist trend of dismantling, in this case applied to the narrative of disability and its containment in the park. Undesign is purposive in that it leaves room for redesign, or the innovative recrafting of humanness such that binaries are eschewed. As we detail in the next chapter, twentieth-century history apprehended and applied the term "disability" to broad and unsteady populations of individuals with diverse conditions, remanding the term disability and its fictions to a plethora of postmodern simulacra. Authors of these stories include scientists, professionals, artists, poets, and proclaimed members of the disability category, among a host of others. Although the conceptual fabric is fraying in some contexts, the dominant narrative and image retain self-appointed or otherwise identified full or partial members of the constructed disability category (in their unchanged corporeal or behavioral form) outside or distant from the gates of acceptance into the house of humanness. What modifications need to be made and if and how these must be enacted have been under the jurisdiction of the disability park, the designed conceptual, spatial, economic, professional, and elite knowledge conglomerate in which members painted into the disability category form the object of scrutiny and work for non members.

Exemplar – Servicebot

Now, as exemplar of redesign vision and praxis, we enlist Servicebot's assistance.

As depicted in the photograph in Figure 1.1, Servicebot is an anthropomorphically designed robot that functions to provide assistance in retrieving, transporting, and placing objects. The original purpose for Servicebot, and thus reflected in her garb, was assistance in carrying a tray in a cafeteria setting. This collaborative robotic project undesigned and redesigned dependence, stigma, and reluctance to eat in public establishments as "cool and contemporary" for people who are unable and prefer not to balance or carry a meal on a tray. Emerging from need and ignited by a collaboration among an engineer, artist, woman designed as disabled by virtue of embodied diagnoses, and faculty in disability studies, Servicebot retrieves cafeteria delicacies, follows a person using wireless technology, or can be remotely summoned, bearing and offloading a full tray of goodies to be consumed with others. Rather than eating behind the ramparts of the disability park, or being branded as dependent, Servicebot users are observed and branded as contemporary (DePoy, Gilson, and Deshpande, 2010).

But, of course, redesign is not simple or provoked by single efforts in isolation from one another. This exemplar is offered to illustrate how one short story of disability in this instance was rewritten, rescripting the dependent and needy character to one who lays claim to admiration.

While this "cool" technology provides an exemplar of a process and object that are physically present, current, fun and concurrent with

Figure 1.1 Servicebot

functional assistance, undesign and redesign must infiltrate multiple domains, as discussed in the art and craft chapters. Consider the brand of "inspirational" ascribed to disability park residents for activity that most would consider mundane for non-residents (Brose *et al.*, 2010). Subtexted in this lexical logo is expected mediocrity. Exposing the underbelly of these stories for their obfuscated meanings of devaluation, while not as obvious or sexy as technology development, is a strategy that is equally critical to undesign and redesign.

Themes of design, undesign, and redesign

Proceeding through the book, the reader will encounter five major themes that are critically engaged and then proposed as one axis of a complex platform for undesign and redesign: language, knowledge production, normal–not normal binary, material and visual culture, and humanness.

Language

The first theme is language and the role of word, image, and symbol in communicating meaning. Language has been a major actor not only in disability history but also in the ancestry and current context of human categorization. As discussed by Hughes (2010) and Bawer (2012), among others, political correctness is a linguistic derailleur of active change as it keeps a theatrical spotlight on futile debate about what to call undesirables while actors continue the status quo in the off-stage shadows.

Another point about language is in order related to our own use of terms and symbols. While we cast doubt on disability as a stable category, we use the term to denote its conceptual existence along with its perceived membership design and branding, albeit ever-changing in response to context. In Part 2, we call for the undesign and redesign not only of the language but of what the words signify.

Knowledge production

Thematically second are the methods, acceptance, use, meaning, and production of knowledge. This ontological and epistemic theme posits knowledge as a fickle narrative, seeking to please its context. Embedded within this theme is the fact–value debate. We take the position that these two words are symbolic, contributing to the lore that knowledge can be objective and axiologically neutral. By objective, we refer to the logico-deductive view of a monistic truth discoverable only through rabid adherence to the rules of empirical inquiry. The principle of axiological neutrality is foundational to logico-deductive thinking, in that what this lens defines as authentic truth is held apart from human value and preference.

Reductionism emerging from deductive logic and monism forms the platform on which medical knowledge stands. Given the advancements that are supported by logico-deductive thinking, we are not suggesting that the proverbial logic baby be jettisoned with the bathwater. We do, however, support limiting reductionism such that it does not ooze into spaces that it cannot explain. In improper places, reductionism leads to what we have referred to as medicalization model of disability and parkesque consequences. These two phenomena are discussed in subsequent chapters.

Normal–not normal binary

Closely related to knowledge production are the binary constructs of normal and abnormal, creators of the "evidence-based" disability park. We detail this theme in Chapter 3, and then meet it throughout this work in various forms. In its current conceptualization and popular parlance, this duo begs for undesign and redesign. In Part 2, we accomplish this critical need with guidance from contemporary, forward thinking designers and artists.

Material and visual culture

Material and visual culture form the fourth theme. As discussed through-out the book, object and image reading are central to ascribing and interpreting meaning and thus contain the ruby slippers, so to speak, to undesign negativity, the park and to redesign a world that can materialize imagination.

Humanness

Finally, all themes for us culminate in defining humanness, its boundaries and its exclusions. In essence, the atypical demands analysis, confronting the most difficult questions about implicit limits of humanness that go unspoken. Chapter 8 directs targeted attention to this seminal theme and sets the context for undesign and redesign of humanness as debated, emancipated from the recesses cloaked by language, democratically nego-tiated, and dynamically in flux.

We now proceed to look at "design and branding past," interpreting their purposes, practices and outcomes for today and tomorrow.

References

Adair, J. E. (2002) *Effective Strategic Leadership* (rev. ed.). London: Pan Macmillan.

Brose, S., Weber, D., Salatin, B., Grindle, G., Wang, H., Vazquez, J. *et al.* (2010) The Role of Assistive Robotics in the Lives of Persons with Disability. *American Journal of Physical Medicine and Rehabilitation*, 6 (89), 509–21.

Claiborne, J., and Aidala, T. (1983) Ethnic Design or Ethnic Slur. *Places*, 1 (2), 18–20. Available online at places.designobserver.com/media/pdf/ Ethnic_Design__942.pdf (accessed January 13, 2014).

de Dampierre, F. (2006) *Chairs: A History*. New York: Henry A. Abrams.

Delbano, A. (2012) Academic Battleground: "The Victim's Revolution," by Bruce Bawer. [Review] *New York Times*, August 23. Available online at www.nytimes.com/2012/08/26/books/review/the-victims-revolution-by-bruce-bawer.html?pagewanted=alland_r=0 (accessed January 13, 2014).

DePoy, E., and Gilson, S. (2011) *Studying Disability*. Los Angeles, CA: Sage.

DePoy, E., Gilson, S., and Deshpande, A. (2010) *Servicebot: Using Technology to Heal Disjuncture: An Innovative Application of Robotics to Improving the Fit Between Bodies and Environments*. Paper Presaented at the 25th Annual Pacific Rim Conference on Disabilities, April, 2010.

Einstein, M. (2012) *Compassion Inc*. Berkeley, CA: University of California Press.

Fast Company (2006) Design Thinking: What is That? *Fast Company*, March 20. Available online at www.fastcompany.com/919258/design-thinking-what (accessed January 13, 2014).

Fry, T. (2011) *Design as Politics*. New York: Berg.

Fukasawa, N., and Morrison, J. (2007) *Super Normal: Sensations of the Ordinary*. Baden: Lars Muller.

Gilson, S., and DePoy, E. (2007) DaVinci's ill-fated design legacy: Homogenization and standardization. *International Journal of the Humanities*, 5. Available online at www.academia.edu/2557400/Da_Vincis_Ill_Fated_Design_legacy (accessed January 13, 2014).

Gilson, S., and DePoy, E. (2012) The Student Body. In A. C. Carey and R. K. Scotch (eds.) *Disability and Community*. Research in Social Science and Disability, Vol. 6. Bingley: Emerald, 27–44.

Goodwin, D. (2007) Guidelines for Group Critique. Available online at www.albany.edu/faculty/dgoodwin/shared_resources/critique.html (accessed January 13, 2014).

Hockenberry, J. (2012) We are All Designers. *TED: Ideas Worth Spreading*, June. Available online at www.ted.com/talks/john_hockenberry_we_are_all_designers.html (accessed January 13, 2014).

Holt, D. B. (2002) Why Do Brands Cause Trouble? A Dialectical Theory of Consumer Culture and Branding. *Journal of Consumer Research*, 29 (1), 70–90.

Horkheimer, M., and Adorno, T. W. (2002) *Dialectic of Enlightenment*, ed. Gunzelin Schmid Noerr, trans. Edmund Jephcott. Redwood City, CA: Stanford University Press.

Hughes, G. (2010) *Political Correctness: A History of Semantics and Culture*. Chichester: Wiley-Blackwell.

Layman, T. (2014) Branding Identifies Corporate Personality. *Atlanta Business Chronicle*, April 20. Available online at www.bizjournals.com/atlanta/print-edition/2012/04/20/branding-identifies-corporate-personalit.html?page=all (accessed January 13, 2014).

Lester, T. (2012) *Da Vinci's Ghost: Genius, Obsession, and How Leonardo Created the World in His Own Image*. New York: Free Press.

Lockwood, T. (2009) *Design Thinking: Integrating Innovation, Customer Experience, and Brand Value*. New York: Allworth Press.

McLuhan, M. and Fiore, Q. (2008) *The Medium is the Massage: An Inventory of Effects*. Berkeley, CA: Gingko Press

Mullins, A. (2009) My 12 pairs of legs. *TED: Ideas Worth Spreading*, March. Available online at www.ted.com/talks/aimee_mullins_prosthetic_aesthetics.html (accessed January 13, 2014).

Owens, K. (2010) Design and Politics by Tony Fry: A Review by Keith Owens. *Academic.edu*. Available online at http://academia.edu/827369/Design_and_Politics_by_Tony_Fry_A_review_by_Keith_Owens (accessed January 13, 2014).

Prestero, T. (2012) Timothy Prestero: Design for people, not awards. *TED: Ideas Worth Spreading*, August. Available online at www.ted.com/talks/timothy_prestero_design_for_people_not_awards.html (accessed January 13, 2014).

Pullin, G. (2009) *Design Meets Disability*. Cambridge, MA: MIT Press.

Riley, C. (2006) *Disability and Business: Best Practices and Strategies for Inclusion*. Lebanon, NH: University Press of New England.

Seldon, A., Bartholomew, J., and Myddelton, D. R. (2007) *Capitalism: A Condensed Version*. London: Institute of Economic Affairs.

Shannon, B. (2007) *Dancing With Crutches*. Pop Tech. [video; 20:23 minutes.] Available online at http://poptech.org/popcasts/bill_shannon__poptech_2007 (accessed January 13, 2014).

Shanon, B. (2011) *Traffic: Shannon Public Works*. [video 15:10 minutes.] Available online at www.youtube.com/watch?v=ezm3_7VZlJA (accessed January 13, 2014).

Terzidis, K. (2007) The Etymology of Design: Pre-Socratic Perspective. *Design Issues*, 23 (4), 69–78.

The Rawness (2008) The Difference Between Style and Fashion. *The Rawness: Human Nature and Sexual Politics*, February 20. Available online at http://therawness.com/the-difference-between-style-and-fashion/ (accessed January 13, 2014).

Turkle, S. (2011) *Evokative Objects*. Boston, MA: MIT Press.

Turkle, S. (2003) Welcome. *MIT Initiative on Technology and the Self*. Available online at http://web.mit.edu/sturkle/techself/ (accessed January 13, 2014).

wikademia.org (2010) http://en.wikademia.org/About_design (last edited on November 3, 2010).

Wolfendale, J., and Kennett, J. (2011) *Fashion*. Chichester: Wiley-Blackwell.

2 History of designing and branding the category of disability

> To study design and its histories is to study the processes of thinking, problem solving, drawing, talking, consulting and responding to a range of practical and aesthetic constraints to create – ideally – the most appropriate solutions under the given circumstances.
>
> (Lees-Maffei and Houze, 2010: 1)

As reflected in the opening quote, historians of design make claim to a wide berth, yet, we still notice the major focus of design history entails the scrutiny of objects and observables as cultural production (Fallan, 2010; Unmaking Things, 2012). As discussed later in the chapter, we suggest that a large analytic girth including the concrete through the conceptual would be most useful for fully mining history to inform the design of humans into categories in general and specifically into the disability division. Thus, in addition to surveillance of the physical world, the design of abstracts such as policy and service systems has an important role in the history of designed disability that has yet to be fully investigated. That is not to say that the "material world" is not a rich source of evidence in itself, particularly when design history moves adjacent to and overlaps visual culture. Yet a wide scope of inquiry provides a rich dataset for analysis not allowed through the more narrow delimitation of design as primarily visual.

An alternative to observing design as a feature of phenomena is the characterization and evolution of design processes as reflected in Table 2.1. The table reflects the amalgamation of thinking from diverse designers and design historians (Baxter, 2013; Candlin and Guins, 2009; Fallan, 2010; Fukasawa and Morrison, 2007; Lees-Maffei and Houze, 2010; Popova, 2012).

Just a basic perusal reveals that over time, design has entered expanding domains, acquired multiple contemporary tools for its craft, met an increasing bevy of contemporary functions, apprehended venues such as the home in which hobby matures into imagination and fabrication, and adopted the dimension of time to activate is own dynamism. From the human intention and process perspective, design has thus morphed from a practice of solving problems and providing answers into one of dynamic

Table 2.1 Comparison of classic and contemporary design

Classical	Contemporary
Problem solving	Problem identification
Responsive and reflective	Provocative and dynamic
Answers questions	Asks questions
Produces what is deemed as a need	Debates need
A single discipline	Pluralistic
An industry	A social service
Functional	Function joins social
Changes the physical world	Changes humanity
A production venue	A consumption venue
A purchase	A thought
Process	Authorship
2D and 3D	4D
Corporate	Proximal
A mano	Technologically enhanced

thought, questioning, and creative irritation (Ebeling, 2011). History not only shows change in design as feature, but in design as a process as well, with contemporary design envisioning the "what if" of creating. We emphasize this important point when we discuss the ideology that can be actualized with the undesign of disability and its redesign as the elimination of a separate disability designation.

Looking back at object conceptualization, production, consumption, use, and eschewal tells the observer not simply about the functionality of object but rather reads (Candlin and Guins, 2009) its cultural context of production. Such an historical focus is extremely useful in illuminating what Fallan (2010) refers to as the actor network, in which diverse designed entities hold divergent and sometimes conflicting meaning to different audiences. Disability as cultural artifact, designed through "the material" over time can therefore be read (Candlin and Guins, 2009) through this theoretical scaffold and diverse methodological approaches, some of which suggest simulating the embodied experience of disabling conditions in order to accurately depict the meaning of design to those who engage with it. As example, Fallan (2010) draws attention to the rollater (or walker) as both form and function, querying the meaning of absence of style from this functional object in a context in which choice, style and aesthetics abound for other populations.

Architectural design provides a succulent symbolic field for investigating the history of designed disability. (CETLD, n.d; Whyte, 2006). For example, the hidden history of disability in higher education built environments in the United Kingdom has been captured in a collection in the British Architectural Library, exposing the inscription of exclusion and segregation in educational design structures. The history of built institutions reveals designed containment and control through the use of colors, spatial management, and navigation (Gilson and DePoy, 2012).

> West Derby Lunatic Asylum from 1846 shows how the order and symmetry of the plan was used to order and rationalise groups of people classed then as 'lunatics'. The labels on the plan show categories such as 'noisy' and 'refractory' that were used to sort residents and inform the design of the spaces they were to inhabit, and the high walls of the 'airing grounds' which shut them in and separate them from each other.
>
> (CETLD, n.d.)

It is curious to note that much of the history of disability as design remains obfuscated by practices which are euphemistically named, even in twentieth century history. As example, is the term "universal design." Inherent in this verbiage, which ostensibly directs the design process to begin with consideration of all bodies, was the veiled attention to those who have been excluded from standard architectural (Architect Design Forum, 2011) and product design proportions and features (DePoy and Gilson, 2011), primarily resulting from impaired bodies.

The most current literature on universal design no longer closets its focus on the atypical as reflected in the title of a recent publication, *Universal Design, Creating Inclusive Environments* (Steinfeld and Maisel, 2012). As disclosed by Titchkosky (2007), the word "inclusion" itself is oxymoronic, in that previously excluded groups must take the stage to be publically displayed for specialized efforts to join an entity. The ostensible aim of increasing participation is thus undermined by keeping the newly included as visible and thus different. Synonymous terms such as "barrier-free design" and "accessible design" further expose the vague and euphemistic nature of universal design as simply a brand name for disability design exclusive to only some bodies. This discussion of words and terms provides an excellent segue to branding. We turn to the history of branding now.

Branding

Branding is multidimensional, taking place over the longitude of history, in multiple geographies, for diverse purposes, and directed at many objects. It has even been suggested that branding predates formal human community, and was essential to its development, given that symbol, label, and myth which inhere in branding practices are instrumental to interaction and necessary to congeal and formalize civilizations. Depicting its centrality to human civilizations, Rush (2005) highlights evidence of human branding in the form of tattooing for spiritual display over 200,000 year ago.

Serving a purpose more earthly than devotional tattooing, and more aligned with contemporary product branding, potters in Ancient Rome marked their work with a thumbprint or image. And illustrating branding for pubic identity in the 1600s, the *fleur de lis* was singed into the shoulders of convicted criminals in France. Each of these purposes has its analog in contemporary intentional and unintended branding practices. Yet, within the context of a global market, branding has expanded way beyond the reach and purposes of its early ancestors.

Contemporary branding as a marketing strategy accompanied mass production in the industrial revolution (Arons, 2011). But according to Blackett (2003) the golden age of branding gained thrust after the conclusion of World War II and continued its hegemony and growth through mass media and now through virtual venues. "Brand mix" is thus more than simple logo, comprising packaging, promotions, and advertising, all relying on the visual and the verbal. Yet, until the 1960s, there was no distinction between branding for the purpose of selling products and marketing the brand itself (Daye, 2006). Contemporary branding practices within marketing contexts sell brands as simulacra in which the brands rather than objects hold the meaning (Kuenstler, 2012). As we discuss throughout the book, multiple forms of contemporary branding cleave humanity into categories, in large part for the purpose of stimulating purchasing and profit.

The purity of simulacra without underlying substance has given rise to branding through multiple intentional methods, including but not limited to place branding (Homadovski, 2012), cause branding (Einstein, 2012), and critical for our focus, the creation and branding of normalcy and its opposite, abnormalcy. Brandscape refers to infusing place and space with meaning in which locations and geographies, from single establishments to nation states, reflect as well as actively shape perceptions of the value of place, those who inhabit or frequent space, and the meaning of place for the continuum of included through excluded. Simply being seen in place in itself confers value or devalue, as space, geography, and location are not neutral (LeFebrve, 1991).

Cause branding is a practice through which profit is maximized by aligning purchasing with social responsibility and then identifying the purchaser as magnanimous, often with a brand item such as a ribbon or rubber bracelet (Moore, 2008). Place branding has joined this choir, with practices such as branding space as green, healthy, for elders only, having stabilized an entryway for medicalization to unobtrusively tiptoe into architectures as cultural narrative (Borsai and Zardini 2012; Edginton, 2010). These obvious to obscured branding practices blur the sequence between brand viewing, brand purchase, and brand occupation (Borsai and Zardini 2012; Einstein, 2012), and have great relevance to the use of abstracts and simulacra for branding humans into groups.

Not surprisingly, medicalization and biomedicalization branding are not just spatial and inscribed in concrete object. Medical and biomedical as brand names posit and reify the abstract myth of normalcy, locate and brand those who do not fit or conform as pathological, disabled, and/or in need of revision (Garland-Thomson, 2009), and then profit from the sales of medical services, spaces, and solutions in obvious through clandestine ways, some intentional and many not so (Borsai and Zardini, 2012; Clarke *et al.*, 2010; Mercola, 2010).

In addition to its form and function, branding has been analyzed by its reflection of intellectual context; for example, modernism, postmodernism, and post-postmodernism. We would, however, suggest that analysis of this variable duplicates an examination of purpose, form, and method, and thus it is omitted from further discussion here. Still, the complexity of branding calls for an organized approach for analysis. Table 2.2 presents a matrix to do just that. Contained in the matrix are critical variables to consider on their own as well as in relation to others. While not the only structure for analytic use, Table 2.2 provides a framework which foregrounds and locates the variables that have been identified in the literature as critical for a multi-dimensional understanding of the processes and outcomes of branding. Table 2.3 provides an example using the matrix.

Using the matrix in Table 2.2, Table 2.3 presents a simple analysis of the design and branding of protective helmets, an example that comes to our aid throughout the book. Even without more detail in the analysis, the complexity of branding can be seen as a function of who develops it, for what purposes, and for what outcomes. As depicted in comparative analyses, the branding can be planned and initiated by multiple individuals and groups

Table 2.2 Analytic matrix for brand analysis

Who or what is branded = Object of branding			
By whom?	For what purposes?	Through what methods?	Outcomes

Table 2.3 Example of analytic matrix for brand analysis

Object of branding = Protective helmets			
Rehabilitation engineers	Professional prescription to enhance function	Brand name and functional appearance	Functional assistance Abandonment
Object of branding = Wearers of protective helmets			
Prescribers	Protection, treatment	Prescription	Protection, through abandonment
Observers	Curiosity, identity	Stereotyping	Devaluation, pity

for diverse purposes and certainly differs by who is branding, branded, why, and how. The outcomes may be diverse, intended or unintended.

Consider the provider who prescribes a protective helmet to decrease the potential of head injury. Object appearance as brand may be operative in derailing the desired outcome of protection, resulting instead in equipment abandonment. Or devaluation, discrimination, and pity, resulting from unintended appearance branding of the helmet and its wearer, may occur from complying with a well-intended wellness goal without considering the stigma associated with the visual (Vara, 2011). Table 2.3 only addresses outcome for the end user of the helmet. But suppose we added outcomes for providers, manufacturers, sellers, health-insurance conglomerates, and so forth, to the mix. Clearly, differential approaches to branding by diverse parties harbor explicit as well as veiled purposes to be considered and create a tumultuous tangle that requires careful and thoughtful scrutiny for analysis and use. Empirically supporting this point is a global study of branding conducted in eight countries, by Torelli *et al.* (2012). These researchers found the interpretation of brand meaning as contextually specific, and thus universal branding (such as the International Symbol of Access) was not useful or efficacious in conveying equivalent meaning, in producing universally predictable response, and thus in meeting a single global branding purpose. The challenge thus remains, for multinational entities to "carefully manag[e] these abstract brand concepts across different cultures" (Torelli *et al.*, 2012: 92).

Meeting Torelli *et al.*'s (2012) challenge, we now turn our eyes once again towards medicalization as a significant context in which designing and branding disability take up residence in diverse global locations. As we discuss later in the book, we have added yet another model of understanding disability to the current compliment, the "medicalization model." Despite the numerous models to characterize disability, we did not find one that foregrounds the role of the medical marketplace in shaping and creating legitimate responses to disability. Further, this nomenclature distinguishes medical from medicalization. For us, while profit may be a significant element of medical intervention, its articulated intended outcomes are the promotion of health and wellness and eradication of illness, as differentiated from the primary aims of medicalization as colonization of the body, accouterments, and space for the purpose of profit. Let us delve into the morass in more detail now.

Medicalization

Not unexpectedly, medicalization has "histories" rather than a single history, given that scholars take divergent approaches to this well-traveled retrospective analysis. Perhaps best known for indicting physicians and their intellectual partners as greedy and insatiable were Szasz, Laing, Goffman, Illich, and Foucault. As eloquently stated by Nye,

these writers accomplished that most beautiful of intellectual opera-
tions: a perfect inversion of the orthodox position. Criminals were
victims of labeling, stereotyping, and racial and economic injustice; the
mad were explorers of new psychological horizons of personal liberty;
and the rebellion against sexual and gender norms was a form of self-
emancipation. In this new scenario, the real villains were the doctors,
psychiatrists, and behavioral scientists who had used their knowledge
and authority to shore up the "establishment" and to segregate and
pathologize the recalcitrant.

(Nye, 2003: 116)

However, looking even further back to the end of the Middle Ages and the
birth of Enlightenment thinking, as religious moral and sin-laden explanations were nudged aside by scientific causal schemes, biology took the lead
in both defining illness and remediating it, to the extent possible at that
point in the development of medical knowledge and technology (DePoy
and Gilson, 2011). This trend created fertile soil for seeding, growing, and
harvesting "normal" and by non-example, "abnormal," which were then
rendered visually into the bell curve, or commonly the "normal curve."

The bell curve was a mathematical and statistical construct developed by
Adolphe Quetelet (1796–1874), a social statistician and mathematician. As
a mathematical construct, Quetelet's bell curve sought to map the "normal
physical, moral, and mental characteristics of the average man." The work
of Quetelet (1842), and subsequently the bell curve, through its centrality
in systematic inquiry, established the binary boundaries of "diverse" and
"not diverse," and located diversity only within categories that were deemed
to be marginal or plus two standard deviations from the mean.

While more extensive epistemic and science history are beyond the
scope of this discussion, we do want to attend to thematic fragments that
were and continue to be instrumental in provoking the design of humans
into binary categories of healthy–not healthy, normal–not normal, beautiful–not beautiful, disabled–not disabled, and thus in potentiating the
entrance and growth of biocapital.

One critical epistemic fragment is the role of the bell curve in positing
knowledge as reality, objective, and ascertainable if logico-deductive rules
of thinking and action are properly enacted. As a descriptive univariate
image the conceptual and visual of the bell curve lies at the heart of logico-
deduction that forms the bedrock for positivism and thus monism, and the
knowledge that is iced on top of this succulent thinking. Defining a
phenomenon both lexically and operationally props open the door to
tautology, reifying a lexical definition by specifying how it is to be counted,
enumerating who meets the definition, creating a visual (curve) of
frequencies and their distribution, and then translating the visual into
"real" binary categories based on most and least typical. While allowing for
prediction, albeit only within an acceptable degree of probability defined

through the lens of the researcher, the numeric quantified affirmation of a single "reality" is a powerful tool serving many purposes. Most relevant for our discussion in this work is the bell curve in service to human bifurcation into pathological and healthy, and thus fodder and a profit center for medicalization.

A second thematic fragment that compliments and is dependent on positivist thinking is the power of scientific narrative in establishing an accepted reality and thus in legitimating practices in concert with that ontology. Illustrating the power of ontology as positivist numeric narrative, Schuster (2011) reminds us of neurasthenia in early twentieth-century history. In his work linking industrialization and modernity to human distress, Schuster shows how happiness entered the criteria for necessary and sufficient conditions for health, despite its previous absence from human health and rights discourses. Thus, happiness became an attribute that humans were supposed to possess in order to be healthy, with its absence named as pathological. Through apprehending knowledge and cultural power, the positivist watershed trend birthed neurasthenia, a vague diagnostic entity, as medical "reality," ripe for assessment, quantification, and capitalism. Rather than looking to more complex consequences of modernity on human wellbeing, the neurasthenic mood state of an individual body became the focus of diagnosis and revision, leaving industrial practices detrimental to human flourishing unchallenged and intact. Despite the disappearance of neurasthenia as formal diagnosis, Schuster (2011) analyzes it as an important history and contemporary analogy within current and more expansive medicalization.

A third instigator, as well as consequence of medicalization, was the repositioning of social control and citizenship status, enacted historically through war and politics. More recently, scientific knowledge and skill power held by a only an elite few unseated battle as the control agent and thus quietly and unrecognized as subjugator, took up residence in the social control palace (Conrad, 2007). The term "biocitizenship" reflects this trend.

Enter professionalization (Ashcraft, Muhr, Rennstam, and Sullivan, 2012). Seizing leadership, authority, and colonization of the body in need of revision, physicians and other medical and health professions captured the legitimacy to define the embodied acceptable, human conditions calling for intervention, methods and even spaces to do so (Borsai and Zardini, 2012). As we reiterate and emphasize, we are not decrying or diminishing the life-saving and -enhancing gifts of scientific knowledge, and health professions. Rather, as we noted above and as a major theme of this work, we see medicine as distinct from medicalization, in that medicine holds as primary the goal of enhancing human health, while medicalization aims to exploit through deception and colonization of the human body. Thus, the context of medicalization, which is characterized by one-hundred-eighty degrees of separation from well-intentioned medical and health practice for us gives rise to designing humans into profit-bearing population segments. The key to unraveling the two and their role in designing and branding humans lies in careful analysis and negotiation of the enormity of causes, processes, and consequences in each, and committing to ongoing dialog among diverse perspectives. For these reasons, we added the medicalization framework to the numerous models of disability for the purpose of depicting the difference between medical and medicalization explanations of disability and hopefully supplanting the term "medical model" with medicalization model. While both share commonalities in the knowledge and praxis dominance of medicine, we make the distinction for clarity, as well as to disengorge the animosity towards the medical model and to redesign it as only one part (and most valuable in responding to medically needy corpuses seamlessly for all bodies), of understanding disability and its social reception. This critical theme underpins our thinking about undesign and redesign of disability as we discuss throughout this work.

Media histories

Illustrative of one of the major themes of this work, media in the visual, auditory, material, and networked culture of the twenty-first century is perhaps the major tool that advertises and thus designs disability for public consumption (Jakubowicz and Meekosha, 2004). Of course, the nature of media and their reach have experienced significant changes as technology sprints ahead (Kovarik, 2011). Once again, visiting the past, Standage (2007) makes the claim that within the technological limitations of the Victorian era, an internet type of system was developed in the form of the telegraph. Unlike early and even mid-twentieth-century media, the telegraph was interactive, worldwide, and a format for immediate communication. Yet, the telegraph was not central to popular culture as it was not omnipotent or visually compelling, despite its reliance on optical material for transmitting text. Still, Standage reminds us that human fascination and desire for immediate communication over a distance are not contemporary artifacts, and thus similar to the intellectual humility of recognizing the birth of the social model of disability in the nineteenth century rather than the 1970s as claimed in referencing. Twenty-first-century hubris touting the current time as the "information age" may also be subdued by history.

In this section, our intent is to delimit the discussion to seminal trends in media history that inform the analysis of disability as designed and branded. Within the twentieth century, media for popular consumption have moved from singular to multi-dimensional, and from carefully crafted behind closed corporate doors to public participatory (Linthicum, 2006). Designing and branding of humans in media thus flow in large part from the capacity of each medium, as engineered or improvised, loquacious or articulate, static or dynamic. Because media are positioned within cultural, social, and techno-logical contexts, they possess great power to shape and transmit information to increasingly broad and diverse audiences. Broadcast and print media, while influenced by social context, deliver messages and meaning. Conversely, social networking and interactive media deliver, create, and contain the tools to recraft story, definition, and interpretation. Given the change in media over the past century, it is therefore not surprising that the processes of disability design and branding have been recast.

Glancing backwards at media before the public involvement in the inter-net, disability design was transmitted through several common themes, some seemingly conflicting but all remanding disability to the extremes of the bell curve, a measured park, so to speak. Explicit themes or those with obvious branding, design disability as deviant bodies, supercrips, and/or pity-worthy. Peeking under even the uppermost veil, however, the observer can see mid- and even late-twentieth-century media branded disability as the half of the human binary in which membership was involuntary and diminished a life.

> From returning veterans learning to renegotiate both the assumptions and environments once taken for granted to the rise of independent living, Hollywood depictions of disability have alternately echoed and influenced life outside the movie theater," said Carter-Long, who curated the series. Twenty-two years after the passage of the ADA and over a century since Thomas Edison filmed *The Fake Beggar*, TCM and Inclusion in the Arts provide an unprecedented overview of how cine-matic projections of isolation and inspiration have played out on the silver screen – and in our lives. When screened together, everything from *The Miracle Worker* to *One Flew Over the Cuckoo's Nest* reveals another layer where what you think you know is only the beginning.
>
> (Harrell, 2012)

Consider these examples of historical disability design and branding. The movies *A Patch of Blue* (1965) and *The Miracle Worker* (1962) design blind-ness as a deficit and visually repugnant to be overcome and cloaked by dark glasses. In a classic scene, Sidney Poitier, who plays the compassionate man, meets Selina, the blind woman, in a park.

> **Gordon**: Here, I bought you a present; take it, put 'em on.
> **Selina**: Glasses.
> **Gordon**: Not quite, they're sunglasses. {She dons the glasses}
> **Gordon**: There, just as I thought.
> **Selina**: What?
> **Gordon**: Now you're a very pretty girl.
> **Selina**: You're pulling my leg.
> **Gordon**: No, I mean it.

Ironside, a television series contemporary of both films about blindness, designed mobility impairment as "supercrip," denying the body in favor of the brain and obfuscating or "sanitizing" inaccessibility (Presley, 2009). Below, the storyline written by Ed Stephan reflects this decontamination.

> Ironside is confined to a wheel chair (an attempted assassination left him paralyzed). With his former assistants Brown and Whitfield (later Belding) and former delinquent (and later lawyer) Mark, he combats crime for the San Francisco police from his mobile office (a van) while leaving a pot of chili cooking back at headquarters.
>
> (Young, 1967–1975)

Over the past fifteen years, however, change has been realized in fictional media, placing embodied impairment designed as part of disability in diverse positions, ranging from monstrosity (Cellania, 2008; Renee, 2011) to typical group member (Haller, 2010), to hot and sexy without anticepticizing impairment. Both extremes and images in between elicit commentary, attention, and in so doing, sculpt cultural tapestries that imagine and reimagine disability.

At the most pejorative endpoint we locate *American Horror Story*. In this television series, embodied impairment languishes among and thus is the face of evil. The horror genre, while ostensibly giving artistic license to symbolize atrocity through the atypical, revives the disabled as monster imagery, maintaining disability design as illegitimate and non-human. Read the excerpt from Wikipedia, which delights in the removal of the extreme atypical from Quasimodo in the 1956 film, rendering him a bit more human than he was portrayed in other visual images.

> Anthony Quinn's portrayal of the hunchback Quasimodo is more human and less horrific than most other portrayals. Instead of having a huge hump and a hideously deformed face, he only has a small curve in his spine and a slightly deformed face.
>
> (Wikipedia, 2013)

Located in intermediate space and returning humanness to impairment, is Pelswick Eggert, the central character in an early twenty-first-century cartoon series authored by John Callahan (2002). Pelswick is described as "a 13-year-old boy who does the same things other 13-year-olds do, except walk" (Petrozzello, 2000). It is curious, however, to read the popular vernacular meaning ascribed to the name Pelswick.

> A derogatory term for any male that has soft qualities. Could be their lack of ability to pick up one night stands at a bar, or their general nerdness. Could also call them Pelz for short. Or someone REALLY deserving the name could be called Captain P, or Lt. P.
>
> (T101mhz, 2010)

The object of gaze, as well as envy, *Push Girls* is a "reality show format [that] has proven itself as a mesmerizing vehicle for examining life's vicissitudes" (Rosenthal, 2013). "Perhaps this entertainment appeals to the voyeur in each of us. *Push Girls* offers a glimpse into a world that may have been eh, pushed aside" (Weinreich, 2012). Thus, consistent with post-modern trends, twenty-first-century popular media bring multiplicity to the design and branding of disability. Although not as frequently addressed in the disability studies literature, non-fiction media texts provide an equally rich data set for analysis of disability design and branding. Similar to popular media, non-fictional media have undergone a transformation from receptive to interactive. Haller (2010) notes that different from being defined by "mainstream" media, interactive social media are platforms for image transformation. Using these media, those with embodied impairments can evaluate, counter, and actively reinvent how they prefer to be portrayed. As example, the BBC currently takes on and provides a forum for dialogue about disability through internet podcast and commentary in numerous corporeal and performance arenas (Rose, 2013).

In 2001, Haller and Ralph wrote, "British companies are still more hesitant in including disabled people in their advertisements." By 2006, Haller and Ralph had a sufficient number of advertisements to serve as the data set for study of disability as symbolic or targeted as a market advertising segment in the UK and the US. And since 2006, change continues, as disability design expands its appearance and scope of symbolism in non-fiction media in general and in advertising in particular. Several themes appear, many reflecting traditional interpretations of disability as tragedy. As example, Vogel (2009) urges employers to recognize and not fear the special needs of employees and family members with disabilities, but rather to brand this population as a potential consumer market to be exploited owing to their rabid product loyalty.

Over the past several decades, however, joining the medicalization of disability, while remaining primarily an object for the stage, disability in contemporary non-fiction media has become well-muscled. To some extent, corporeal impairments, as long as they are attached to bodies that have acceptable traits such as facial beauty, intellect, humor, or even cuteness, brand the owner as unique, desirably diverse, emotionally strong, and even heroic. We offer in evidence the large number of TED Talks on disability.

> TED is a nonprofit devoted to Ideas Worth Spreading. It started out (in 1984) as a conference bringing together people from three worlds: Technology, Entertainment, Design. [TED] bring[s] together the world's most fascinating thinkers and doers, who are challenged to give the talk of their lives.
>
> (TED Conferences, n.d.)

Given the mission, it is curious that a search of TED Talks using "disability" as key term unearthed 1,495 results. The omnipresence of disability within the TED world elevates disability branding and design to innovation, perseverance, and object of admiration. As an example, in 2012, Aimee Mullins became the brand ambassador for L'Oreal of Paris, symbolizing the juxtaposition of beauty with atypical embodiment (Mullins, 2012). Expanding previous discussions in which she exposes the term "disability" as a most unfortunate and demeaning brand for embodied difference (Mullins, 2009), in her 2012 video she redesigns disability as "reinvention" (Mullins, 2012).

The title of Alberto Cairo's (2011) talk, telling the narrative of his transformation from provider to activist, is "There Are No Scraps of Men," a powerful text in which lives are redesigned and disability is rebranded as "change agent and teacher." Design and branding through TED does not remain contained in the non-profit TED arena. Corporate partners include American Express, Delta, Gucci, Samsung, Levi's, General Electric, and Google Chrome, all of which companies become branded as luminaries through their connection with "ideas worth spreading."

Although one often thinks of the logo as the primary branding mechanism, we would suggest that language trumps this abstract and thus provides a major undesign, redesign, and thus rebranding tool set. In her 2009 TED talk, Mullins critically focuses on the language of disability, suggesting that the term disability be replaced by the word "adversity." Given that synonyms for adversity shown on one web-based thesaurus include "bad break, suffering, hard knocks, and even the devil's own luck" (Thesaurus.com, 2009), we see adversity as the conceptual doppelganger of disability, without anything gained by substituting what sounds like a mirror image for disability for itself. However, Mullins does raise the language scepter for thought and discussion.

Given the critical role of language in branding, we now look to turnings in history that have given rise to contemporary naming. As we have already discussed, post-modern thinkers foregrounded language as simulacra interpreted through local ideology and value. It is curious to note that post-modernists and conservatives share the end result of language as cultural production although each group navigates to this endpoint through vastly different arguments (Hicks, 2004; Lind, 2004).

In this context-setting chapter, we enter and navigate the linguistic design park through political correctness to provide the historical grounding for language as label and branding iron. According to Hughes, political correctness,

> started as a basically idealistic, decent-minded, but slightly puritanical intervention to sanitize the language by suppressing some of its uglier prejudicial features, thereby undoing some past injustices or "leveling the playing fields" with the hope of improving social relations.
>
> (Hughes, 2010)

Other scholars characterize political correctness as the enculturation of Marxist economic ideas used as a strategy to seize control over language, which would then be translated into thinking and action with the aim of creating a classless society (Lind, 2004). Because the truth-value of words and narrative are rejected, for both ends of the political spectrum, words become a means of interpretive control, allowing the speaker or author to imply value, devalue without taking the responsibility of telling the "truth." According to Lind, decimating the common meaning of words allows the communicator to "declare certain groups virtuous and others evil *a priori*" (p. 6).

We would suggest that political correctness has different aims for diverse individuals and groups. For some, it designates relief through the removal of pejorative branding, while for others, the word "logo" is nothing other than code for what is already devalued (DePoy and Gilson, 2011). Consider person-first language for example. It is only invoked for conditions which are undesirable, pretending that hiding the descriptor behind personhood apron strings rebrands the subject as human. Applied to branding disability, terms such as "person with a disability," "individual with a cognitive impairment," "person with AIDS" (which has even earned its own acronym) try to masquerade as respectful, but serve two major purposes, branding and derailment of fundamental undesign and redesign beyond linguistic repartee.

Much literature in disability studies, as well as other fields, is devoted to words as labeling and thus never moves to actions. Yet, in its inertia, language about language is powerful in perpetuating the status quo and thus, paradoxically, provokes negative action as maelstroms which capture speakers and listeners. The etic onlooker who is not caught in the semantic current, however, can recognize the potency of lexical labeling to enjoin undesign and redesign and thus to make change. Similar to iconic logo (Holt, 2002), lexical brands obtain cultural status and are recognizable for their interpretive power, particularly in a global context in which branding in itself can remake meanings.

In the next chapter, we take on two iconic brands, normal and abnormal, and examine how they have not only crafted identity designs, but have captured the epistemic and ontological world of the design science of disability.

Summary

In this chapter, we dove backwards into historical seas. We examined and analyzed the chronological trajectories of design and branding in diverse fora, applying more generalized revelations to understanding disability through the thematic crafts of visual, linguistic, and knowledge production. We further elucidated the theme of the medicalization model of disability, distinguishing it from the "medical" model, and suggesting that the term "medical" is a misnomer for understanding embodied disability designs and the actions engendered. The chapter concluded with analysis of brand euphemism in the form of policed linguistc descriptors, assigning disability to bodies and then labeling these corpuses as devalued.

References

Architect Design Forum (2011) Accessibility v. Universal Design. Archinect Discussion Forum, November 20. Available online at http://archinect.com/forum/thread/28141674/accessibility-v-universal-design (accessed February 15, 2014).

Arons, M. de S. (2011) How Brands Were Born: A Brief History of Modern Marketing. *The Atlantic,* October 3. Available online at www.theatlantic.com/business/archive/2011/10/how-brands-were-born-a-brief-history-of-modern-marketing/246012/ (accessed February 15, 2014).

Ashcraft, K. L., Muhr, S. L. Rennstam, J., and Sullivan, K. (2012) Professionalization as a Branding Activity: Occupational Identity and the Dialectic of Inclusivity-Exclusivity. *Gender, Work and Organization,* 19 (5), 467–88.

Baxter, P. (2013) The Evolution of Design – From 2D to 3D to 4D. *IDG Connect,* June 3. Available online at www.idgconnect.com/blog-abstract/1904/the-evolution-design-from-2d-3d-4d (accessed January 14, 2014).

Blackett, T. (2003) *Brands and Branding.* New York: Economist Intelligence Unit.

Borsai, G., and Zardini, M. (2012) *Imperfect Health: The Medicalization of Architecture.* Montreal: Lars Mueller.

Cairo, A. (2011) Alberto Cairo: There are no Scraps of Men. *TED: Ideas Worth Spreading,* December. Available online at www.ted.com/talks/alberto_cairo_there_are_no_scraps_of_men.html (accessed January 14, 2014).

Callahan, J. (2002) John Callahan's Pelswick. Nelvana. Available online at www.pelswick.com (accessed January 14, 2014).

Candlin, F., and Raiford G. (2009) *The Object Reader.* London: Routledge, 2009.

Cellania, M. (2008) Coney Island Freaks of Yesterday and Today. *Mental_Floss,* February 15. Available online at http://mentalfloss.com/article/18052/coney-island-freaks-yesterday-and-today (accessed January 14, 2014).

CETLD (n.d.) Exploring Aspects of the History of Disability and Architecture. Using the British Architectural Library Collections. Centre for Excellence in Teaching and Learning Through Design. *So What is Normal? Resources on Disability and Architecture for Higher Education.* Available online at www.sowhatisnormal.co.uk/histories (accessed January 14, 2014).

Clarke, A. E., Mamo, L., Fosket, J. R., Fishman, J. R., and Shim, J. (2010) *Biomedicalization.* Durham, NC: Duke University Press.

Conrad, P. *The Medicalization of Society: On the Transformation of Human Conditions into Treatable Disorders.* Baltimore, MD: John's Hopkins University Press, 2007.

Daye, D. (2006) History of Branding. *Branding Strategy Insider,* August 14. www.brandingstrategyinsider.com/2006/08/history_of_bran.html (accessed September 16, 2012).

DePoy, E., and Gilson, S. (2011) *Studying Disability.* Los Angeles, CA: Sage.

Ebeling, M. (2011) Mick Ebeling: The Invention that Unlocked a Locked-in Artist. *TED: Ideas Worth Spreading,* March. Available online at www.ted.com/talks/

mick_ebeling_the_invention_that_unlocked_a_locked_in_artist.html?quote=95
2 (accessed February 15, 2014).

Edginton, B. (2010) Architecture as Therapy: A Case Study in the Phenomenology of Design. *Journal of Design History*, 23 (1), 83–97.

Einstein, M. (2012) *Compassion, Inc: How Corporate America Blurs the Line between What We Buy, Who We Are, and Those We Help.* Berkeley, CA: University of California Press.

Fallan, K. (2010) *Design History: Understanding Theory and Method.* New York: Berg.

Fukasawa, N., and Morrison, J. (2007) *Super Normal: Sensations of the Ordinary.* Zurich: Lars Müller, 2007.

Garland-Thomson, R. (2009) *Staring: How We Look.* New York: Oxford University Press.

Gilson, S. F., and DePoy, E. (2012) The Student Body. In A. C. Carey and R. K. Scotch (eds.) *Disability and Community.* Research in Social Science and Disability, Vol. 6. Bingley: Emerald, 27–44.

Haller, B. A. (2010) *Representing Disability in an Abelist World.* Louisville, KY: Avacado Press.

Haller, B. A., and Ralph, S. (2001) Profitability, Diversity, and Disability Images in Advertising in the United States and Great Britain. *Disability Studies Quarterly*, 21, no. 2. Available online at http://dsq-sds.org/article/view/276/301 (accessed January 14, 2014).

Haller, B. A., and Ralph, S. (2006) Are Disability Images in Advertising Becoming Bold And Daring? An Analysis of Prominent Themes in US and UK Campaigns. *Disability Studies Quarterly*, 26 (3). Available online at http://dsq-sds.org/article/view/716/893 (accessed January 14, 2014).

Harrell, D. (2012) Inclusion in the Arts partners with TCM to Examine Hollywood's Depiction of People with Disabilities. Alliance for Inclusion in the Arts, July 24. Available online at http://inclusioninthearts.org/inclusion-in-the-arts-partners-with-tcm-to-examine-hollywoods-depiction-of-people-with-disabilities (accessed January 14, 2014).

Hicks, S. R. C. (2002) *Explaining Postmodernism: Skepticism and Socialism from Rousseau to Foucault.* Tempe, AZ: Scholargy.

Holt, D. B. (2002) Why Do Brands Cause Trouble? A Dialectical Theory of Consumer Culture and Branding. *Journal of Consumer Research*, 29 (1), 70–90.

Homadovski, A. (2010) Place Branding in the Culture of Design. *Prostor*, 18 (1), 190–203.

Hughes, G. (2010) *Political Correctness: A History of Semantics and Culture.* Chichester: wiley-Blackwell.

Jakubowicz, A. and Meekoshak, H. (2004) Detecting Disability: Moving beyond metaphor in the crime fiction of Jeffrey Deaver. *Disability Studies Quarterly*, 24(2). Available online at http://dsq-sds.org/article/view/482/659 (accessed February 15, 2014).

Kovarik, B. (2011) *Revolutions in Communication: Media History from Gutenberg to the Digital Age.* New York: Continuum.

Kuenstler, W. (2012) *Myth, Magic and Marketing: An Irreverent History of Branding From the Acropolis to the Apple Store.* Havertown PA: Zolexa.

Lanzavecchia, F. (2008) Pro Aesthetics Supports. *Designboom*, September 3. Available online at www.designboom.com/design/pro-aesthetics-supports-by-francesca-lanzavecchia (accessed February 15, 2014).

Lees-Maffei, G., and Houze, R. (2010) *The Design History Reader*. New York: Berg.

Lefebvre, H. (1991) *The Production of Space*. Malden, MA: Wiley-Blackwell.

Lind, W. (ed.) (2004) *Political Correctness: A Short History of an Ideology*. Washington, DC: Free Congress Foundation.

Linthicum, E. (2006) Integrative Practice: Oral History, Dress and Disability Studies. *Journal of Design History*, 19 (4), 309–18.

Mercola, J. (2010) How to Brand a Disease – and Sell a Cure. *Mercola.com*, October 29. Available online at http://articles.mercola.com/sites/articles/archive/2010/10/29/disease-branding-for-the-sake-of-drug-marketing.aspx (accessed January 14, 2014).

Moore, S. (2008) *Ribbon Culture*. New York: Palgrave.

Mullins, A. (2009) Aimee Mullins: The Opportunity of Adversity. TED Talks, *TED Partner Series*, Oct. Available online at www.ted.com/talks/aimee_mullins_the_opportunity_of_adversity.html (accessed January 13, 2014).

Mullins, A. (2012) Meet L'Oréal Paris Brand Ambassador: Aimee Mullins. *YouTube*, January 12. Available online at www.youtube.com/watch?v=MGPsP-aF4DM (accessed January 14, 2014).

Nye, R. (2003) The Evolution of the Concept of Medicalization in the Late Twentieth Century. *Journal of History of the Behavioral Sciences*, 39 (2), 115–29.

Petrozzello, D. (2000) Disabled? Not This Kid. *Daily News Entertainment*. October 23. Available online at http://articles.nydailynews.com/2000-10-23/entertainment/18143698_1_pelswick-kids-paralyzed (accessed February 15, 2014).

Popova, M. (2012) Designers on Top: MoMA's Paola Antonelli on the Evolution of Design. *Brain Pickings*, July. Available online at www.brainpickings.org/index.php/2012/07/16/designers-on-top-paola-antonelli-eyeo (accessed February 15, 2014).

Presley, G. (2009) Why I Never Like the Ironsides TV Series. *Seven Wheelchairs: A Life Beyond Polio*, October 19. Available online at http://sevenwheelchairs.blogspot.com/2009/10/why-i-never-like-ironsides-tv-series.html (accessed February 15, 2014).

Quetelet, L. A. (1842) *Treatise on Man, and the Development of His Faculties*. Edinburgh: W. and R. Chambers. Available online at https://archive.org/details/treatiseonmandev00quet (accessed February 15, 2014).

Renee (2011) Ableism and Adelaide in American Horror Story. *Womanist Musings*, November 11. Available online at www.womanist-musings.com/2011/11/ableism-and-adelaide-in-american-horror.html (accessed January 14, 2014).

Rose, D. (2013) Goodbye – Ouch is on the Move. Ouch: it's a disability thing. BBC. www.bbc.co.uk/blogs/ouch/.

Rosenthal, G. (2013) *Push Girls*, Season 2. Produced by Gay Rosenthal Productions. Sundance Channel. Available online at www.sundancechannel.com/series/push-girls (accessed January 14, 2014).

Rush, J. (2005) *Spiritual Tattoo: A Cultural History of Tattooing, Piercing, Scarification, Branding, and Implants*. Berkeley, CA: Frog.

Schuster, D. (2011) *Neurasthenic Nation*. Piscataway, NJ: Rutgers University Press.

Standage, T. (2007) *The Victorian Internet: The Remarkable Story of the Telegraph and the Nineteenth Century's On-line Pioneers*. New York: Walker.

Steinfeld, E., and Maisel, J. (2012) *Universal Design: Creating Inclusive Environments*. Hoboken, NJ: Wiley.

T101mhz (2010) Pelswick. *Urban Dictionary*, November 7. www.urbandictionary.com/define.php?term=Pelswick.

TED Conferences (n.d.) About TED. Available online at www.ted.com/pages/about (accessed January 14, 2014).

Thesaurus.com (2009) Adversity. In *Roget's 21st Century Thesaurus*. Thesaurus.com. Available online at http://thesaurus.com/browse/adversity?s=ts (accessed January 14, 2014).

Titchkosky, T. (2007) *Reading and Writing Disability Differently*. Toronto, ON: University of Toronto Press.

Torelli, C. J., Özsomer, A., Carvalho, S. W., Hean Tat Keh, and Maehle, N. (2012) Brand Concepts as Representations of Human Values: Do Cultural Congruity and Compatibility Between Values Matter? *Journal of Marketing*, 76 (4), 92–108.

Unmaking Things (2012) About. Unmaking Things: A Design History Studio. Available online at http://blog.rca.ac.uk/unmakingthings/the-history-of-design (accessed January 14, 2014).

Vara, S. (2011) Breaking the Stigma. *Brand Marketing Integration*, January 10. Available online at http://kherize5.com/breaking-the-stigma (accessed February 15, 2014).

Vogel, N.O. (2009) Diversity, Disability and Branding. *Worklife Matters*, Spring, 17–18. Available online at www.consultspringboard.com/2009/diversity-disability-branding (accessed January 14, 2014).

Weinreich, R. (2012) The Good, The Bad, And the Sexy: Push Girls on the Sundance Channel. *Huffpost TV*, May 6. Available online at www.huffingtonpost.com/regina-weinreich/push-girls_b_1571181.html (accessed January 14, 2014).

Whyte, W. (2006) How do Buildings Mean? Some Issues of Interpretation in the History of Architecture. *History and Theory*, 45, 153–77.

Wikipedia (2014) The Hunchback of Notre Dame (1956 Film). *Wikipedia: The Free Encyclopedia*, January 7. Available online at http://en.wikipedia.org/wiki/The_Hunchback_of_Notre_Dame_%281956_film%29 (accessed January 14, 2014).

Young, C. (1967–1975) *Ironside*. [TV series] Produced by Harbour Productions Unlimited, Universal TV.

3 Designing and branding disability as abnormal

We have already introduced you to Quetelet and his masterpiece, the normal curve. In this chapter, we delve into normalcy and its non-example, not normalcy, examining its history, creation, espousal in contemporary empirical thinking, and its power in the design of human categories and humanness.

The etymology of the word "normal" is to some extent unremarkable. In the 1500s, "typical, common" was the accepted usage until the mid-sixteenth century, when normal was applied to spatial proportions. Nevertheless, lexical materials for normal all referred to conformity to some sort of standard (Barnhart, as cited in Harper, 2001–2013). Curiously, the term "normal school," while one might have expected it to mean learning to teach to the average, actually referred to model teacher education, implying excellence, but then more recently falling back to educating teachers in theory and techniques of teaching the typical. As we discuss immediately below, the history of normalcy holds a much more illustrious narrative than the word "normal" itself, with the exception of the normal school.

"Abnormal" has a colorful but still benign origin. We did find the meaning and onomatopeia of the 1942 analogy, abnormous (1742), titillating, as it implies magnitude and sounds large, while denoting the small parcel of real estate and the tail ends of the bell curve. The Latin word, *abnormis*, brings deviance to the term, defining abnormous as "deviating from a rule," (Harper, 2001–2012). The early Greek lexical ancestor of abnormal was *anomalos*, from an- "not" plus *homalos*, from *homos* "same." Thus, within the family tree of contemporary abnormal lurks implicit non-membership in humanity, since those who were labeled with this term were "not the same" as other humans.

A little more history

According to McBride and Nief (2011), each generation has its distinct view of what is normal. Interestingly, the authors refer to this shared experience as a mindset, illuminating the power of differential context in creating expectations and degrees of conformity. In disagreement, Ernst (2006) claims that until the eighteenth century, the concept of normal was purely descriptive and not encased in moral judgment. On the surface it might appear as if these two perspectives are contradictory, one suggesting that context provides expectations that could be violated and thus judged, and the other remanding normal exclusively to description. Yet, we would suggest that understanding the evolution and current picture of normal and its obverse, over time, live within both description and axiology and thus inhabit a world of judgment about who and what behaviors, experiences, and appearances legitimate membership in either segment of the binary (DePoy and Gilson, 2004; 2011). The entity of the "normal school" highlights this point, as it provided a desirable of what education should be, ergo axiology, while describing learning techniques and outcomes (description).

Proceeding into the twentieth century, normal moved even further into the moral realm, prescribing what should be on the basis of what is most frequent (DePoy and Gilson, 2012; Fendler and Muzaffar, 2008) or what Hacking (2006) referred to as "probabisation." We introduced this point in the previous chapter, in our brief discussion of Quetelet and the bell curve, and now look through an epistemic lens for edification of normal as surreptitious designer and brander of human desirability.

While Quetelet brought the bell-shaped curve to explanations of social phenomena, Abraham de Moivre actually is credited with its "discovery" in the eighteenth century as an artifact of probability (Bellhouse, 2011). In his own words, De Moivre first elevated the bell curve into the realm of divine design.

> And thus in all cases it will be found, that although chance produces irregularities, still the Odds will be infinitely great, that in process of Time, those irregularities will bear no proportion to the recurrence of that Order which naturally results from Original Design.
> (Gaither and Cavazos-Gaither, 2012: 364)

Building on De Moivre's work, Gauss and LaPlace advanced the math of the normal distribution (Ernst, 2006), elucidating the typical symmetrical curvilinear shape that emerges from measures of natural occurrences (Goertzel and Fashing, 1981). Classical and contemporary scholars examining the application of mathematical theory to social science suggested that Quetelet, in his effort to impose order on social and human experience, failed to distinguish equations of chance from a more concrete existence of an empirical world. Moreover, reflecting Aristotelian thinking, Quetelet assumed that God aimed for a single central point in creating humans, without ever hitting the bull's eye. Conceptually, calculating the mean score of human attributes would therefore reveal the ideal human with the extreme scores defining the most distal limits of humanness beyond which human status is not conferred. Measured extremes such as excessive intelligence strength and so forth, although considered anomalous for the time, were considered as harbingers of future ideals (Goertzel and Fashing, 1981), and ultimately the objects of eugenics.

And thus, the bell curve became simulacrum (Smith, 2001), absorbing and communicating diverse meanings depending on its landscape. Within the fertile narrative of scientific method, the curve ostensibly denotes a distribution of scores (Figure 3.1). It is, however, curious that Pearson (Goertzel and Fashing, 1981) found numerous data sources in which scores were not normally distributed, despite claims to the contrary. The absence of this fabled distribution was met with diverse mathematical meanderings, many which promoted the current psychometric practice of jettisoning items from newly developing instruments because the distribution of responses does not mirror the bell curve (DeVellis, 2011).

Because the foundation of logico-deductive nomothetic inquiry is translation of abstract into measurement, and given that measurement is validated according to normal distribution of item scores, how nomothetic inquiry creates its reality from symbol by verifying or falsifying constructed indicators of concepts that are advanced in theory becomes transparent (DePoy and Gilson, 2007: 6).

In addition to placing items within the statistical cradle of the bell curve, experimental methods seek to verify or falsify their theoretical surroundings and thus in this logico-deductive tradition, theory must frame

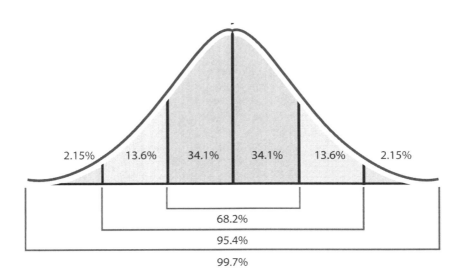

Figure 3.1 The bell curve

hypothesis testing (DePoy and Gitlin, 2011). Statistical and conceptual structures within experimental methodologies do however, allow for "story" in the conclusion section of the research report, giving the bell curve its interpretive and often prescriptive pulpit. Contrary to monistic claims made by experimental researchers who hang their ontological hats on the bell curve, the logico-deductive methodological tradition is bounded on one end with preference for a particular theory and then delimited on the other with narrative about the meaning of the numbers yielded by investigator choice of statistical tool.

In his most recent work, Orrell (2012) suggested that the story told by the bell curve is one of deceptive beauty. Accordingly, the search for symmetrical order as an aesthetic in both science and mathematics seduces researchers into simplifying and limiting their understandings of the universe that they seek to detail.

Affirmed by Byers (2011), the acceptance of logico-deductive methods as the basis of scientific "truth" and elegance is both simplistic and erroneous.

> It seems strange to call science a mythology since the story that science tells about itself is precisely that it, an activity pursued by human beings, is objective and empirical; that it concerns itself with the facts and nothing but the facts... And yet science is a human activity. This is an obvious statement but it bears repeating since part of the mythology of science is precisely that it is independent of human beings; independent of mind and intelligence... How do human beings create a system of thought that produces results that are independent of human thought?
>
> (Byers, 2011: ix–x)

In his classic work, Tufte (2001) lodged a similar concern related to the graphic depiction of scientific data. While Tufte espouses the truth value of statistical calculations for supporting theory, he warns the statistician to avoid chart junk, referring to hyper-designed visual graphics which obscure accuracy and thus supplant truth with fiction.

Yet, unless the reader of the deductive knowledge is aware of its interpretative and human nature and adorned visual presentation, the bell curve can uncritically design and then brand humans into topoi of normal and not normal camps. Consider the example of grade inflation. Last year, in the University of Maine, we were asked to eliminate the practice of grade inflation in our courses. Subsumed in this term is the notion that student test scores will follow a normal distribution, with most students receiving mediocre grades, some failing and some achieving excellence. Why not expect and hope that all students will engage in demonstrable and reportable learning achievement and thus teach to that expectation? This short story of limited expectations is repeatedly reified in too many arenas of human striving, a number of which set the expectancy bar too low and thus ransack esteem.

> The bell curve powerfully shapes how we think of human perform-ance: If lots of students or employees happen to show up as extreme outliers – they're either very good or very bad – we assume they must represent a skewed sample, because only a few people in a truly random sample are supposed to be outliers.
>
> New research suggests, however, that rather than describe how humans perform, the bell curve may actually be constraining how people perform. Minus such constraints, a new paper argues, lots of people are actually outliers.
>
> (Vedantam, 2012)

Given the mythic nature of the bell curve (Goertzel and Fashing, 1981) as well as its variations in visual design (Tufte, 2001), the extent to which statistics that ostensibly provide empirical evidence of claims are anchored on this imagery is cause for skepticism regarding the truth value of scien-tific narratives in words, images and/or numbers. This point provides a segue to thinking about science from a paradigmatic contemplation.

We first visit with Sheldrake (2012) to engage with his vexation about the nature of science and its current failure to move beyond its inherent mate-rialism. In agreement with Byers (2011), Sheldrake suggests that the anachronistic constraints of science reify the reality of the existence of substance, eschewing as yet undiscovered what cannot be physically or conceptually palpated. Superimposed on this understanding of the universe is the asserted vulnerability to the influences of context that science experiences. In synthesizing the dogma of the bell curve, the context-embedded nature of scientific knowledge and the adherence to materialism, predictive norms and their opposites are thus suspect and open for interrogation. Yet the norm as a social entity, not a scientific one, is depicted in the designed visual of the apex and proximal surroundings of the bell curve.

In his classic philosophical work on the nature of norm and pathology, Canguilhem (1989) purported that branding an individual as normal, while accepted as a statistical "truth," is polemic, political, contextual, and regressive with regard to social change. That is to say, the bell curve designs individual normalcy as commonality within contextual boundaries of age and place, and thus maintains the status quo by prescription (Reynolds, 2012). Accordingly, pathology is constructed in relation to normalcy, tauto-logically reified by counting what it is not, and then served up for twenty-first-century branding practices (Perry, 2007).

Consider post-traumatic stress disorder (PTSD), for example. Concern with response to severe trauma has been documented throughout history (Anders, 2012). The World War I term "shell shock," a phrase which is devoid of the contemporary scientific shine of current mental health diagnoses, was replaced by PTSD in 1980 to name and frame response to trauma as a disease state. Yet only recently have the traumatic criteria been revised to expand this brand of illness to a broad swath of individuals who claim that the process of maturation in itself was traumatic, particularly if one's parents were portrayed as harsh. Changing the name brand to denote pathology swelled and ripened the market segment for picking by the medical and pharmaceutical industries (Anders, 2012). And of course, this diagnosis often procures an invitation into the permanency of the psychiatric disability park.

Until recently, transforming the "pathological" or aberrant back to the desirable of normalcy did little to advance or improve what is common, retaining the status quo of "what is" as both normative and desirable. "No doctor proposes to produce a new kind of man" (Canguilhem, 1989: 258). However, contemporary normalcy, while still languishing in its status quo lounger, is being challenged by genetic redesign as well as rebranding. Perry (2007) urges rebranding for market purposes, mentioning the potential of renaming to reduce stigma of the not normal or pathological as part of stimulus for the acceptance of purchasing body revision. Still inherent in revision is the undesirability of the "outliers" or attributes that subsist on the very edges of the bell curve until they are changed (Spuybroek, 2012; Wallesch and Schlote, 2010).

Naming and framing outliers

With the bell curve as mascot, we now can move into a discussion of design and branding of outliers. As a statistical phenomenon, outliers are observations that are translated into scores that indicate extreme deviance from the average or the mean. They are interpreted and addressed in several ways. First, outliers often are considered to be an anomalous function of measurement error and eliminated from a set of scores in order to achieve a normal distribution (Motulsky, 2010). Second, one can pay attention to outliers as non-examples or extremes of a construct being measured and address them as such, leaving them to rest or demanding their relocation towards central tendency. A third perspective is that the presence of numerous outliers indicates a "non-normal" or kurtic distribution, raising the possibility that the theory being tested is invalid and new theory needs to be developed. These three approaches mirror thinking and action processes related to the atypical human and thus the design and branding of disability.

Disregarding or expelling the outlying individual is analogous to the statistical practice of eliminating extreme scores. We see this mathematical, methodological construct translated into practice in institutionalization and other manipulations of humanness such as preventing birth, involuntary treatment, assisted suicide, all forms of structural, institutional violence, referring to harm perpetrated by social organizations and cultural conventions (Iadicola and Shupe, 2013). We revisit institutional violence in more depth in Chapter 8.

Scrutinizing as different and thus designing the outlying body and behavior (Price, 2011) as fodder for revision reflects the second statistical trend. Exemplified here is social phobia that includes shyness and embarrassment measured beyond ±2 standard deviations from the mean.

> Social phobia is a strong fear of being judged by others and of being embarrassed. This fear can be so strong that it gets in the way of going to work or school or doing other everyday things. Everyone has felt anxious or embarrassed at one time or another. For example, meeting new people or giving a public speech can make anyone nervous. But people with social phobia worry about these and other things for weeks before they happen.
>
> (NIMH, n.d.)

And finally, the third approach, questioning theory as relevant, useful, and valid activates the cynic, charting a course for undersign and redesign of disability and its branding.

Normal and abnormal designs and brands

We now sharpen the focus of this chapter on disability as designed and branded as abnormal humanness or beyond. So far, we have discussed the history and origin of normal and abnormal, finding the bell shaped curve as the primary brand recognition for dividing humans into binary categories. Before we look at specific exemplars, we want to remind the reader that both the medical and medicalization models of disability espouse the monistic truth value of the bell-shaped curve. We make this claim on the basis of the logico-deductive hegemony of research methods that are enacted and named "best evidence" in these fields (Cochrane Collaboration, 2012).

Table 3.1 contains lexical and visual brands that identify normalcy and abnormalcy in three arenas: statistics, medicine, and the disability park

Table 3.1 Brands of normal and not normal

Statistical brands	Medical model brands	Park brands
f or v	within normal limits (WNL)	eligible
percentile (%)	unremarkable	special
σ^2 : SD	neurotypical	delayed
mean: x	deformity	families and children
z score	functional	exceptional
$P = 0.05$	disorder	age appropriate

(education and other services). As we introduced in Chapter 1 and rein-troduced once again above, we refer to the third category as the disability park (DePoy and Gilson, 2011) suggesting a post-modern vision of services (including the knowledge and policies that guide them) as theme parks of a sort. For us, this viewpoint does not indicate that services are unnecessary, frivolous, or malicious. Rather, we chose this vernacular to identify that despite the professionalism and altruism of those who provide services, their situation in an economically driven context captures and swirls the service recipients as well as the providers in a complex economic waltz, most often with the profit motive obfuscated below the "helping" stage. And as we indicated above, disability is the default brand for not normal even in philosophical discussions of rights. For example, Talbott asserts that robust rights or those that posit freedom from tyranny should be conferred on all adults who are normal. The two referents for those not included in his thinking are children and people with disabilities:

> It is important for me to say something about persons with disabilities because throughout I have characterized the human rights as the rights that should be guaranteed to normal human adults. What do I mean by normal? My use of normal is not meant to exclude those with disabilities. It is rather meant to emphasize that normal cognitive, emotional, and behavioral development is sufficient for achieving autonomy in my consequentialist sense of the term-that is to have good judgment and self-determination.
>
> (Talbott, 2010: 322)

We wonder how Talbott distinguishes disability, given his not so veiled reference to normal cognitive, emotional and behavioral development as non-example of disability.

We return to our discussion of the park in subsequent chapters, but encounter it here as the basis for understanding it as a perimeter that both reflects and shapes norms and their attainment.

Although statistics are most typically the vernacular used in research literature, the symbols and the meanings designed by them are seen in the public domain. The symbol, f, and its equivalent, v, brand the number of appearances made by a phenomenon, with the most frequently occurring observations ascending to the apex of the bell curve. X, σ, %, and z collaborate by reducing raw scores to numbers denoting the nature and scope of normal and the valleys beyond.

Consider the design of intelligence and its non-exemplary brand, intellectual disability. While the history and detailed discussion of intelligence quotient (IQ) are not our aims here, we ask for temporary participation from IQ and its verbal relatives in our work to illustrate the process of design and branding based on the elegant visual symbol of the bell curve.

Intelligence tests typically situate the normal or mean intelligence quotient score at 100 with a standard deviation (or $z = 1$) of 15. Those who score two standard deviations below and above 100, (70–130) are considered normal, typical and within normal limits (WNL) while those scoring below 70 and above 130 are not normal, but rather are branded as abnormal (Figure 3.2).

Of course, it is most desirable in contemporary times to score above 130 and thus be known as supranormal. Parkscapes such as Mensa International seek members who sport the "super" brand, the genius, so to speak, who scores at or above the ninety-eighth percentile or better than ninety-eight percent of his/her age cohort.

> The Mensa Admission Test takes two hours to complete and includes two tests featuring questions involving logic and deductive reasoning. If you score at or above the 98th percentile on either of the two tests, you'll qualify and be invited to join Mensa.
>
> (American Mensa, 2013)

Unlike their unremarkable, age appropriate, or delayed counterparts, the lucky but abnormal few who score in the stratospheric level of the bell curve are designed as gifted and talented, with children in the United States and other countries, as well frequenting places of educational stardom: "Children and youth with outstanding talent who perform or show the potential for performing at remarkably high levels of accomplishment when compared with others of their age, experience, or environment" (US Department of Education, 1993, cited by NSGT, 2014). In the United Kingdom, the supranormal IQ holders are now rebranded as Potential Plus UK members, implying innate but perhaps unrealized as yet endowments.

On the "sub" end of the curve, we find the brands names "exceptional" and "special." According to the Council for Exceptional Children (2011), low IQ score-holders, signified by a raw IQ score of more than two standard deviations below the mean, are designed by the undesirable comparative location of their scores as persons with intellectual impairments. Within

Figure 3.2 Intelligence test distribution

the servxice park, these individuals are branded as exceptional and special, a curious lexicon to obscure debasement. Children with IQ scores in this subterrain in the United States are placed in special education designed by numeric score and "eligibility" on the basis of inferior academic perform-ance despite the many attributes that they bring to home and community (NICHCY, 2012). Similar to others who have suggested that the brand of low IQ packs its own behavioral baggage, the bullet ant who resides in the Amazon rain forest tells a foreboding story. This ant is a fascinating crea-ture with no natural predator. As it languishes in its imposed complacency, it succumbs only to a fungus which creates the ant's behavioral death knell by intoxicating it with atypical social and motor behaviors. For us, the metaphor is one of withering without the opportunity for challenge and healthy competition and thus is the question raised by the perilous insect as teacher. As presented in the narrative below, in the Special Olympics, everyone is a winner without regard to performance. No competition exists and thus what is set into motion is institutional intoxication and abatement for the unsuspecting participant as well as the park observers.

Now look at the texts below describing Special Olympic athletes in contrast to their Olympic counterparts.

Special Olympics: Who we are

Athletes are the heart of Special Olympics. Our athletes are children and adults with intellectual disabilities from all around the world. They are finding success, joy and friendship as part of our global community. They're also having lots of fun.

(Special Olympics, 2012)

10 characteristics of Olympic athletes worth copying

1   Winning isn't everything, but wanting to win is. Olympians have a "whatever-it-takes" attitude. They've made the decision to pay any price and bear any burden in the name of victory.
2   Olympic athletes embrace conflict for growth. When most people run into an obstacle, they seek escape. Olympic athletes have a plan to push forward when this happens and learn all they can from the challenge. They know facing adversity is part of being successful.
3   Olympic athletes are held accountable on so many levels. One of the biggest problems is that most people have no means of accountability or a support system in place when it comes to what they're trying to accomplish.
4   Olympic athletes are learning machines. They spend hours prac-ticing, studying their competitors, watching videos of their performances and session after session with their coaches and mentors. If the average person adopted just a fraction of their work ethic, the results they could achieve would be endless.

5   Olympic champions know very good is bad. For the average person, to be classified as very good is something to be proud of. For the great ones, it's an insult.

6   Olympic athletes make "do-or-die" commitments. When most people are burned out from the battle, Olympians are just getting warmed up. It's not that they don't fatigue, but their commitment to their dream of winning the gold keeps them going.

7   Olympic athletes are consistently great. The reason they are so consistent is because their actions are congruent with their thought processes. They have a very clear mental picture of what they want, why they want it and how to move closer to their target objective.

8   Olympians are coachable. Most people will only accept the amount of coaching their egos will allow. Champions like Olympic athletes are well-known for being the most open to world-class coaching. The bigger the champion, the more open-minded they are.

9   Olympians compartmentalize their emotions. In other words, they have the ability to put aside anything else going on at that very moment and focus only on the task in front of them.

10 Olympians think big. Ask most people what they're thinking at any given time, and you might be surprised to learn how many think about just getting by. That's called selling yourself short. Olympians are fearless and focused on manifesting their ultimate dream of bringing home the gold.

(TheTandD, 2012)

As illustrated above, intelligence quotient (IQ) is an eloquent yet surreptitious use of the bell curve, earning equivocal reviews. Look at Hunt's text below for his simple yet precise explanation of IQ and its purposes.

If you want to go beyond saying people are different, you have to offer some way of measuring differences. There is an imperative to develop such measures of a society wants to assign different roles to different people based on their personal characteristics. ... Not everyone can have what they want. Students have to be selected, jobs have to be filled and when behavior problems arise, mental competence must be assessed.

(Hunt, 2011: 3)

Alfred Binet was one of the first to step up to this challenge, designing intelligence as an age-related ability to solve problems, branding intelligence with the term "mental age." Over the many years that intelligence has been fashioned as numeric, theories of intelligence have changed the underlying constructs of the object of measure (Hunt, 2011). Yet, the bell curve holds its position constant, designing and branding intelligence as a symmetrically distributed comparative human trait inferred through observing selected human performances (Figure 3.3).

Moreover, this numeric address in the geography of intelligence is an expansive brand for life, assigning value, opportunity, rights and responsibilities, and direction outside its cognitive arena, depending on one's scored location on the curvilinear cul de sac. It is therefore not surprising to find such heated and ongoing debate about the meaning and reflection of human intelligence. Many scholars disdain numbers as designers and reflections of humans' capacity to think. Consider the classic work of Gould (1996), which although criticized for inaccuracy by some, was powerful in exposing the foibles of inferring how smart one is by a numeric score on a test. Gould is not the first and certainly not the last scholar to throw darts at designing human intelligence through measurement.

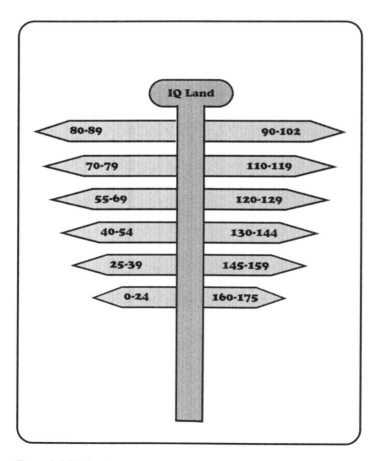

Figure 3.3 IQ land

Of course, the bell curve does not restrict its design and branding to intelligence. Consider the field of abnormal psychology. Look at the description of one of the seminal scholarly journals in the field to walk through the "abnormalscape" of psychology.

The *Journal of Abnormal Psychology®* publishes articles on basic research and theory in the broad field of abnormal behavior, its determinants, and its correlates. The following general topics fall within its area of major focus:

- psychopathology – its etiology, development, symptomatology, and course;
- normal processes in abnormal individuals;
- pathological or atypical features of the behavior of normal persons;
- experimental studies, with human or animal subjects, relating to disordered emotional behavior or pathology;
- sociocultural effects on pathological processes, including the influence of gender and ethnicity; and
- tests of hypotheses from psychological theories that relate to abnormal behavior.

(APA, 2014)

Normal and abnormal make multiple appearances on this textual screen, reifying the existence of the binary as observable and quantifiable in human behavior (Davis, 1995).

Within the medical and medicalized models of disability discussed in Chapter 2, the terms normal and abnormal are omnipresent, inhabiting all arenas of human performance and experience. It is therefore curious that disability lives in the abnormalscape, given the epidemiological claims of its typical and frequent appearance as humans age. We enter vision as our final piece of evidence.

From an early age, one becomes familiar with the chart in Figure 3.4. This icon designs humans into categories of "age appropriate visual acuity" (American Optometric Association, 2013). A brand of 20/20 means "you can see clearly at 20 feet what should "normally" be seen at that distance. If you have 20/100 vision, it means that you must be as close as 20 feet to see what a person with normal vision can see at 100 feet."

Once again, inherent in these normative designs is the bell curve. But in the case of vision, vintage enters the picture, bringing in statistics of association between age and acuity along with the emblematic brand that separates groups from one another, $P=0.05$, 0.01 or 0.001. These statistical brands indicate that differences between and among groups are not a chance occurrence, within an investigator-selected degree of certainty (DePoy and Gitlin, 2011).

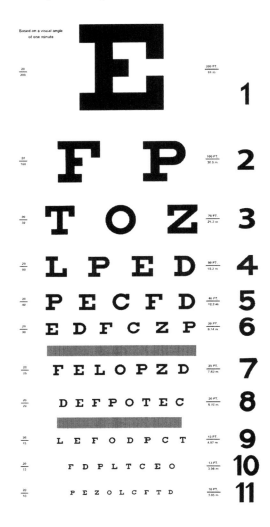

Figure 3.4 Eye chart
Source: © Shutterstock

Before leaving the normal/abnormal theme, attention to contemporary reinvention of the terms is briefly introduced. Early twenty-first-century art and design have apprehended the normal moniker to denote the choreography of a typical or "normal" day and the objects that are designed to activate and excite. As example, consider the short video hosted on Vimeo which depicts:

Winner of "Best Director" award at Nokia N8: Direct and Project. Shot entirely on the Nokia N8 mobile phone, "Normal Design" explores what happens when mundane activities take on an unusual rhythm.

(Anderson, 2011)

Phrases such as the "new normal" introduce normal as relative rather than fixed. As example, new normal is ascribed to revision of American lifestyles in a failing economic climate as well as to a TV sitcom starring gay parents.

Rebranding normal and its non-example present an opportunity for redesign, as we discuss in subsequent chapters.

Summary

In this chapter we have examined normal and abnormal as designers and branders of a human binary. The normal or bell-shaped distribution formed the statistical foundation as well as visual simulacra for bifurcating and affirming these two grand categories of humanness and what lies beyond. Significant consequences become attached to addresses outside the normal half of the binary from captivity in the disability park to denial of human rights. The chapter concluded with a teaser introduction of reinvention of the normal brand.

References

American Mensa (2014) Take the Admission Test. American Mensa. Available online at www.us.mensa.org/join/testing (accessed January 14, 2014).

American Optometric Association (2013) Visual Acuity: What is 20/20 Vision? American Optometric Association. Available online at www.aoa.org/x4695.xml (accessed January 14, 2014).

Anders, C. J. (2012) From "Irritable Heart" to "Shellshock": How Post-Traumatic Stress Became a Disease. *IO9: Secret History*, April 4. Available online at http://io9.com/5898560/from-irritable-heart-to-shellshock-how-post+traumatic-stress-became-a-disease (accessed January 14, 2014).

Anderson, J. (2011) Normal Design. *Vimeo*, January 19. Available online at http://vimeo.com/19021923 (accessed January 14, 2014).

APA (2014) Journal of Abnormal Psychology: Description. American Psychological Association. Available online at www.apa.org/pubs/journals/abn/index.aspx (accessed January 14, 2014).

Bellhouse, D. R. (2011) *Abraham De Moivre: Setting the Stage for Classical Probability and Its Applications*. Boca Raton, FL: CRC Press.

Byers, W. (2011) *The Blind Spot*. Princeton, NJ: Princeton University Press.

Canguilhem, G. (1989) *The Normal and the Pathological*. New York: Zone.

Cochrane Collaboration (2012) The Cochrane Collaboration. Available online at www.cochrane.org (accessed January 14, 2014).

Council for Exceptional Children (2014) Disability Terms and Definitions. Available online at www.cec.sped.org/Special-Ed-Topics/Who-Are-Exceptional-Learners (February 15, 2014).

Davis, L. (1995) *Enforcing Normalcy: Disability, Deafness, and the Body*. London: Verso.

DePoy, E., and Gilson, S. F. (2004) *Rethinking Disability: Principles for Professional and Social Change*. Pacific Grove, CA: Wadsworth.

DePoy, E., and Gilson, S. F. (2007) The Bell-Shaped Curve: Alive, Well and Living in Diversity Rhetoric. *International Journal of Diversity in Organisations, Communities and Nations*, 7 (3), 253–9.

DePoy, E., and Gilson, S. F. (2011) *Studying Disability: Multiple Theories and Responses*. Thousand Oaks, CA: Sage Publications.

DePoy, E., and Gilson, S. F. (2012) *Human Behavior Theory and Applications: A Critical Thinking Approach*. Thousand Oaks, CA: Sage Publications.

DePoy, E., and Gitlin, L. (2011) *Introduction to Research* (4th ed.). St. Louis, MO: Elsevier.

DeVellis, R. (2011) *Scale Development: Theory and Applications* (3rd ed.). Los Angeles, CA: Sage.

Ernst, W. (2006) *Histories of the Normal and the Abnormal Social and Cultural Histories of Norms and Normativity*. Abingdon: Routledge.

Fendler, L., and Muzaffar, I. (2008) The History of the Bell Curve: Sorting and the Idea of Normal. *Educational Theory*, 58 (1), 64–82.

Gaither, C. C., and Cavazos-Gaither, A. E. (2012) De Moivre. In *Gaither's Dictionary of Scientific Quotations* (2nd ed.). New York: Springer.

Goertzel, T., and Fashing, J. (1981) The Myth of the Normal Curve: A Theoretical Critique and Examination of its Role in Teaching and Research. *Humanity and Society*, 5, 14–31.

Gould, S. (1996) *The Mismeasure of Man*. New York: Norton.

Hacking, I. (2006) *The Emergence of Probability* (2nd ed.). Cambridge: Cambridge University Press.

Harper, D. (2001–2012) Normal (adj.). *Online Etymology Dictionary*. Available online at www.etymonline.com/index.php?term=normal (accessed January 14, 2014).

Hunt, E. (2011) *Human Intelligence*. New York: Cambridge University Press.

Iadicola, P., and Shupe, A. (2013) *Violence, Inequality, and Human Freedom*. Lanham, MD: Rowman and Littlefield.

McBride, T., and Nief, R. (2011) *The Mindset Lists of American History: From Typewriters to Text Messages, What Ten Generations of Americans Think Is Normal*. Belmont, CA: Wiley.

Motulsky, H. (2010) *Intiutive Biostatistics*. New York: Oxford University Press.

NICHCY (2012) Categories of Disability Under IDEA. National Dissemination Center for Children with Disabilities, March. Available online at http://nichcy.org/disability/categories (accessed January 14, 2014).

NIMH (n.d.) Social Phobia (Social Anxiety Disorder). National Institute of Mental Health. Available online at www.nimh.nih.gov/health/topics/social-phobia-social-anxiety-disorder/index.shtml (accessed January 14, 2014).

NSGT (2014) Giftedness Defined. National Society for the Gifted and Talented. Available online at www.nsgt.org/articles/index.asp (accessed January 14, 2014).

Orrell, D. (2012) *Truth or Beauty*. New Haven, CN: Yale University Press.

Parry, V. (2007) Disease Branding: What it is, Why it Works, and How to do it. *Pharmaceutical Executive*, October, 22–4.

Price, M. (2011) *Mad at School*. Ann Arbor, MI: University of Michigan Press.

Reynolds, T. (2012) Beyond Inclusion: Rethinking Normalcy, Identity, and

Disability in Theological Terms. YouTube, March 9. Available online at www.youtube.com/watch?v=WgMGxJr5JuQ (accessed February 15, 2014).

Sheldrake, R. (2012) *Science Set Free.* New York: Random House.

Smith, M. (2001) *Reading Simulacra: Fatal Theories for Postmodernity.* Albany, NY: State University of NY Press.

Special Olympics (2012) Who We Are. Special Olympics. Available online at www.specialolympics.org/Sections/Who_We_Are/Who_We_Are.aspx (accessed January 14, 2014).

Spuybroek, L. (2012) The Ages of Beauty. In J. Brouwer, A. Mulder, and L. Spuybroek, *Vital Beauty.* Rotterdam, Netherlands: V2 Publishing.

Talbott, W. (2010) *Human Rights and Human Well-Being.* New York: Oxford University Press.

TheTandD (2012) 10 characteristics of Olympic athletes worth copying. *Times and Democrat,* August 6. Available online at http://thetandd.com/characteristics-of-olympic-athletes-worth-copying/article_6fb3c3b8-e00b-11e1-8b68-0019bb2963f4.html (accessed January 14, 2014).

Tufte, E. (2001) *The Visual Display of Quantitative Inforamtion.* Cheshire, CT: Graphics Press.

Vedantam, S. (2012) Put Away The Bell Curve: Most Of Us Aren't 'Average'. Retrieved from NPR, May 3. Available online at www.npr.org/2012/05/03/151860154/put-away-the-bell-curve-most-of-us-arent-average (accessed January 14, 2014).

Wallesch, C. W., and Schlote, A. (2010) WHODAS II – Practical and theoretical issues. *Disability and Rehabilitation,* 32 (8), 685–6.

4 Axiological design

Designing and branding, meaning, value or devalue

> The last few decades have belonged to a certain kind of person with a certain kind of mind – computer programmers who could crank code, lawyers who could craft contracts, MBAs who could crunch numbers. But the keys to the kingdom are changing hands. The future belongs to a very different kind of person with a very different kind of mind – creators and empathizers, pattern recognizers, and meaning makers.
>
> (Pink, 2006: 1)

These sage words that open this chapter are excerpted from Daniel Pink. And while kneaded by multiple uses and handling, this quotation remains fervent to further our analysis of design and branding. In essence, design and branding are interwoven processes of making meaning that ascribes value and worth.

Meaning making is a well-traveled term that in itself has multiple interpretations. Kurzman (2008) defines meaning making as a set of processes through which humans seek to understand their world. He parses meaning making into two divisions, individual-methodological and cultural. Individual-methodological refers to the idiographic processes of differential perception and response to sensory stimuli, such as words, symbols, tastes (Scott, 2011), and so forth. Collective perception and reaction from which only outliers are exempted is its cultural associate. Unlike the idiographic phenomenon, a large percentage of the responses within the cultural division involves the communal conferral of value on the sensory stimulus, rendering value as topos. For this reason, business and design schools have begun to join hands (Pink, 2006; School of Visual Arts, 2012), and those which resist have been cajoled to move into the twenty-first century if they are to influence public perception and behavior (Walters, 2011).

Making meaning through design

As discussed in Chapter 2, theories of design have expanded from planned properties of aesthetic appearance to a process in which the object of scrutiny (be it abstract or concrete) is only a small part of the dynamism and the reach of design. As theorized by Kazmierczak (2003) the three linchpins of design, the intended purpose, the actual construction, and the receipt of the designed entity, leave large spaces for diverse meanings to be fabricated by all involved in the process and thus introduce meaning making itself into the fundamental definition of design. Through this lens, the designer may be any of those involved in the three elements including the recipient of the designed entity. Applied to the construct of disability, the diagnostician, the observer, and the individual sporting the disability label are all involved in the process of human design through the attribution of meaning to each creation and its brand.

Communicating meaning and value through branding

Einstein's (2012) analysis of corporate social responsibility and cause related marketing reveal the contemporary power of branding in not only showcasing personal identity, but also in creating brand communities in which shared values are imparted and bestowed. These communities demonstrate membership legitimacy "by integrating members into the group and helping them properly use their brand" (Einstein, 2012: 19–20).

Thus, unlike its predecessors, twenty-first-century branding has moved beyond advertising the features of a product to the role of axiological icon. Observing the brands that are selected or involuntarily imposed bathe the branded in wash of value to devalue (DePoy and Gilson, 2011; 2013). Successful brands not only sell, but additionally communicate reputation, standing, and status (Berntson, Jarnemo, and Philipson, 2006; Blackett, 2003). As an example, brands:

> provide an easy way for youth to compensate for their feelings of anxiety by acting as a substitute for value; the right label can confer a superficial layer of prestige and esteem upon teens, which can act as a temporary shield against criticism and self-doubt.
>
> (Tokuhama, 2011: 34)

A key question raised by Kurzman's (2008) distinction between individualist and collective meaning is who is in the branding driver's seat? In other words, who creates the stimulus, manipulates its receipt and interpretation, for whom, to whom, and for what purposes? And then, what happens to the uncooperative outliers who cannot be swept into a collective vision? In her classic but often contested work, Klien (2009) sketched branding as a practice usurping the sale of objects, replacing it with the sale of identities. Let us consider two exemplars to illustrate, autism spectrum disorders (ASD) and mental illness.

Autism spectrum disorders

In this section, it is not our intent to debate the essence, cause, scope or even existence of ASD in detail. For those who seek this knowledge, we direct you to the myriad works that contain this discussion (Autism Speaks, 2012; Feinstein, 2012; Jordan, 2009; Parent Dish, n.d.). Here, however, we employ autism to exact a critical examination of the multiple factors that design and branding bring to shape the meaning of predominant medicalized disability texts. Thus, autism, Asperger's syndrome and other syndromes "on the spectrum" accompany us through analysis of disability design and branding as axiology and as meaning-making. ASD has an illustrious past and present, with branders as well as branded arguing about its essence as unique, desirable, pathological or iatrogenic.

Looking historically, Kanner popularized Bleuler's term, autism, among psychiatric designers in the 1950s to refer to youth who demonstrated atypical behaviors that often included self-imposed social isolation. At a time when science and medicine were climbing the fashionable explanatory ladder, behavior on the outskirts of the bell curve was not seen simply as eccentric but was subjected to measurement and designed as denigrated pathological syndromes ordaining medical treatment.

But after being criticized for attributing biological cause to autism, Kanner and associates ultimately acquiesced to the accepted intellectual climate of the time, and dangled, in front of expert audiences, the psychodynamic explanatory carrot of refrigerator mothering as the root of autism. Until psychodynamic pathology fell from paradigmatic grace in psychiatric circles, the carrot elicited attention and thus the maternal parent was designed as the perpetrator of harm to the victimized withdrawn child. By the 1990s, the ascent of genetics and neurobiology (Carlson, 2011; Massachusetts General Hospital, 2012) redesigned the construct of autism, not only exonerating the mother but elevating her to valued brand labels of caregiver and advocate for a child branded as disabled despite the identical circumstances of parenting a child with unusual behaviors.

The current diagnosis of ASD is inferred from behavioral aberration, but depending on one's lens and valuation, it is outfitted with varied meanings. Just from a descriptive standpoint, the most contemporary, "hot off the press" behaviors necessary for being branded with ASD have finally emerged from closeted negotiation by the individuals who were appointed to pen the fifth edition of the American Psychiatric Association's *Diagnostic and Statistical Manual of Mental Disorders* (DSM). The text below reads as a publisher's advertisement, selling the new edition of the DSM to willing buyers with the grand narrative promising better science than the previous edition.

> One of the most important changes in the fifth edition of the Diagnostic and Statistical Manual of Mental Disorders (DSM-5) is to autism spectrum disorder (ASD). The revised diagnosis represents a

new, more accurate, and medically and scientifically useful way of diagnosing individuals with autism-related disorders.

(APA, 2013)

We return to a discussion of this taxonomy later in this chapter, but for now, we offer the DSM as evidence in support of the tautological design of autism that can thus be read as many meanings because of its circular reasoning. As we have discussed in previous chapters, tautology is quite profitable for those who know how to use it. The tautologist creates a construct on the basis of observation, names the essential observed criteria, and then counts their existence as empirical support for the reality of the phenomenon that he/she defined through initial observation, thereby reifying the existence of the branded entity that began with defining what was already observed. No cause is provided in DSM-5 nor is treatment specified. Consider the diagnostic process to illustrate. The purity of description thus offers the brand name for a range of valuation and speculation regarding why ASD occurs. The ASD criteria in DSM-5 stipulate:

> People with ASD tend to have communication deficits, such as responding inappropriately in conversations, misreading nonverbal interactions, or having difficulty building friendships appropriate to their age. In addition, people with ASD may be overly dependent on routines, highly sensitive to changes in their environment, or intensely focused on inappropriate items. Again, the symptoms of people with ASD will fall on a continuum, with some individuals showing mild symptoms and others having much more severe symptoms. This spectrum will allow clinicians to account for the variations in symptoms and behaviors from person to person.
>
> Under the DSM-5 criteria, individuals with ASD must show symptoms from early childhood, even if those symptoms are not recognized until later. This criteria change encourages earlier diagnosis of ASD but also allows people whose symptoms may not be fully recognized until social demands exceed their capacity to receive the diagnosis.
>
> (APA, 2013)

Even within description, the numbers of individuals who fit these criteria depend on meaning making; in other words, how each criterion is interpreted and then determined to meet eligibility factors that were already observed and diagnostically branded. The authors of this new edition, DSM-5, changed the criteria for ASD contained in previous editions, redesigning them as both more prevalent and potentially latent, despite the same youth exhibiting the identical behaviors that under the earlier design would not have secured an invitation into the park. So the circular thinking is political and axiological, bringing profound change in meaning to those who have not changed at all with the exception of new branding.

Just as diagnostic criteria to label behaviors pathological do not remain stationary and static, values attributed to the branded causes are equally as mobile. Autism spectrum disorders ascribed with pathological meaning are not as desirable in public or professional standing as those that move into the diversity suite. Thus, branded individuals lose even more worth as the behaviors move further from the mean of the behavioral bell curve as a result of the changes in measures and naming.

It is therefore not surprising that there is a growing backlash against devaluation of medicalized brands of ASD. This effort, rebranded as "neurodiversity," emulates the design of previous civil rights and anti-discrimination movements. At the center point of the neurodiversity texts lies the claim that autism is the medicalization and thus discrimination and devaluation of human difference, eccentricity, and plurality.

> the neurodiversity claim contains at least two different aspects. One aspect is that autism (or at least high-functioning autism) is not to be treated like a disability or a handicap but rather as a natural variation. The other aspect is about conferring rights and in particular value to the neurodiversity condition, perhaps again to high-functioning autism. This condition is not just natural and not pathological, but also valuable. The political claim of the neurodiversity movement goes beyond just giving rights to autistic persons similar to rights to handicapped people; it also claims for recognition and acceptance ... some of them (people with ASD diagnoses) are being harmed by it, because of the disrespect the diagnosis displays for their natural way of being.
>
> (Jaarsma and Welin, 2011: 20)

We find it curious that in denying the disability emblem, those who claim the name of neurodiversity unintentionally malign members trademarked as belonging to the disability club which they wish to escape, designing the meaning of "the handicapped brand" as one even those at the most rural ends of the bell curve do not want to wear.

Casok's poetry exemplifies the heart of neurodiversity design and highlights the devaluing subtexts contained in the disability brand.

Autistic Rap

My mum misses me, my family dissess me.
Society dehumanises me. Despises me. Criticize me.
They are fossilized. I do not apologise.

I am ridiculed, violated, bullied. Ignored.
I am stared at, laughed at spat at.
What have I done to you? I mind my own business.
I do not listen. I do not see or give you the third degree.
I am holistic, simplistic certainly not materialistic.

My disability is your prejudice, systemic injustice.
Your presumptions and assumptions.
Intolerance of my difference.
Your misperception I take objection.

I am not a disorder, im not a symptom. Its not catching.
Im not a label or a vegetable or a crystal angel.
Im not a lost soul or out of control.
Im not from outer space, or a charity case.
I am suppressed not possessed.
Institution is not a solution.

I don't have a condition, im not an exhibition.
Im not an artist or a musician, or on a hostile expedition.
Maybe I will become a politician.

Im not an Einstein or like Rain man.
Im not Pinocchio or Peter pan.
Im not ill, I don't want your pills
Or your out of date text book skills.

Im not a zoo exhibition or a freak show,
Im a feeling human from head to toe.
I can get lost in the worlds beauty
So don't make me fit in your reality.
Why should I conform
To what you think is the norm

Like a Big Brother contestant
All we want is acceptance.
The world loves Happyfeet Nemo and Shrek
So should I paint my face green and be on Star Trek?

I create employment and opportunity,
I educate the world in diversity.
You cant bleed the devil out of me,
People like me have influenced history.
You need me.

So don't cure me.
Don't pity me just let me be.

(Casdok, 2007)

Arguments against neurodiversity branding maintain the corporeality of autism and have attached yet another brand, pervasive developmental disability (PDD) to the range of behaviors that render an individual eligible for both. Individuals who have been branded with ASD or PDD are lieges of their own unique service system, one that provides alternative space for individuals who do not neatly fit into a world unwelcoming to those who reside beyond ±2 standard deviations away from the structural and functional neurological mean. Even virtual space joins a safe retreat imbuing places and resources with the ambiguous meaning of segregated comfort.

> The role of Internet-based information forums, the establishment and maintenance of interest and activist groups on both sides of the aisle has been significant, especially for the neurodiversity contingent. The neurodiversity movement is comprised in large part of people who are themselves autistic and are unable or uncomfortable navigating and initiating more traditional information collectives, which generally requires just the sorts of communication and social skill sets those with autism characteristically lack.
>
> (Cohen, 2010)

We would be remiss not to mention the myriad other causes proposed for ASD, many of which have been dismissed as bogus by legitimate knowers, including mumps, measles, and rubella vaccine, mercury, gluten, and other dietary allergies, viruses, ingested substances, both prenatally and postnatally, and so forth. While many of these explanations have been discredited through scientific narrative, many still hold meaning for believers and attract affinity groups even on Facebook.

Each explanation designs ASD differently and assigns a continuum of value through devaluation to those who display the formal ASD brand name. Again, we are not taking a position on the viability of neurodiversity, genetic, or other explanations but discuss ASD and its various designs as seductive of depth of thought.

First, with regard to genetic design of ASD, we raise the issue of violation of the "normal" chromosomal design for identified conditions, and wonder if "standard genetic composition" is analogous to the construction of the normal curve, albeit through a sophisticated system of visual and textual signifiers about the human genome. Second, what and who are included in calculating the genetic "norm"? What and who are excluded? What should be considered as extreme and unhealthy variation and what is merely a behavioral or visual burp? How should the environment be designed to welcome and facilitate flourishing the full range of ASD brands? These questions hover and emerge throughout the book until they are fully activated in Part 2.

Before we leave ASD, we present two compelling pieces of evidence for the power and place of market strategies in diverse branding, one a logofied "pride" T-shirt (Figure 4.1), and the other a cause-branded credit card designing ASD as the object of charity.

Figure 4.1 "Pride" T-Shirt

Source: Photograph by Stephen Gilson. Available from National Symposium on
   Neurodiversity at Syracuse University;
   http://neurodiversitysymposium.wordpress.com/wear-your-support-for-neurodiversity

We now turn to the brand name, psychiatric disability, for further analysis of axiological design and branding of disability.

Psychiatric disability

This region of designed disability is complex and raises some points that are similar to the discussion of ASD, including the cause-marketed credit card (APA, 2012) and the pride T-shirt (NAMI, 2014). Of particular overlap is the design of behavior into the normal and abnormal binary hosted on a third-dimensional backdrop of longitudinal maturation that prescribes how humans should generally act as they age (DePoy and Gilson, 2012). Curiously, the logo on the National Alliance on Mental Illness T-shirt reads "Normal's Overrated" (Figure 4.2).

Despite the fashion and spending themes, we chose to enter into the domain of psychiatric disability, in particular, the spectrum of "depressive" disorders, for a different set of explorations than we encountered in ASD.

Figure 4.2 Got a T-shirt

In this section, we analyze the roles of pharmaceuticals, the mental health park, the medicalization model of disability, and media branding in the perpetuation and axiological design of sadness as pathology, chronicity, and the crafting of the "mental patient."

> Depression may be described as feeling sad, blue, unhappy, miserable, or down in the dumps. Most of us feel this way at one time or another for short periods. True clinical depression is a mood disorder in which feelings of sadness, loss, anger, or frustration interfere with everyday life for weeks or longer.
>
> (Berger and Zieve, 2012)

Inherent once again in the definition above is the bell curve, as the object of treatment is visualized only in undesirable contrast to normal fluctuations of mood. Consistent with our discussion of ASD, we do not take a position on the truth-value of depression, its prevalence, incidence or even the accuracy of the many explanations for human feeling and behavior. Rather, this diagnostic repertoire foregrounds the complex issues involved in the axiological branding and design of mood as pathology and who benefits or does not from redesigning atypical mood towards "normalcy."

There is no dearth of popular, clinical, and critical literature on depression (Dunner, 2007; Neurocritic, 2009; NIMH, 2009). In his watershed book, *Listening to Prozac*, Kramer (1997) brought his query of the role of psychoactive drugs to public recognition. Although Kramer did not refute the presence of depression as a disease state, his more profound concern was the effect of Prozac in redesigning personalities into valued mood pastiches. Building on this work, many scholars have moved in diverse directions, from eschewing depression as pathology at all to supporting it's physiological existence and thus its multiplicity of causes as environmental, psychological, chemical, genetic and so forth. On the heels of causal legitimacy are treatments ranging in scope from basic psychotherapy and pharmacology to bee-sting therapy (Novalla, 2012).

Our concern in this chapter is not with the existence of human sadness and despondency, which we do not question, but rather with two major value themes, the design and branding as disability in the name of profit and the crafting of the undesirable "mental patient."

Design and branding mood as disability

The impending revision of each DSM has incited as much criticism as applause. In 2007, Horowitz and Wakefield (2007) lobbed serious indictments at mental health providers and pharmaceutical companies for their role in pathologizing, devaluing, and branding "normal" levels of human emotion as disability. (Once again, implicit in this claim is the lowly pedigree of the disability brand name, one that no one wants to wear.)

More recently, the inclusion of grief in the DSM-5 as mental illness rather than human response to loss has heightened accusations of the purposive swelling of the potential population who can be designed as sick and relocated from mourning loss into the psychiatric park for prolonged psychotherapy and psychoactive medications (Gever, 2012). Orr (2010) claims that this trend is designed as a form of pharmaceutical governance so to speak: "the biopsychiatric imaginary of brain dysfunction as the fundamental context for understanding psychic distress legitimates biological intervention as an appropriate, even exemplary, technique for regulating disorderly mentalities" (p. 355).

Referring to the shift from psychosocial to medical informatic language in an earlier edition of the DSM-III (APA, 1980), Orr's (2010) work is particularly convincing in exposing the lexical branding underbelly of meaning making in biopsychiatry. This linguistic turn met the purposes of aligning psychiatry with medicine, designing mental disease, legitimating professional surveillance of human behavior, and thus serving to flag an algorithmic treatment and thus control of human thought.

Dumit's (2012) ideas take Orr's (2010) work several steps further into the expansive material design of mentation and human health. The brand "at risk" opens the door for medicalization of potential loss of health for sturdy individuals who have not yet succumbed (Koch, 2012). Scientific narratives design health as a temporary valued condition to be preserved by the pharmacological industry. Changing the meaning of health to a state that needs to be maintained by prescription and regular ingestion of drugs increases the demand for pharmaceuticals.

Different from vaccines, which are intended to commit suicide by eradicating the undesirable conditions for which they are developed, at-risk status engorges the market through pseudo-scientific trickery. As example, advertising hosted by pharmaceutical companies masquerades as "scientific" questionnaires for the public both for self-diagnosis and then to legitimate to prescribers the need for drugs for what might, in the future, plague those who score in the at risk range. These surreptitious questionnaires are convincingly designed as authoritative, driving healthy people to beg for medication from health care providers to avoid sliding down the proverbial chute into mental illness (Manninen, 2006).

We logged onto WebMD (WebMD, 2013) to examine the depression screening instrumentation. We both completed it. The unconsidered context in this so-called screening tool for Stephen was his fall resulting in a fracture of his lumbar spine last year. The first page locates age and membership in male/female only categories, eliminating contemporary gender diversity from consideration. Moving to the second page, the question of previous diagnosis with depression is accompanied with what we see as an "infomercial" regarding the prevalence of depression. The meaning we attributed to it was to link the respondent to an affinity group or brand community (Einstein, 2012), decreasing the perceived stigma of revealing, to one's intimates, providers, and even Facebook friends, symptomology designed as depressive. Proceeding to the next page, the item reads, "Lately, have you been feeling down, depressed or hopeless most of the day?" Besides committing the double-barrel structural error of basic survey item construction, visual culture comes to town as an image of a woman appearing saddened. In our test case, a simple check affirming losing pleasure in activity that was once enjoyed, losing sleep, presence of muscle tension, pain, and increased fatigue, decrease in physical activity, all which are a function of Stephen's injury, begot the following "individualized report":

> Although your answers aren't like the ones usually provided by people suffering from major depression, they are similar to answers often given by people suffering from minor depression, dysthymia or other types of depression. However, only your doctor can properly diagnose and treat you. Please see your doctor so that you obtain a complete evaluation and diagnosis.
>
> Based on your responses, you are experiencing depression-like symptoms that are having an adverse impact on your life. Depression can be a debilitating condition that increases irritability, restlessness,

fatigue and feelings of worthlessness, and sadness, while decreasing sex drive, energy levels, and sleep. It can also hurt physically, with symptoms of persistent pain such as headaches, back pain, and digestive problems.

Liz then completed the instrument and received the identical report, despite different responses. The only variation in our reports was the recommendations to gender-specific screening tests for other conditions.

Again, we are not maligning the proliferation of information on the web, but using this exemplar to illustrate the design and branding of mental illness in the form of marketing disguised as science.

The crafting of the "mental patient"

By crafting of the mental patient, we refer to the meaning making of a mental health diagnosis as a reason for lifelong medication and mental health park containment (Manninen, 2006). Enter our friend and colleague, Jasmine, of course deidentified owing to stigma and negative evaluation. Jasmine was a promising academic, who had just received her PhD in philosophy. Moving to a new academic position away from family and friends, she sought mental health counseling for loneliness and mood fluctuations, and was ultimately diagnosed as bipolar disorder by her well-intended counseling professional. Jasmine was referred to a psychiatrist for medication management.

Over a two-year period, Jasmine's mood stabilized to what she described as the color gray. Along the longitudinal walk, Jasmine developed tremors, fatigue, and several other serious iatrogenic complications, including the inability to engage in writing and research necessary to acquire tenure and promotion. Rather than halting the onslaught of harmful consequences perpetrated by psychotropic drugs, additions amounting to a pharmaceutical buffet were prescribed, many to mediate the side effects of the original drug that was meant for healing. We were not surprised when Jasmine left work on long-term disability support and remains unemployed, yet medicated, three years later. Jasmine's counseling provider sent her home with some gifts, bipolar awareness factsheets to be distributed to family and friends, further branding her as a lifelong patient.

The story is not new or unique. Ostensibly purported as restoration to mental health, the patient is pharmaceutically captured, "chronisified" and then branded as of little or no value to the workplace. Such "patients" coalesce, inhabiting the mental health park or what we refer to as the psychiatricscape. By psychiatriscape we mean the physical, virtual, and conceptual spaces designated for individuals branded with psychiatric disability. These include housing, day treatment or "clubs," and institutions, the design of which is becoming a specialty within architecture. We were not surprised to find a website for the Design in Mental Health

Network (www.dimhn.org). This membership organization hosts an architectural specialty devoted to redesign of the institutional built environment into a psychiatricscape, now elevated to a health promotion practice through the creation of mood space (Spuybroek, 2012).

Now look at examples of virtual psychiatriscapes, such as the Depression and Bipolar Support Alliance (www.dbsalliance.org), affinity groups, complete with iPhone applications to design and affix disability branding to mood:

> StrengthofUs provides opportunities for you to connect with your peers and offer support, encouragement and advice and share your real world experiences, personal stories, creativity, resources and ultimately, a little bit of your wonderful and unique self. It is a user-generated and user-driven community; so basically it's whatever *you* make it. Everything here has been developed and created by and for young adults with you specifically in mind... because we think you're worth it! We hope every time you visit, you find hope, encouragement, support and most of all, the strength to live your dreams and goals.
>
> (strengthofus.org/)

> **DBSA** [Depression and Bipolar Association] **Wellness Tracker**
> Wellness involves your whole health – emotional and mental, as well as physical. The DBSA Wellness Tracker is a free, innovative, and user-friendly online tool that allows you to keep track of your emotional, mental, and physical health.
>
> Stay on track with DBSA Wellness Tracker. It's easy, takes only a few minutes a day, and, like the other tools in the Facing Us Clubhouse, it's free.
>
> (DBSA, n.d.)

Before we leave the domain of mental illness, we bring your attention to a contemporary form of meaning making and positive valuation of psychiatric disability, the fashionable. As an example, Mad Couture Catwalk not only reifies mental illness but stylizes it and designing eccentricity and creativity in its branding. The text under a photograph of a red and silver-slivered cape reads "Madness" and "genius" – especially creative genius – have long been thought to go hand-in-hand" (George-Parkin, 2012).

Reading further in the text, well-known clothing designers such as Yves Saint Laurent and Donatella Versace are branded as mentally ill, designing a high-brow, highly valued brand community that many would aspire to join. As we discuss below, the valuation of diverse disability labels and brands is dynamic, embedded within contexts that create differential hierarchies of meaning to disability brands. We refer to this phenomenon as the pecking order of pedigree.

The pecking order

Because worth, membership, acceptance, respect, and legitimacy are a matter of value, we address these important branding mechanisms in this chapter. Applied to disability, pecking order of pedigree refers to the designed and branded ordering of conditions on the worth continuum.

Disability pedigree is not a simple, monistic phenomenon. Context and purpose design value through mechanisms, only some of which are transparent and/or logical. So we approach this discussion from proximal to distal contexts to the extent possible. We also remind you that even within individual brand names such as ASD, diverse meanings and statuses inhere, depending on the density and extremity of the atypical, the brand owners, and the causal attributions.

Proximal contexts

By proximal, we refer to the valuation of diverse types of embodied notions of disability by disability brand communities. A more prevalent term to describe such groups in the current disability studies literature is "disability culture." Brown's narrative quoted below captures the basic elements that are common to most assertions of disability culture.

> People with disabilities have forged a group identity. We share a common history of oppression and a common bond of resilience. We generate art, music, literature, and other expressions of our lives and our culture, infused from our experience of disability. Most importantly, we are proud of ourselves as people with disabilities. We claim our disabilities with pride as part of our identity. We are who we are: we are people with disabilities.
>
> (Brown, 2003: 80–1)

In our own scholarship, we do not use the term "disability culture" for several reasons. First, in our earlier research when we were exploring disability as a social–cultural entity (Gilson and DePoy, 2004), we were unable to support the presence of, and identification with, disability culture in a diverse group of individuals across age and diagnostic spectra. Second, as reflected in the text above (Brown, 2003), the logic of disability as non-corporeal is internally contradictory with claimed membership in a group on the basis of an embodied impairment. Third, moving back to our current work, this book analyzes disability as designed and branded and thus the term "brand community," not disability culture, is both systematically supported and logically consistent with contemporary thinking.

The hierarchy of disability type first became apparent to us at a disability studies conference, a proximal context. Essentially, despite the rhetorical espousal of non-embodied models of disability, the hierarchy is composed of medicalized disability branding, much of it occurring through objects designed as disability paraphernalia. Highest in the pecking order tend to be those with the most widgets on electric wheelchairs, and blindness and deafness that are observably apparent and branded by accouterment. The second tier of acceptance includes ambulatory people with observable atypical gaits, amputations, or other recognizable impairments, along with disability park objects such as crutches, canes and prostheses. Attendees without visible trappings of impairment were met with limited enthusiasm. It was curious that many in the peripheral tier of unobservable branding asserted their disability legitimacy, authentic membership and attempted to climb the hierarchical ladder by orally branding themselves as owners of non-visible impairments such as psychiatric diagnoses, learning disability, autism, and so forth.

Clearly, gatherings of impairment brand communities sought credibility in proximal settings, connection, and political power through vocalizing disability identity, a technique used by many groups who have been subject to discrimination. As we discuss in subsequent chapters, rights movements in the mid and even late twentieth-century achieved some successes from declaring pride in their diversity, yet in the twenty-first century, we see design and branding as the more relevant power tools for social change.

Moving distally, the tables turn somewhat, but not a full 180 degrees. Wheelchair users, individuals who are blind, and those who are deaf are most privileged by the policy hierarchy as they are the primary recipients of accommodations and accessibility responses. Yet so-called equal rights for these three subgroups is mythic, as accommodations must be requested, their conferral is poorly enforced, and even a cursory response to improve access is excused from the table if affordability is raised as a barrier to expanding participation. The euphemisms in the United States, "undue hardship and reasonable accommodation" refer to the accommodator's financial status and capabilities, not to the individual requesting access. So the right to participate is usurped with what is deemed reasonable in light of what the accommodator claims to be able to afford and for whom. Moreover, attitudes, employment and equivalence of opportunity for these three groups remain restricted. Unlike the tarnished views of soldiers in the 1970s in the United States, attitudes towards veterans branded as disabled have been polished and now temporarily shine, until there is a profound request for access to employment. So we place veterans atop the temporary rhetorical hierarchy only.

The group of individuals branded with ASD seems to be up and coming on the disability funding hierarchy. Within the past ten years, funding for autism research and programming have exponentially increased, with National Institutes of Health, Obama, Maternal and Child Health in the lead and many clamoring for a piece of this lucrative pie (Associated Press, 2012). But the value stamped on ASD brand holders is oxymoronic and context dependent. The funding hierarchy is not designed to preserve neurodiversity, but rather to eliminate it. So while ASD is a hot topic and is well funded, this news is not good for those who perceive the ASD brand community as diverse rather than undesired.

Members of athletic groups branded as disabled or parathletes are making significant headway up the food chain as they gain recognition and raise debate about cyborgs and post-humanism (Scott, 2011). As example, until his fall from grace, Oscar Pistorius was a respected public figure. We are not surprised, given that he was not pitiable or villainous, and did not invoke aesthetic or existential anxiety, Harlan Hahn's terms for two responses respectively, "what if I looked like that," and "what if I were like that?" (Sandahl and Auslander, 2005). Similarly, Aimee Mullins started her career as an athlete, running on Cheetah legs.

So who is missing from the pecking orders in each of these contexts? We would suggest that individuals with intellectual and psychiatric impairment branding remain weighted down on the bottom rungs by negative valuation and stigma, particularly given the assumption that both of these groups are not viable wage earners. In addition, and to some extent differentiating psychiatric from intellectual impairment branding, the degree to which the condition is thought to be a choice of its owner is a major variable in how individuals fare on the pecking order. Those with intellectual impairment emblems are pitied and infantilized, while individuals with labels such as depression, except within the psychiatriscape and in public politically correct dialog, are often considered as counterfeit when they do not just "get over it."

The twenty-first-century post-postmodern world has transposed the branding hierarchy in some domains, particularly in the arts and entertainment arenas. For example, although controversial regarding legitimacy and morality, the presence of mobility props in Lady Gaga's (2009) video, *Paparazzi*, not only materialized but earned the brand "disability chic" (Stewart, 2013). *Push Girls*, a reality TV show on Sundance Channel chronicling four women who use wheelchairs for mobility, is now moving into its second season. Next, look at the text below describing actor, Mitch Longley, as a "wheeler," quite the linguistic turn, reflecting a move away from negative stigma and piteous stereotype to designed as desired and sexy.

> It's not easy to get fans, not to mention Hollywood execs, to look past the wheelchair and see the hunk and talent underneath, but Mitch Longley has made this far-fledged dream a reality. Since his breakout role in 1991 in the soap opera Another World, prefaced by a stint as a model and muse for Ralph Lauren (appearing in several print ads in the early 1990s), Mitch has been a regular face on network television ever since. And one of the few wheelers to make this happen (this guy really needs a website).

> (Tiffiny, 2013)

As reflected in this chapter, design and branding are omnipresent and potent in the chronological context of the twenty-first century. We suggest that both have been used in diverse ways for centuries to reflect and confer human valuation. Yet, not until the market economy became hegemonic were these strategies visualized as axiological change agents. In Part 2, we propose the beauty and power of design and branding if harnessed for advancing human flourishing and equivalence of value.

Summary

This chapter mined the potency of design and branding for creating and ascribing value texts. We began with the language theme, examining diagnostic lexicons as conferring the range of value to devalue. We then moved through visual culture and other design crafts as axiological, illustrating the pecking order of brand names, logos, objects, and spaces. The chapter concluded with twenty-first-century disability chic, in which disability branding is looking up, providing a trailer for what is to come in Part 2.

References

APA (1980) *Diagnostic and Statistical Manutal of Mental Disorders III* (3rd ed.). Washington, DC: American Psychiatric Association.

APA (2012) Bank of America. American Psychiatric Association. Available online at www.psychiatry.org/join-participate/member-benefits/bank-of-america (accessed January 15, 2014).

APA (2013) Autism Spectrum Disorder. Fact Sheet. Arlington, VA: American Psychiatric Publishing. Available online at www.psychiatry.org/autism (accessed January 15, 2014).

Associated Press (2012) Autusm Research May be About to bear Fruit. *Fox News*, April 10. Available online at www.foxnews.com/health/2012/04/10/autism-research-may-be-about-to-bear-fruit/#ixzz2GwRwa4rT (accessed January 15, 2014).

Autism Speaks (2012) Large DSM-5 Study Suggests Most Children Will Keep ASD Diagnosis. *Autism Speaks*, October 2. Available online at www.autismspeaks.org/science/science-news/large-dsm-5-study-suggests-most-children-will-keep-asd-diagnosis (accessed February 15, 2014).

Berger, F. K., and Zieve, D. (2012) Major Depression. *A.D.A.M. Medical Encyclopedia, PubMed Health*, August 3. Available online at www.ncbi.nlm.nih.gov/pubmed health/PMH0001941 (accessed January 15, 2014).

Berntson, A., Jarnemo, C., and Philipson, M. (2006) *Branding and Gender: How Adidas Communicate Gender Values*. Master's Thesis, Business Administration, Karlstad University. Available online at www.diva-portal.org/smash/get/diva2:5954/FULLTEXT01 (accessed January 15, 2014).

Blackett, T. (2003) *Brands and Branding*. New York: Economist Intelligence Unit.

Brown, S. (2003) *Movie Stars and Sensuous Scars: Essays on the Journey from Disability Shame to Disability Pride*. Lincoln, NE: iUniverse.

Carlson, E. A. (2011) The Body as a Biological and Genetic Entity. *Social Research*, 78 (2), 349–58.

Casdok (2007) *Autism Rap.* Available online at http://motherofshrek.blogspot.co.uk/2007/08/autistic-rap.html (accessed January 15, 2014).

Cohen, K. A. (2010) Neurodiversity: Conflicting Perspectives on Autism. *Verstehen: McGill's Undergraduate Sociology Journal.* Available online at http://mcgillverstehen2010.weebly.com/neurodiversity-conflicting-perspectives-on-autism.html (accessed January 15, 2014).

DBSA (n.d.) DBSA Wellness Tracker. Depression and Bipolar Support Alliance. Available online at www.dbsalliance.org/site/PageServer?pagename=wellness_tracker (accessed January 15, 2014).

DePoy, E., and Gilson, S. (2011) *Studying Disability.* Los Angeles, CA: Sage.

DePoy, E., and Gilson, S. (2012) *Human Behavior Theory and Applications: A Critical Thinking Approach.* Thousand Oaks, CA: Sage.

DePoy, E., and Gilson, S. (2013) Disability Design and Branding: Rethinking Disability for the 21st Century. In L. Davis, *The Disability Studies Reader* (4 ed.). New York, NY: Routledge, pp. 477–88.

Dumit, J. (2012) *Drugs for Life.* Durham, NC: Duke University Press.

Dunner, D. L. (chair) (2007) Preventing Recurrent Depression: Long-Term Treatment for Major Depressive Disorder. *Primary Care Companion Journal of Clinical Psychiatry*, 9 (3), 214–23.

Einstein, M. (2012) *Compassion Inc.* Berkeley, CA: University of California Press.

Feinstein, A. (2010) *A History of Autism: Conversation with the Pioneers.* Malden, MA: Wiley.

George-Parkin, H. (2012) Do Fashion Design and Mental Illness Go Hand-in-Hand? *Styleite*, April 15. Available online at www.styleite.com/media/madness-genius (accessed January 15, 2014).

Gever, J. (2012) DSM-5 Critics Pump Up the Volume. *Medpage Today*, February 29. Available online at www.medpagetoday.com/psychiatry/dsm-5/31416 (accessed January 15, 2014).

Gilson, S., and DePoy, E. (2004) Disability, Identity, and Cultural Diversity. *Review of Disability Studies*, 1 (1), 16–23.

Horowitz, A., and Wakefield, J. *The Loss of Sadness.* New York: Oxford University Press.

Jaarsma, P., and Welin, S. (2011) Autism as a Natural Human Variation: Reflections on the Claims of the Neurodiversity Movement. *Health Care Analysis*, 20 (1), 20–30.

Jordan, R. (2009) Medicalization of autism spectrum disorders. *British Journal of Hospital Medicine*, 70 (3), 128–9.

Kazmierczak, E. T. (2003) Design as Meaning Making: From Making Things to the Design of Thinking. *Design Issues*, 19 (2), 45–59.

Klien, N. (2009) *No Logo.* (10th anniv. ed.) Toronto, ON, Canada: Random House.

Koch, B. (2012) The Medicalization of Nerdiness. *Soc'ing Out Loud*, February 1. Available online at http://bradleykoch.blogspot.co.uk/2012/02/medicalization-of-nerdiness.html (accessed February 15, 2014).

Kramer, P. (1997) *Listening to Prozac.* New York: Penguin.

Kurzman, C. (2008) Meaning-Making in Social Movements. *Anthropological Quarterly*, 81 (1), 5–15.

Lady Gaga (2009) *Paparazzi.* Retrieved from Youtube, November 25. Available online at www.youtube.com/watch?v=d2smz_1L2_0 (accessed January 15, 2014).

Manninen, B. (2006) Medicating the Mind: a Kantian Analysis of Overprescribing Psychoactive Drugs. *Journal of Medical Ethics*, 32 (2), 100–5.

Massachusetts General Hospital (2012) New Genes Contributing to Autism Discovered; Genetic Links Between Neurodevelopment and Psychiatric Disorders. *Science Daily*, April 19. Available online at www.sciencedaily.com/releases/2012/04/120419121525.htm (accessed February 15, 2014).

NAMI (2013) Welcome to Strength of Us. National Alliance on Mental Illness. Available online at http://strengthofus.org (accessed January 15, 2014).

NAMI (2014) House M.D. T-Shirt Partnership. National Alliance on Mental Illness. Available online at www.nami.org/Template.cfm?Section=House_T-Shirt_PartnershipandTemplate=/ContentManagement/ContentDisplay.cfmand ContentID=72825 (accessed January 15, 2014).

Neurocritic (2009) Myth of the Depression Gene. *The Neurocritic*, June 18. Available online at http://neurocritic.blogspot.com/2009/06/myth-of-depression-gene.html (accessed February 15, 2014).

NIMH (2009) *Men and Depression*. Bethesda, MD: National Institute of Mental Health, January 21. Available online at www.nimh.nih.gov/health/publications/men-and-depression/causes-of-depression.shtml (accessed February 15, 2014).

Novalla, S. (2012) Bee Venom Therapy Update. *Science-Based Medicine*, June 20. Available online at www.sciencebasedmedicine.org/bee-venom-therapy-update (accessed January 15, 2014).

Orr, J. (2010) Biopsychiatry and the Informatics of Diagnosis. In A. Clarke, L. Mamo, J. Fosket, J. Fishman, and J. Shim (eds.), *Biomedicalization, Technoscience, Health and Illness in the US*. Durham, NC: Duke University Press, pp. 352–79.

Parent Dish. (n.d.) Celebrities and Other Famous Folks with Autism. Available online at http://gblsharing.app.aol.com/pop-up (accessed February 15, 2014).

Pink, D. L. (2006) *A Whole New Mind: Why Right-Brainers Will Rule the Future*. New York: Penguin.

Sandahl, C., and Auslander, P. (eds.) (2005) *Bodies In Commotion: Disability and Performance*. Ann Arbor, MI: University of Michigan Press.

School of Visual Arts. (2012) Masters in Branding. SVA Branding Studio. Available online at branding.sva.edu (accessed February 15, 2014).

Scott, J. (2011) The Architecture of Humanism: A study in the History of Taste. In M. F. Gage, *Aesthetic Theory: Essential Text for Architecture and Design*. New York: W.W. Norton, pp. 179–96.

Spuybroek, L. (2012) The Ages of Beauty. In J. Brouwer, A. Mulder, and L. Spuybroek (eds.), *Vital Beauty: Reclaiming Aesthetics in the Tangle of Technology and Nature*. Rotterdam: V2 Publishing.

Stewart, D. (2013) Questions About the High Fashion and Domestic Violence in Lady GaGa's Video. *Jezebel*, January 3. Available online at http://jezebel.com/5285868/questions-about-the-high-fashion—domestic-violence-in-lady-gagas-video (accessed January 15, 2014).

Tiffiny. (2013) SCI Superstar: Mitch Longley. *Spinalpedia*, January 3. Available online at www.spinalpedia.com/blog/2013/01/page/5 (accessed January 15, 2014).

Tokuhama, C. (2011) Consumption, A Modern Affliction: Branding Culture, Youth Identity and College Admission. *Journal of College Admission*, (210), 32–8.

Walters, H. (2011) Design and Business Education: The System is not Good Enough. *Observatory*, May 31. Available online at http://observatory.designobserver.com/feature/design-and-business-education-the-system-is-not-good-enough/27658 (accessed January 15, 2014).

WebMD (2013) Depression Assessment. WebMD. Available online at www.webmd.com/depression/depression-health-check/default.htm (accessed January 15, 2014).

5 Designing individual and collective identity

With guest author Aimee Mullins

In this chapter, we enter the world of identity through popular culture and media, both crucial elements of creating identity in the 21st century visual and material culture. Because of her prominence and public identity, we rely on Aimee Mullins as guest author to reflect these constructs and how her interactions, interests, history, and personal and public tensions have evolved throughout her life. As Aimee states, "to those who observe me, I am both disabled and not-disabled enough to neatly fit into an expected disability identity category."

Aimee has engendered a full scope of responses as she waltzes in public life with diverse and changeable heights made possible through innovative prosthetic design and her own creativity. Although Aimee does not fully agree with us, as you will read in her words below, we see her presence in fashion, beauty, and film as one of several important beacons informing critical undesign and redesign of disability. Her influence and potential to elicit change is a function of her own insights and her hold on the gaze of the public eye.

Defining terms

Before beginning our conversation with Aimee, we erect a definitional and theoretical scaffold to set her life and narrative within the scholarly trajectory of this work. The usage of the term "identity" dates back to the late 1500s, denoted to mean "sameness" (Harper, 2001–2013). Curiously, contemporary usage serves single as well as hoarded masters, in locating identity as both an interior uniqueness and exterior brand:

- sameness of essential or generic character in different instances;
- sameness in all that constitutes the objective reality of a thing: oneness;
- the distinguishing character or personality of an individual: individuality;
- the relation established by psychological identification.

(Harper, 2001–2013)

There has been a large literature on the nature of human identity, its causes, and to some extent, its absence (Popova, n.d.). We build on the work of Olson (2012) as the basis for organizing a discussion of identity that is relevant to the scope of disability identity design and branding. The construct of identity addresses the following questions:

- Who am I?
- What is constant about me?
- How do I come to know who I am? How do others come to know who I am? How do these perspectives differ from one another?
- How am I similar to others and to whom? Different from others and from whom?
- What else could I be?
- At what point am I no longer myself?
- How do I fit within personhood?

Each question is not only pertinent to understanding the scope of disability design and branding but is crucial for informing undesign and redesign as well.

"Who am I" and constancy refer to one's sense of self. For those who espouse the construct of enduring identity, this sense is considered both deeply personal as well as shaped by context (Regehr, 2006). Distinguishing features can be stable or fleeting, or even fickle (Hutson, 2013), observable or invisible, shared, or kept in a secret compartment. As stated by Popova (n.d.) in her perusal of various perspectives bearing on identity constancy,

> Here is an omnibus of definitions and insights from notable cross-disciplinary thinkers, from philosophy to neuroscience to literature, underpinning which is a shared sentiment that "character" is fluid and *responsive to context*, rather than a static and unflinching set of traits.
>
> (Popova, n.d.)

The epistemic questions (How can one come to know self and others? How does one document and communicate this knowledge?) are fodder for much debate, often resulting in stalemate. Can one know oneself, and through what evidence? Can one know another, and through what evidence? Responses to these questions, the tasks of coming to know the nature of one's own personhood, the humanness of others, and the data verifying diverse identity theories have captivated human thinking and deliberation since ancient times. It is curious that despite the absence of consensus, the contemporary story told by measurement is well oiled and frequently inscribed as the evidence-based means to design constancy of identity in the service of prediction. Applied to disability design, enumerators look at prevalence and incidence of pathological condition or impairment as the basis for formulating disability identity, even when professing to espouse identities constructed by social expectations rather than numerically configured as embodied impairment (DePoy and Gilson, 2011).

We do not even begin to reply to the identity questions above, given proportions of this leviathan. Rather, the queries stand as a portal to conceptualizing identity as a multi-faced phenomenon that has been explored and theorized through perspectives ranging in scope from the microcellular to the ethereal interactive. Identity makes its appearance in this chapter because of its centrality in disability and diversity dialog, and its enmeshment with design and branding of personhood, character, membership, and self-reflection.

One concept within identity theory that helps organize further analysis of its scope is identity negotiation. Brought to disability in large part by Goffman (1961), identity negotiation theory places identity on an interactive stage. Thus identity is contrived as multifaceted with private, public, socially specific, intimate, expectancy, and role elements (Ting-Toomey, 2011). Because identity negotiation theory crafts identity as dynamic and ranging from publicly conferred to privately coveted, it directs us to conceptualize identity both as designed and agentic in its own potential for undesign and redesign. What resonates with identity for our scholarly agenda is the power of person branding through the eyes and words of others, along with the gift of identity negotiation of self-knowledge, design, and self-projection through observable and conceptual emblems. Aimee Mullins eloquently speaks to these points as she both eschews disability identity for herself while accepting it for others who choose its power to craft membership and legitimacy. Before hearing her words, we take another short foray, this time into the literature on disability identity.

Disability identity: self selected or assigned design?

The literature on disability as personal and collective identity is well known within disability studies, but not a frequent speaker beyond its boundaries. Here, we provide just a brief overview of the tenets as the basis for understanding how individuals design themselves and are stylized by others as disabled. Because we discuss the role of spaces, objects, policies, (Linton, 1998), and other entities in the scope and craft of current disability design in other chapters, we aim this chapter at the stories of embodied atypical as both captured and imposed identity.

As a brief review, countering the embodied deficit identity of self-proclaimed or otherwise-named members of the disability club, individuals fitting into the embodied atypical (including diverse conditions that may not be visible) have requisitioned disability as a defining characteristic, one that endowed and thus ostensibly redesigned the devalued body with pride and esteem. Similar to other minority pride movements, proponents of disability identity espoused it in diverse configurations from fully corporeal, assigned as brand name in the format of a diagnosis, to individual-personal through chosen group solidarity.

Johnstone (2004) proposed six categories of disability identities appearing in the literature: socially ascribed, disempowering; overcompensating; identities that shift focus away from disabilities; empowerment; complex; and common identity. This work reflects the state-of-the-art disability studies thinking in 2004, yet for contemporary analysis, two hollows appear, the missing articulation of a definition of disability, and disability as a function of unknowns.

We suggest that omitting a clear lexical description of disability relegates it back to the body despite contestations to the contrary, an unintentional, logical burp, symptomatic of much of the disability studies literature (DePoy and Gilson, 2011). The second fissure, anonymous assigners of identity, is particularly significant to observe and repair for understanding disability design and branding. Yet, even with these empty spots, the literature on disability identity in the latter half of the twentieth century was groundbreaking, successful in part in burglarizing disability from the medicalized institution and attempting to land it's reconceptualization in the laps of those who were object and subject of medical diagnostic deficit explanations.

Visit with Linton for an example. In her seminal work, she stated,

> We are as Crosby, Stills and Nash told their Woodstock audience, "letting our freak flags fly." And we are not only the high-toned wheelchair athletes seen in TV adds but the gangly, pudgy, lumpy and bumpy of is, declaring that shame will no longer structure our wardrobe or our discourse. We are everywhere these days … We are all bound together, not by this list of our collective symptoms but by the social and political circumstances that have forged us as a group.
>
> (Linton, 1998: 4)

Disability identity moved to a different location as the literature evolved and expanded in complexity, sophistication and dissonance. Haller, Dorries and Rahn (2006) acknowledged the critical importance of the language theme in print and electronic media in changing disability imagery and valuation, albeit a process that has not yet met its goal of eliminating stigma.

While not yet actualized, we agree with Murugami's vision:

> a person with disability has the capability of constructing a self-identity not constituted in impairment but rather independent of it, and of accepting impairment as a reality that he or she lives with without losing a sense of self.
>
> (Murugami, 2009)

In the current visual culture and advanced market economy, disability identity is filling a niche as it goes into business, illuminating the importance of design and branding as strategies for undesign and redesign. Consider Lime Connect as exemplar:

> Lime Connect is looking to Re-Brand disability. They feel that employers historically have seen disability hiring as something "good to do." Individuals with disabilities attend schools like Princeton, Duke, and Georgetown. They are quality candidates. The team at Lime Connect sees a disability as a characteristic, not a definition.
>
> (Lime Connect, 2011)

The last sentence in the quote from Lime Connect links us to our guest, Aimee Mullins, who is introduced through Blinn's (2009) words in his review of Graham Pullin's (2009) book, *Disability Meets Design*. Given her view on beauty and adornment as transformative, we expect that Aimee may not agree with all that Blinn has said, but the story that he weaves in this short excerpt raises the seminal issues to which we believe Aimee speaks.

> While the gorgeous carved legs that she modeled for Alexander McQueen were striking, it was the functional but aesthetically unorthodox "cheetah" legs that brought her to public prominence and allowed her to transcend preconceptions by competing with Division I athletes and then setting Paralympics records.
>
> Perhaps the trouble with expecting prosthetics to transcend human preconception on a fashionable basis alone is that culture itself transcends fashion. Indeed, fashion trends are often originated by those of sufficient social status to ignore preconceived trends (think rock and roll style). Consequently the best lifestyle improvement for the "impaired" is to allow them the facility to excel within society...Aimee Mullins' legs exist because of a complex interaction between scientists, engineers and every human being who has ever added value to the world economy. The transformative moment for the culture was when a talented and charismatic figure like Mullins met Ossur's Flex Foot Cheetah leg.
>
> (Blinn, 2009)

Talking with Aimee Mullins

The discussion with Aimee occurred in early 2013. We took the liberty of organizing the interview in three sections: an overview of personal and public identity today, how she arrived at this point, and her current life and thinking.

Let's listen

Being thought of as beautiful is new for me. I will take it as long as I have it. It is a step up. A couple years ago, just to fess up, I was president of the women's sports foundation. The black-and-white image taken by Harold Shotz of me in my sprinting legs appeared in an issue of *Sports Illustrated*. I was away, before internet was everywhere. When I returned I learned that there was this hubbub from the leadership about some anonymous feminist blogger who wrote an attack on the *Sports Illustrated* piece. She claimed that I was being objectified. Rather than being lauded for my accomplishments she was distressed that the photo essay was too sexy. Her concern was with the objectification of my body as sexy? Wait a minute!!!! That someone thought this photo was too sexy to be representative as an athlete was a step up for me. That you can look at an image of a woman wearing two prosthetic legs and see "too sexy" is a huge step up. It was only five years ago that Aunt Millie and the massage therapist were saying, you would be so pretty if it weren't for your legs. The women's foundation took the image off their website. I was livid.

You can't have it both ways. You cannot lambaste the idea that we have societally accepted conventions of what is attractive and then at the same time throw darts at people you think fit that vision. The legs, the McQueen legs and glass legs are so beautiful. Now I am going the other way from awww...so sorry to how beautiful...The man, a shoe designer, who worked on my wooden legs came up totally emotional, for him it was a touchstone in his career. It transformed what he thought about shoes as prosthetic.

I have been with the same man for twenty-two years, and we have chosen our lifestyle. He is beautiful and is a beautiful person. In certain parts of the world to be thirty and unmarried is unheard of. So when I was in Egypt to give a talk this guy in the audience, who was an entry level physician for this company, cornered me, wanting to know why I was not married. He lamented, "oh he won't marry you because of your legs." Wait another minute. I had just been paid a nice sum of money to speak on whatever I wanted to speak about and this man felt sorry for me? So I will take the step up. Oh my God, I am being objectified and it is a step up to be objectified like every other woman. It was the first time I had that thought. It is not my aim nor my preference that women be objectified for their bodies but that is a separate issue. I'll take the step up. Otherwise I am somebody's inspiration, "Good for you." Wow, despite those legs they let you on the runway with Naomi Campbell? I am not saying that someone who owns words like crip and disabled does not have a right to do that. There is a hallmark of this society, it is personal choice and customized lifestyle.

Looking back

My father emigrated here and my mother is one of many siblings. We were not affluent at all as they both worked in several jobs to make ends meet. I was very much a tomboy and much more comfortable being boyish, in every sense of the word, gawky and awkward. I had braces and head-gear that moved my jaw. I had to do all those stretches that kids did when you had plaster casts on both legs. But I have vivid memories of a shoebox that shaped my identity.

This old shoebox contained treasures that belonged to my mother, but which she sparingly used. She had been a Franciscan nun for five years of her life, prior to getting married, so she was not indulgent, vain, or self focused. I had a childhood where it was constantly reinforced that everyone else came before me. I did not know what beauty meant, I did not know what was meant by ugly feet or a good ass until I was twenty-three. But I had an understanding as I was playing in that makeup box. I felt different. I was mesmerized by Cleopatra and Liz Taylor with those incredible eyes. When I played with that box, I could transform myself. I loved Joan of Arc and Amelia Earhart. I loved women who seemed iconic and looks were certainly part of that for a young girl. I could be them. And the idea of transformation stayed with me.

When I left small-town PA I had four years of Washington DC around kids who came from wealth. From them I learned that the world works through connections but I did not fully understand how to do that until I started working in fashion when I was twenty-three. My first fashion cover was actually fifteen years ago.

I remember ten years ago, I was bemoaning a situation to Billy Jean King, about being used as a poster child. What she said was powerful "I don't know what you are talking about. Pressure is a privilege. The good news is you have a brain and a voice and have been given the platform to say what you think. You do not need to stand for anyone else other than you. If I do not say these things, others will say them for you. If you can see it, you can be it. No one ever gives you your power, you have to take it."

On that note, I remember the first time I read someone's academic assertions about me . . . There was this guy who really wrote things that were shocking. He was writing about the objectification of people with disability and used me as the prime example, "she was cyborgyzed, narcissistically complicit on her own subjugation." It was so personal, it was a personal attack. I am not some dead historic figure, I am alive and living my life. There are people who would love to believe I would like to be subjugated in a kind of an erotic way. Really the only one who objectified me in this way is this guy. I was purely a figure to be dissected and analyzed from afar. He did not treat me like a human being.

I have had a public life for over twenty years so my life is there. I have carefully rejected the triumph over tragedy narrative. It is a template for lots of people and that is their prerogative but being a threat to people, making them a little uncomfortable with what box to put me in took my insides some time to catch up. In my younger days, I did have a deep desire to be understood, but I had to abandon that and I am fine with it now to the point of wanting to entitle a book of my memoirs "The Provacateur." I think I can be that voice without bludgeoning those who disagree with me. I feel more beautiful now because I am myself.

This idea of transformation brought me to knowing that acting was going to be the first thing I wanted to do. It is such a relief to be someone else. It was escape and I could escape from the hero or freak dichotomy by changing my design.

I believe that people have good intentions so I try to find elegant gracious ways to counter being dehumanized. A couple years ago I was asked to do an AMA on Reddit. It is a terrifying thing to say ask me anything. Someone asked a question and pointed out to me, your success is based on your good looks, your level of education and your financial wealth. What would you say to that? I basically wrote in a kinder, gentler way asking this questioner, what is the point of saying that, I am not disabled enough and I don't deserve what I have achieved? I did not have a community, I never met other amputees until I was eighteen. I am living my life, exploring things that are interesting to me. If the world did not think what I was doing was interesting, I would not have a career. Listen first to the statement and then to the question and finally what I wrote back.

> I LOVED your TED Talk about your many pairs of legs (It's not fair having twelve pairs of legs) and it completely changed by view on people with physical disabilities. Whenever I get the opportunity, I send the link to people so they can watch it also, it is by far one of my favorites. However, someone pointed out to me that your success was due to your good looks, level of education and financial wealth. That, if you were the victim of a land mine in Cambodia, you would not be looking at your disability as an opportunity for growth. Any thoughts on that?

First, thank you for the kind words about that TED Talk ... glad it had such an impact on you. Okay, this is another tricky question for me, one that I honestly have avoided answering until NOW. I did say AMA so here we go.

The particular response of the kind of haters you mention surprised the hell outta me, because it's such troll-y behavior. What is their point, really? Obviously, we ALL use whatever skill sets we have to do what we can, and no, I'm not from Cambodia, and I didn't become an amputee from an exploded landmine. This might shock them to hear this, but I have never pretended to be those things, and I'm not going to beg forgiveness from them for not being those things. Where I come from is on the record, although I have never flaunted it because it's background, and doesn't have to do with the ideas explored in that TED Talk. My father emigrated here with very little resources outside of his grit and determination, and my mother is one of eleven children – again, no affluence or connections to speak of. Both my parents worked multiple jobs. As any child from an immigrant household can tell you, education is paramount. I used my significant time spent in hospitals as a child to read everything I could get my hands on, and then I wrote my own stories and plays. Making honor roll with straight A's was expected (demanded, really... if I wanted to have any sort of extracurricular life), so I am also really proud of attaining my "level of education," which was afforded to me via a full academic scholarship. That was a real victory for me because then I could use my savings from the paper route I had since age twelve to pay rent and eat and afford basic car insurance/gas money in college. I also had an after-school job since the age of fifteen and worked full time during my summer "breaks" since that time too. I started my babysitting and snow-shoveling "businesses" when I was eight, so by high school I was looking to transition to something approaching minimum wage. (Once a hustler... always a hustler!) And that is really what building this multifaceted "career" has been – a very long, continuous hustle. The "financial wealth" you mention has really only happened in the last two years, and that's the truth. I have had the kind of wealth that matters way before that – I had fabulous adventures and love and was lucky enough to meet extraordinary people (and people who would let me borrow great clothes) who gave me the emotional and psychological support to keep going with my instincts. But it took me ten years of eking it out to actually make any money from anything, which is partially why this patchwork career developed as it did... I had to keep all plates spinning at once to just be able to break even (and there were plenty of years where I didn't quite muster that).

It's all there as plain as day, but it amazes me that people think it just dropped out of the sky for me... like my opportunities just "materialized" without an extraordinary amount of work and persistence on my part. There were no athletes with prosthetic legs running in the NCAA before me; no Wheaties box deals or sponsorships for "people like me," no matter how many world records we set. Outside the singular case of Jim Abbott, there weren't any athletes with "disabilities" before me who were able to convince an agent to take them on as a client. I actually had the very first agent I interviewed with (one of the most powerful sports agents ever at IMG) write me this past summer, to talk about Oscar Pistorius, and they told me that I was ten years before my time, and they knew it. They knew there was very little financial opportunity they could secure for me then, even if I did have plenty of charisma and talent. "There was just no market for you yet, you had to go out and create it." There sure as hell weren't any runway models with prosthetic legs, and no agents with open arms in that industry either. I honestly did not make one dime in modeling until I signed my global contract with L'Oréal Paris last year. How easy do you think it was to get an agent/manager in the acting business? Re: getting all these pairs of legs, I did what any hustler would do. I traded what I had to get what I wanted. I offered up myself as a guinea pig to test and abuse and be abused by the newest technology around, and I had a brain and a voice;

I had a press kit three inches thick that proved I could get my ideas published and get attention for the products I was wearing. That, and I came up with a lot of the ideas incorporated into the products being developed. (And no, my brain doesn't wear lipstick.) Of course, I was decent at drawing, painting and sculpting, and I learned how to paint my face when I was a kid, using my mom's makeup to try and feel as powerful as I imagined Cleopatra felt with that eyeliner, or Marilyn with those red lips. (I wasn't allowed to go out of the house like that though. Only on Halloween. WERK. My Vampire Queen look is still one of my best.) I was a proud tomboy so I had physical confidence in my body, which translates to a certain tangible power as well.

So what are we really talking about here, with these people who want to devalue my ideas – you don't have to agree with them or like me, but you do have to take the ideas on their own merit – what they're essentially saying is that somehow I didn't really "earn" it, am I right? (I guess "it" is their idea of "success," by the way.) Their argument is as ridiculous as saying that Obama would never have been President of the United States if he didn't have charm, charisma, good looks and his level of education. Not to mention his ability to get other people to join his cause by fundraising. Uh, yeah . . . you're right. And so? What is their point? what, he didn't work for all those things? He didn't DEVELOP charm, elegance in social situations, the ability to communicate authentically with people? It's not like he was the first intelligent, charismatic, determined black man to run for political office. And yet he's still the first black President, the pioneer of uncharted waters. Is he just luckier than most? Would his luck be different if he wasn't raised by a single mother, or if his grandparents didn't want to be there to help raise him, or if he didn't get a scholarship to go to Columbia, or how about if he didn't marry someone as charismatic and intelligent as Michelle? Should he apologize for what his particular basket of luck looks like? If luck is when preparation meets opportunity, he earned every ounce of that "luck." We make our own luck with whatever we got – and I've worked my butt off.

The monster under the bed in this line of attack from the haters you mention is this, and I wonder about it: maybe I'm just not disabled enough for them. Maybe they need me to flaunt my struggles a bit more, to talk about how hard it was/is for me, to give them a full plate of "tragedy" before they can accept and award me my "triumph." And you know what? Not interested. I don't need to prostrate myself for those people to feel like my story is palatable enough for them. In fact, I'm fine being a bit of a threat to those people. What a welcome relief to being someone's inspiration porn – co-opting a photo of me and turning it into a poster with some attached slogan under it like "what's your excuse?" is really a bummer. I would NEVER say that. Some people have very good excuses at certain times in their lives, myself included. (Maybe they're living in Cambodia and stepped on a landmine and they are banned from accessing ANY public education.) We have legitimate reasons to sometimes feel things we wish we didn't have to feel; we are not robots. (oh, how the themes all come together!) In my opinion, what's always been missing in the broad narrative around disability is some GLAMOUR. Some fun, frivolity, light, a bit of benevolent mischief, and honest to goodness glamour!! So I'm trying to bring some of that.

Back to today

You ask why I was selected by L'Oreal? Why now? How did my background and being an amputee factor into their decision? Well, they picked me because I wrote a good essay about beauty. As one result of my TED Talk of February 2009, I was approached by an anthropologist, Elizabeth Azoulay, to contribute to a collection entitled *100,000 Years of Beauty*, beginning with prehistory and then moving to the classical age, to modernity and then future.

They asked if I would concentrate on the future of beauty. The premise of the book was that how beauty was conceptualized was specific to time and location. We have liked different appearances, rubinesque, heroine chic, stretching our necks with rings, our lips with plates, and so forth. This anthropologist placed beauty and body adornment as a common thread of transformation. In her view, humans have always asserted the right to transform themselves, claiming invention of identity.

So I wrote the essay, the future of beauty. It contained two images of me, both in my sprinting legs. As an aside, writing this chapter was the spark for the substance of my second TED Talk about words. Fast forward to L'Oreal. My essay received a lot of buzz in Europe. L'Oreal contacted me to get to more academic understandings and explorations of beauty and how humans define and create it, how we assign labels for it. So I was asked to serve on a panel of five women all who contributed to this book. Interestingly, what people wanted to talk about was architecting their own bodies. Taking this object, a prosthetic that always represented something morose, I could bring some frivolity to it, some glamour some fun, by deliberately going outside the medical establishment and finding people who were not in the historical business of what it should be, and so I was now claiming the right to direct this part of my real estate.

So afterwards, a few women approached me from the L'Oreal Foundation to ask me to speak in a forum. The conversation was about beauty and individuality. We talked about why beauty is homogenized, why is everyone seeking to look the same as everyone else who is considered to meet the standard of beauty.

At the L'Oreal Foundation, Global Women's Forum, I got a standing ovation for the idea of the right to claim your body. I remarked that technology, science, and things like the internet have never made this more possible. We are not beholden to traditional buckets of identity. You can get everything on-line no matter where you live. It used to be that you had to come to New York, to go and be with the tribe, but not anymore.

I got this ovation and the senior ranking person and twelve others at L'Oreal took me to dinner. The new CEO for Maybelline came to see me next month with a team. They said, I think this is what the postmodern woman is, she takes what she wants and likes from different aspects from qualities of other lifestyles. So I was hired. For me to say because I am worth it took me fifteen times before I actually got to the reality of it, and mean it without being defensive. In my head I had all these subtexts, to squirm out and diminish myself. Is disability value added for L'Oreal? Of course, but it is because I can speak. It is value added in the sense of diversity. Do I think that amputees or people who use wheelchairs see my face and say I am going to buy L'Oreal. No, I think a woman will see the commercial, and would be intrigued with knowing that I don't fit the standard and can still be celebrated as beautiful. This is how the primal marketing works. I have had letters from gay teenage boys as well, who identify with me for alternative options.

Ten years ago, I was put up for the Lancôme spokesperson but it was too weird for them back then. So why now? I think people have explored concepts of beauty, where the future of beauty is going and they were intrigued by my ideas. And then they did market research. While I may not be the household name, I have a cult following but in way more diverse bases than say Beyonce, in the art world, design tech world, singularity, posthumanism, cyborg girl. Today I think what we are actually seeing much more diversity in images of what society puts a stamp on as beauty. In each of the last four seasons we have seen transgendered people walking in major runway shows. There has never been more of connection between high-end fashion and literal translation on the street. The cool kids that have vision to see beauty in that image already understand me. For me it would be remarkable to be seen and understood by someone in a drugstore in Topeka or in Bogota or Jaipur. Maybe they will never see an edgy fashion magazine. Everything I did until then was edgy, not "walk into your drugstore and see me next to Beyonce's head." But unlike yesteryear, to be taken seriously as an athlete in 2013 you can have long hair and you can wear lipstick. You see X-Game athletes in bubblegum pink. Even traditional ideas like femininity are not beholden or limited. Normal is total bullshit, there is none. I am not setting out to make some statement about what is normal and what is disability because I never ascribed disability identity to myself. I identify more with people who like B-grade horror movies than with other amputees. So I think that when people are vilifying me, I am both assailable and have transcended the hit of inspirational despair. I am seen as both disabled and not disabled. The tension between what I want to assert and what is thrust upon me is great, as Billy Jean King said. But, would L'Oreal have assigned me to a global contract if I could not stand as a face who could not sell makeup, amputee or not? I do not think so. And what a change from ten years ago.

I understand those kids in their early twenties. They know that a job is not going to be there for forty years of their lives. They have to think of themselves as people who can cross pollinate, take what they learned from their career over there and put it to use over here. These changes are reflected in images, fashion and changing perspectives on beauty. They are liberating.

But getting down to business basics, the numbers of tubes of foundation that are sold by my image and brand compared to others is amazing. They are renewing my contract because I am making them money. Marketing can transform how we think about diversity. So of course it makes sense to use the market for innovation and change.

Summary

In this chapter we explored identity and disability identity as an artifact of visual culture. While beauty is not the point of this book, it speaks to visual couture and the power of the market economy in designing and branding personhood. Aimee Mullins' words comprised much of the chapter as Aimee's ideas and life reflect the centrality of the visual and material, as well as the transformative potential of both for future vision. As she herself said, ten years ago, an amputee would not have been employed as a spokesperson for a corporation that sold beauty to the public.

References

Blinn, R. (2009) Book Review: Disability Meets Design. Retrieved from *Core 77*, December 24. Available online at http://m.core77.com/blog/book_reviews/book_review_design_meets_disability_by_graham_pullin_15597.asp (accessed January 16, 2014).

DePoy, E., and Gilson, S. (2011) *Studying Disability*. Los Angeles, CA: Sage.

Goffmann, I. (1961) *Encounters*. Indianapolis, IA: Bobs_Merrill.

Haller, B., Dorries, B., and Rahn, J. (2006) Media labeling versus the US disability community identity: a study of shifting cultural language. *Disability and Society*, 21 (1), 61–75.

Harper, D. (2001–2013) Identity (n.). *Online Etynmology Dictionary*. Available online at www.etymonline.com/index.php?allowed_in_frame=0andsearch=identity andsearchmode=none (accessed January 16, 2014).

Hutson, M. (2013) Gray Matter: Our Inconsistent Ethical Instincts. *New York Times*, March 30. Available online at www.nytimes.com/2013/03/31/opinion/sunday/how-firm-are-our-principles.html?_r=0 (accessed January 16, 2014).

Johnstone, C. J. (2004) Disability and Identity: Personal Constructions and Formalized Supports. *Disability Studies Quarterly*, 24 (4). Available online at http://dsq-sds.org/article/view/880/1055 (accessed January 16, 2014).

Lime Connect (2011) Re-Branding Disability. *Virginia Business Leadership Network*, December 13. Available online at http://vabln.org/2011/12/re-branding-disability (accessed January 16, 2014).

Linton, S. (1998) *Claiming Disability: Knowledge and Identity*. New York: New York Univerity Press.

Murugami, M. W. (2009) Disability and Identity. *Disability Studies Quarterly*, 29 (4). Available online at http://dsq-sds.org/article/view/979/1173 (accessed January 16, 2014).

Olson, E. (2010) Personal Identity. *Stanford Encyclopedia of Philosophy*. Available online at http://plato.stanford.edu/entries/identity-personal/#WidIss (accessed January 16, 2014).

Popova, M. (n.d.) What Is Character? Debunking the Myth of Fixed Personality. *Brain Pickings*. Available online at www.brainpickings.org/index.php/2012/03/02/character-personality (accessed January 16, 2014).

Pullin, G. (2009) *Disability Meets Design*. Cambridge, MA: MIT Press.

Regehr, G. (2006) The Persistent Myth of Stability. *Journal of General Internal Medicine*, 21 (5), 544–5.

Ting-Toomey, S. (2011) *Understanding Intercultural Communication*. New York: Oxford University Press.

6 Market segment

Designing and branding the disability park

Figure 6.1 The disability park

In this chapter, we discuss the scope of design and branding of diverse disability-specific entities, or what we have referred to as the "disability park" (DePoy and Gilson, 2011). As introduced in previous chapters, the disability park is a set of large diversified thematic corporations, knowledge productions, and other entities designed to define, attract, and contain the population segments of eligible persons branded as disabled and their peripherals such as family. Logo, slogan, label, space, narrative, and other strategies distinguish and ascribe public perception of the worth and humanness to those who are the objects of attraction, invitation and capture in park environments.

Although the application of theme-park theory to disability may seem caustic or farcical to some, our intention is not to diminish the good works of those who seek to engage in "helping and healing." Rather, it is our intent to use a themed lens to examine disability responses as twenty-first-century marketplaces that recruit and then vet customers, guide their entrance, navigation, long-term consumption, and loyalty. Glance back to Chapter 4 in which T-shirts, slogans, and even iPhone applications are sold as park paraphernalia. Such scrutiny is an essential precursor of informed disability undesign and redesign. As detailed in Part 2, we see the park, not those who work within it, as the primary locus for major change. Similar to other institutionally inscribed beliefs and practices, it is plausible and even most likely probable that park employees and invited guests are not cognizant of the park and its surreptitious stronghold.

Of particular analogic importance to this discussion, because of the aim of theme parks in large part as selling "experience," is the concept of the "experience economy" (Pine and Gilmore, 2011). Looking back at the emergence of the "experience economy," Pine and Gilmore (2011), although not the first authors to present these ideas, gave them form and substance while situating them within a longitudinal continuum of market development. They suggested a trajectory of business and marketing aims moving from motivating consumption by product feature to provoking ongoing consumption through memorable experience culminating in transformation. Because the consumer perceives personal benefit through the experience he/she continues to frequent the service, being seduced not by product or service purchase, but rather by belief that the experience is transformative.

More recent work has posited that experience and thus transformation is interactive and co-created (Bakhtiari, 2013). We would suggest that the concept of the experience economy not only followed the service economy chronologically but has come full circle in framing the disability park as transformative with interactive rhetoric, albeit controlled by park policies and praxis, not the consumer. In a recent interview, Pine discussed how health services contributed to his theorizing.

> What does customization turn an experience into? What happens when you customize and design an experience that is exactly the experience someone needs right now?" And I realized the next stage would be to turn it into a life-transforming experience – in other words, an experience that changes us in some way, transformation. A transformation is when you use experiences as raw materials to guide your customers to change.
>
> (Summers, 2012: 17–18)

Let us see what happens when we transplant Pine's words into disability service lingo as person centered planning.

What is **person-centered planning**?
We're glad you asked! Person-centered planning is a process-oriented approach to empowering people with disability labels. It focuses on the people and their needs by putting them in charge of defining the direction for their lives, not on the systems that may or may not be available to serve them. This ultimately leads to greater inclusion as valued members of both community and society.

Person-centered planning involves the development of a "toolbox" of methods and resources that enable people with disability labels to choose their own pathways to success; the planners simply help them to figure out where they want to go and how best to get there.

(Cornell University, 2013)

The parallels in both verbatim quotes are remarkable. Both provide an experience, both sell transformation, and in both the experience is ostensibly co-created. At this point, one might argue that services and business serve different masters. However, Bessant and Maher (2009) claim that the business viscera of the service sector, once recognized, provides the rationale for the critical need to systematically and intentionally bring marketing innovation to the service domain. Their arguments are compelling, as they identify the competition among services that emerges not always from consumer choice, but rather by budgeting cutbacks in which health and disability services compete with other public sector needs such as criminal justice, roads, education, and so forth, for limited dollars and thus survival.

Building on the earlier work of Leadbetter, (2004), Bessant and Maher (2009) propose that services be "co-created." Following this trend, numerous service "parks" have expanded the experience of service consumption to what has been branded participatory planning. Consider the example provided by Rabinowitz and Berkowitz (2013):

when the story is told, it becomes clear that the well-intentioned professionals in charge had totally misunderstood or ignored some fundamental fact about the community or the target population. Since they assumed they knew what was needed, they planned the whole thing themselves... and failed miserably.

For every horror story, however, there's a story about an intervention where everything went right. In many of these cases, you'll find that the target population – and often the larger community as well – was included in the planning of the intervention from the beginning... In its simplest terms, a participatory approach is one in which everyone who has a stake in the intervention has a voice, either in person or by representation. Staff of the organization that will run it, members of the target population, community officials, interested citizens, and people from involved agencies, schools, and other institutions all should be invited to the table. Everyone's participation should be welcomed and respected, and the process shouldn't be dominated by any individual or group, or by a single point of view.

That's the ideal. The reality may often be quite different.

(Rabinowitz and Berkowitz, 2013)

We see the influence of the experience economy on participatory strategies. In essence, participation is staged by well-intended service providers. Service users branded as participants are distinguished from experts, are invited, and then "educated" in specific knowledge seeking and planning strategies (McIntyre, 2008). Thus, the process is both controlled and choreographed by provider employees of the park and their collaborators many of whom are university faculty engaged in the knowledge generation and transmission enterprise. Aims such as consumer "buy-in," investment, "ownership," and "voice" typically trump the purpose of obtaining sound knowledge on which to ground services or determine if they are even needed and for what purposes? Although the rhetorical goals of participation are noteworthy, we would suggest that the differentials in resources and power create a participatory process which animates the experience economy to achieve politically correct, semantically respectful segregated service park survival, growth, and institutionalization as the resolution to "disability problems." Nevertheless, much can be learned about design, undesign and redesign using such successful park strategies. This discussion awaits us in upcoming chapters.

Getting into the park: One way turnstiles

Figure 6.2 Getting in and staying in: one way only

While there are multiple forms and locations of disability parks globally, the basis of invitation and attendance for most is created by adherence to the medical and/or medicalized model of disability. Look at Table 6.1 for exemplars of the scope of target branding for disability park entry.

Just a smattering of eligibility criteria reveals the expansive reach of the service park. Simply being poor renders one a psychiatriscape park invitee in Washington State. Of course, these eligibility criteria are not static, and thus they illuminate the competing trends that have emerged as the global economy increases its hegemony in the world of diagnostic branding. Not surprisingly, movement in and out of favor complicates an understanding of the behest to pass through park turnstiles. The first major trend discussed is a two-part expansion. As the continued engorgement of the list of legitimate medical (or other "at risk") disability designs proceed, what was considered the territory of normal is eroded. A brief revisit of the most recent published edition of the American Psychiatric Association *Diagnostic and Statistical Manual* (DSM), the bible of psychopathology, so to speak, which often results in life-time captivity in psychiatriscape, reveals its literal as well as conceptual weight gain. Literally, the book grew from 134 pages inscribing 182 disorders as mental illness in 1968, (American Psychiatric Association, 1968) to 265 conditions scribed on 494 pages in 1980 to a whopping 947 pages capturing over 300 conditions and variations thereof in 2013 (American Psychiatric Association, 2013).

Table 6.1 Examples of eligibility criteria

Developmental disability[1]	SSDI[2]	Mental Health Services[3]
Developmental delay	Musculoskeletal conditions	Medicaid recipients are automatically enrolled in a local mental health managed care plan which is called the Regional Support Network (RSN). RSNs coordinate mental health services offered within their service area through contracts with community mental health agencies.
Down syndrome	Cardiovascular conditions	
Too severe to be assessed	Senses, skin, and speech issues	
Intellectual disability	Respiratory conditions	
Cerebral palsy	Neurological conditions	
Epilepsy	Mental disorders	
Autism	Immune disorders	
Other intellectual disability, or neurological condition	Various syndromes	

Sources:
[1] Maryland Department of Mental Hygiene (n.d.)
[2] Laurence (n.d.)
[3] Washington State Department of Social and health Services (n.d.)

Conceptually, we refer to the DSM as an increasing heavyweight in conferring a diagnostic brand as a one-way ticket into the psychiatric park. Behaviors previously considered odd or eccentric such as overeating (Clausen, 2012), hoarding (Mataix-Cols *et al.*, 2010) and worrying about body odor have now been branded as bonafide medical conditions begetting invitations to consume services and products in the psychiatric mart (OCD Center of Los Angeles, 1999–2012).

A second part of the expansion lies in the world of specialized human rights policy. We distinguish these instruments from the policies and constitutions that are designed to protect all citizens. As discussed in subsequent chapters, while these policies may have been intended to redress historical discrimination and exclusion, they shoot themselves in their ostensibly purposive foot by quarantining only certain "vulnerable" populations and thus painting them as outside of citizen rights for all. Such mechanisms increasingly envelop an enlarging part of citizenry under the external feathers of policy's protective wing, segregating a growing group and branding them as park residents. As example, the Americans with Disabilities Act Amendments Act (ADAAA) of 2008 diverted its focus from eligibility squabbles to strategies to protect those who do meet park criteria. Thus, individuals who may have encountered barriers to the hippodrome specific to rhetorical human rights protection no longer do.

> In short, the ADAAA and its final regulations now shift the focus of virtually every situation that implicates the ADA [Americans with Disabilities Act]. Before the amendments, the interpretation of the ADA largely focused on whether an individual was substantially limited in a major life activity and, therefore, disabled under the ADA. Under the ADAAA's broader construction, the focus is not directed toward the actual definition of disability, but rather on discrimination and reasonable accommodation.
>
> (Nowak and Radelet, 2011)

In addition to individual policies expanding their reach, the proliferation of specialized human rights policies around the globe is another method through which individuals are summoned to disability stadia. Not only are policies emerging within nation states, but global assertions of rights such as the UN convention in the Rights of Persons with Disabilities are making their debut (UN General Assembly, 2007).

Note that we have referred primarily to specialized human rights policy under the expansion trend. We would suggest that these policies serve several masters. First, the rhetorical support for non-discrimination is contained within these policies without the muscle to enforce them. Thus, this implementation scheme is inconsistent and does not distribute fiscal or other resources unless legal action is sought and upheld. However, rather than taking the route of assertion that all people should be protected by existing human rights policy, these extra strata of group-specific policies spotlight and thus brand specific bodies simply through defining eligibility. While well-meaning, we would suggest that human rights policies which contain and name a subgroup design its members outside the boundaries of acceptable humanness, ripe for viewing, branding, and invitation into conceptual and built parkscapes, and in essence serving the disability park system without malintent.

Now, let us consider the second major policy trend, contraction. While it may seem oxymoronic to suggest two opposing trends, a further examination reveals that contraction occurs in a parallel universe adjacent to expansion. Contraction or limitation trends within the distribution of public resources for those who fit the medicalized model of disability. So while still branded as disabled, maintaining and growing the park invitation lists persists while the provision of concrete resources diminishes with budget cuts, rightfully frightening eligibles who do not see or have not been exposed to other alternatives to support participation and equivalence of opportunity for flourishing. As example, a recent post on federal budgeting read:

> *most federal programs will be slashed by at least 8.2 percent.* That means that more than $1 billion will be chopped from special education, the White House said. Meanwhile, housing for people with disabilities will be reduced by $14 million and the U.S. Department of Labor's office focusing on disability employment will be cut by $3 million.
>
> (Diament, 2012)

Once an individual enters the park portal, many do not exit. While long-term and even lifelong services in the current world of standardized expectations, built environments, and mass produced products as well as nomothetic theories which prescribe "normality" as desirable may provide benefits, we would suggest that holding the disability park intact in perpetuity does little to undesign segregation, stigma, and inequality of opportunity for choice and participation. Incarcerating target segments through policy and service offerings siphons off energy necessary for more profound integrative social change outside the park. Consider this simple example, with names changed to protect the guilty.

> The Special Adaptive Skiing program at Snow Mountain is free, conducted by volunteer skiers, and is only available on weekends. To enter this disability park, an individual must have a physicians note verifying a medical pedigree, and must complete a long form which asks invasive questions such as "how do you handle frustration, what medications are you currently taking" and so forth.

Unpacking the multiple implications and effects reveals the negative consequences of this disability playground. Most proximal and different from what is ever considered acceptable for non-disabled skiers who want to take lessons is the invasion of privacy through medicalized, presumptive questioning that has nothing to do with skiing. Second, the failure of the program to charge for lessons reifies the assumed link between poverty and embodied disability. (We already saw this relationship from a different stance in Table 6.1 above, assuming poverty as an associate of mental illness). We always wonder why lessons are not free for those who cannot afford them rather than for an inferred essentialist expectation of poverty on the basis of embodied condition label.

Second, hiding under the volunteer zeal is the assumption that skiers in the disability park do not need certified instructors perhaps because they are not capable of advancing in sport.

Moving to more distal consequences, while well intended, these volunteers assuage the responsibility of Snow Mountain to provide lessons by certified instructors on the days when non-adaptive skiing counterparts can participate, and thus the status quo of segregation continues. Failing to provide equality of opportunity is one part of the park which maintains it as well as perpetuates the design of adaptive skiers as apart from an environment in which all skiers can participate. The performance of adaptive skiers is too often named inspirational, exceptional, or another euphemism that splays open the expected incapacity of the embodied atypical. Think back to Chapter 5, in which Aimee Mullins exposed the expected mediocrity inherent in such inspiration fables.

Now extrapolate what the disability ski playground teaches to other areas of life such as health, education, employment, and civic participation. Although not articulated and made transparent, disability parks use successful market strategies in their design and sustainability. Let us consider these now.

Iconic branding

A simple definition of icon is image or visual. However, its synonyms tell a different story. Words such as "idol," "painted image," "representation," and "hero" betray the power potency of visual symbol and foretell the role of icon as grand manipulator. What elevates a brand to iconic status is its perfusion into culture such that the brand itself not only functions as recognition but holds meaning prestige. According to Alexander, Bartmanski, and Giesen (2011), icons tell tales which engage participation from those who are not fully aware of the depth of the chronicle. Stories can be transmitted or embellished and tailored by co-creation. Yet, despite their power and cultural centrality, iconic brands have been overlooked or sidestepped by scholarship in social sciences and even in the humanities outside of the realm of design thinking.

We would suggest that this theoretical and praxis void is no longer useful in the twenty-first-century visual and material culture, particularly when analyzing the disability park. At diverse levels of exposure, from internal through external-visual to abstract imagery (e.g., the language theme) park rangers promulgate their own or endorse omnipresent iconic brands for multiple purposes. When the dialog about branding is broached it is embedded within an altruistic "helping" tenor, a strategy that we would consider a conceptual brand in itself that tells one tale but misses the depth of the full narrative. "The people running these brands paint themselves as perpetual underdogs, fighting against the blandness produced by modern marketers and the standardization of modern life" (Berveland, 2009).

Once again, we remind the reader that we are not criticizing helping, nor maligning professions, providers, and those who seek to improve life for residents of the disability park. Rather, we aim to increase the volume of the whisper such that iconic branding can be used not simply to maintain the status quo but to engage co-creators in undesign and redesign thinking and action to achieve what we see as equivalence of worth and participation opportunity in the world among all bodies. Iconic brands, if directly encountered and deliberately put to work, can be champions of positive social change.

The classic example of the iconic disability brand is the wheelchair symbol, named the international symbol of access (ISA), and presented in Figure 6.3. We discuss this symbol in more detail in Chapter 9, but raise it here because of its ubiquity.

The scope of this iconic brand is universal, recognized as the designator which weaves a complex story about disability and/or accessibility, not simply about wheeled mobility. Read what Ben-Moshe and Powell, and Imre have to say.

Figure 6.3 The international symbol of access
Source: Shutterstock

Some may argue that the awareness raised is done with a negatively connoted tool, namely an individual's needing specific adaptations to access particular spaces. Yet the existence of the ISA simultaneously testifies to attempts to facilitate disabled individuals' full participation in society. However, at the same time this symbol often directs persons needing accommodations to "special," often segregated, locations. If universal design principles had been carried out fully we would have no need for such a symbol, because places and objects would have been designed from the start for a diverse population.

(Ben-Moshe and Powell, 2007)

Yet current urban planning is inscribed by a "design apartheid" where urban planners, architects and related officials are guilty of constructing spaces that exclude disabled people and prioritize the dominant values of the temporarily able-bodied community.

(Imrie, 1996)

For us, the ISA symbolizes the disability park invitation, entrance, and containment but certainly not access. To the contrary, identifying the park with a symbolic wheelchair assigns identity and as suggested by Titchkosky (2007), exclusion by the branded nature of inclusion.

As further illustrated by the ISA, branding is not restricted to a logo designed for a product, but rather occurs in the meaning made by signifiers. The image of the blue-and-white cartoon of a wheelchair functions as iconic simulacra in multiple arenas including but not limited to products, spaces, ideas, services, and even sounds (Licht and O'Rourke, 2007). Thus, the park and all designed as part of it can be amalgamated under a single essentialist image.

The ISA however, takes on numerous personas and thus has a wide interpretive reach functioning in obscure ways. In addition to its hegemony in reifying both a user group and their assigned environmental containers, the ISA brands empathic volunteerism and charitable efforts attached to the park and then not so altruistically, restricts the conceptual public perception of access to the simple solution of erection of a ramp in one entry way even if it is the trash outlet. Our recent voyage to La Antigua Guatemala provides consummate sampling of the little figure's secrets. Figure 6.4 displays this curious story which tattles on its participants.

Despite impassible cobblestone streets peppered with pot-holes and barriers to topple even the most surefooted athlete, the ISA made its frequent appearance in the oddest places, flush on the streets, often under barriers that if not avoided could decapitate any person over three and a half feet tall. Because the icons seemed to have no discernible purpose to the novice visitor, even in identifying ramped building entrances, we consulted the web on our cell phone for clarification. Look at Rudy Giron's experience and explanation.

Figure 6.4 The international symbol of access on La Antigua streets and sidewalks
Source: Photograph by Stephen Gilson

Even though I said before that people enjoy walking and strolling La Antigua Guatemala, I sort of lied. See walking is still the best way to get to know and to enjoy La Antigua. But the problem is that the sidewalks are uneven, there are all kinds blocking part of the sidewalk and many people hit their head with the concrete or rock window sills. Sometimes the sidewalk gets broken by a driveway or the cement cover of the water meter is missing and there is huge hole where you break your foot.

However, if you are handicapped, La Antigua Guatemala could be a nightmare. There aren't wheelchair ramps in the corners; the sidewalks are too narrow; and you still have to deal with all the problems listed above. *La Antigua sin barreras* (La Antigua Guatemala Without Barriers) was a project/NGO which tried to fix the sidewalks and make them wheelchair/handicap friendly. Whichever block they were able to fix, they placed a tiny handicap white-and-blue tile. You can see how small the tiles are by looking at this other photo. I don't know whatever happened to La Antigua Guatemala Without Barriers project, but for sure they were not able to fix all the sidewalks around Antigua Guatemala. Too bad, because by fixing the sidewalks for the handicapped, they were fixing the sidewalks for everybody else.

(Girón, 2007)

Investigating further did not reveal the workings and participants of the Sin Barerras project. Yet, parallel (International Volunteer Headquarters, n.d.)

programs bespeak the misplacement of volunteerism in construction efforts that require substantive skill to produce enduring results.

> Volunteers are not required to have experience with construction work, but a reasonable level of fitness and strong dedication to the work at hand will go a long way to ensuring you get the most out of your volunteer project.
>
> (International Volunteer HQ, n.d.)

We wonder what construction projects in the private sector would invite builders with no experience or skill to complete a task.

Inside the park

The disability park is not a single location but rather comprises the sum of abstracts and palpables (which we have neologized as "concretuals" to denote that objects take on parallel dynamic motion alongside ideas) that design and brand disability, its membership, and its meaning. In this part of the chapter, we discuss the scope of the park and leave its action processes to the chapters that take up design craft in Part 1 and to undesign and redesign chapters within Part 2.

The park design

As we have noted, the park is an amorphous contemporary system of hubs and spokes that seems locally situated. However, its appearances, entrance and egress, practices, movement patterns, activities, economics, signs, signifiers, and governance are controlled elsewhere and are remarkably similar across geographies and functions, particularly in the United States and other developed countries.

As example, the other day, we went to purchase a back support brace for sports activity at a retail store. Unexpectedly, the store was an easily recognized disability park, arranged as a typical medicalized space located in a shopping mall. Within the space were the telltale attributes of parkesque environments. On the window, the names of the park workers were stenciled followed by tentacles of credentials, denoting professional certification as orthotists and prosthetists despite the claim that the inventory was for anyone's choice and comfort. A push plate for the automatic door had the ISA symbol proudly centered, and directions adjacent to the door commanded wheelchair users to access the device. We walked through the wide door without using the automatic feature and immediately found ourselves in a waiting room with a plate glass sliding window separating the office staff from the park users. Waiting for service, we were entertained with brochures for Special Olympics (another park environment as we discuss later), adaptive ski programs, and so forth, all advertising to the target market of atypical bodies. When the receptionist engaged with us, she did so from behind the glass and asked us to make an appointment to see one of the professionals for assessment. We decided to leave and take our business elsewhere, shopping in a non-parkesque environment, the internet. How curious that the park appeared in the shopping center, given the multiple online and built retail outlets in which one can purchase supportive back braces.

Similar to the park description above, disability service climate has a recognizable climatic design, typically presented and portrayed as altruistic, professional, and helping. As we have asserted throughout this work, we do not dismiss or vilify these important aspects of disability services for the current context of a standardized world in which all bodies do not neatly fit and act. However, the park picture is not as simple as making life better for its customers and without alternative vision and redesign, this aim may never be fully actualized.

Service park design transmits many muffled messages to the user and observer. For example, unlike environments that are accessed by choice and thus aim to compete for success, in the park, one expects to wait, as communicated by the omnipresent "waiting room." Park climate and design tell many stories, some not articulated as clearly as others. According to Evenson and Dubberly,

> *designing for service* is a meta activity: conceiving and iteratively planning and constructing a service system or architecture to deliver resources that choreograph an experience that others design. When a company provides the optimal mix it will have produced a resonating service system and delivers an experience advantage.
>
> Designing for service is a process that brings together skills, methods, and tools for intentionally creating and integrating (not accidentally discovering and falling into) systems for interaction with customers to create value for the customer, and, by differentiating providers, to create long-term relationships between providers and customers.
>
> (Evenson and Dubberly, 2010)

Thus, Evenson and Dubberly reveal the design of service parks to achieve multiple aims including service provision, but also aligned with the experience economy's foci on commerce and loyalty (Pine and Gilmore, 2011).

Now look at the definition of service provided by Gadrey, as cited in Evenson and Dubberly:

> a service may be defined as a change in the conditions of a person or a good belonging to some economic unit, which is brought about as the result of the activity of some other economic unit with the prior agreement of the former person or economic unit.
>
> (Evenson and Dubberly, 2010)

Gadrey goes on to explain that a service should first be considered a process, and geometrically represents service as a triangular entity connecting three primary points: service provider, customer/client/user, and transformation of a reality. Consistent with literature on the disability industry published by Gill as early as 1992, perhaps an alternative shape with the customer restrained within a conceptual and physical perimeter would more accurately depict the park.

Service parks are designed for broad purposive scopes, including economic advantage, consumption, containment, as well as good intentions to facilitate individual function. Looking at park design through sign and signifier, economic hegemony is visible through "environmental simulacra." This term was popularized by Galician (2004) referring to theme parks not easily distinguishable from the reality they represent. Applied to the service park, and its current fiscal and sociopolitical context we suggest that these simulacra appear as spaces, images, and products that convince users and others in the life of users of service necessity while simultaneously serving to capture a market segment not only as temporary guests, but as life-long loyal customers.

Similarly, policies governing park elements, while rhetorically claiming the major purpose of services to facilitate maximum functionality and independence for users, synchronizes this aim with institutionalizing a market segment. As example, consider the term "assistive technology" and federal US policy (the Assistive Technology Act was passed in the United States in the late twentieth century) as simulacra. Park invitees use assistive technology while nondisabled people who employ identical products use technology or, as Seymour (2008) asserts, fashionable technology. Notice that branded in the term "assistive" explicates the need for help. This brief reference to technology provides a segue to the next section, shopping in the park.

Shopping in the park: Products branded for disability

Unlike retail commerce outside the park, shopping within is most frequently done with medical insurance dollars. We would suggest that this revenue source is both a blessing and a curse, and we unpack it in more detail in Chapter 13. Here, we examine the design itself.

Because of disproportionate underemployment of park users, medical insurance provides a safety net so to speak for needed items and services. Yet, medicalizing the disability park payor sustains the medicalization model of disability and all of its disadvantages as well. Moreover, because medical insurance begets medical products and services, the medical deficit, as well as other parts of identity of the product user are controlled, fixed and branded by the buyer while the park prospers.

Similar to spaces in the service park, products eligible for medical insurance coverage look the part. They have a telltale stigmatizing patina and are often situated adjacent to medical equipment, blurring the line between disability and illness, and reifying the medicalization model of disability.

Consider assistive technology once again as example. Assistive technology is defined in the US legislation, the Improving Access to Assistive Technology for Individuals with Disabilities Act of 2004, as:

> technology designed to be utilized in an assistive technology device or assistive technology service. The term "assistive technology device" means any item, piece of equipment, or product system, whether acquired commercially, modified, or customized, that is used to increase, maintain, or improve functional capabilities of individuals with disabilities.

Despite medical equipment not being included as assistive technology in the Act, and only two appearances of the word "medical" in the entire Act itself (both unrelated to assistive technology), numerous programs funded under this Act apprehend medical equipment as part of the assistive technology collection. As example, MassMatch, the federally funded assistive technology program in Massachusetts provides the following text on its website:

> Most medically necessary AT is provided by public or private health insurance, and falls under the term "durable medical equipment" (DME).
>
> Examples of DME include manual and power wheelchairs, catheters, and orthotics. This section provides information on how to pursue your DME needs from insurance sources. It includes information on appealing denials – an often necessary and effective step toward acquiring DME – as well as information on care coordination and advocacy services.
>
> (MassMatch, n.d.)

Five of the thirteen catalogs listed as assistive technology on the MassMatch website advertise and sell medical equipment. The first listing is A-Med Health Care – urological, bowel management, suction and tracheal, skin and wound care, hygienic aids (MassMatch, n.d.). What does this gallery of medical products have to do with the purpose of technology centers articulated within and funded by the Tech Act and its amendments?

While the Assistive Technology Act and its amendments do not specify medical devices as part of assistive technology, the vagueness inviting "concretuals" contributes to the indistinct divider between disability designed as embodied and its close relative, medical diagnostic condition. Further, we would suggest that this legislation despite its rhetorically progressive and expansive definition of disability is a fundamental illustration of a park conceptual. The medicalization model of disability is not clearly articulated in the definition of disability, but is implied within its functional referents and vocabulary such as "deterioration."

> (A) INDIVIDUAL WITH A DISABILITY – The term 'individual with a disability' means any individual of any age, race, or ethnicity –
> (i) who has a disability; and
> (ii) who is or would be enabled by an assistive technology device or an assistive technology service to minimize deterioration in functioning, to maintain a level of functioning, or to achieve a greater level of functioning in any major life activity.

Moreover, similar to the "retail" back support shop discussed above, the legislation sanctions and funds segregated service parks which even in many cases transmogrify into medicalized settings without reproach from the Act.

Park literature such as rehabilitation catalogs and brochures are consistent with park design and branding as well. As we mentioned above, while detained in the waiting room of the "retail" back support store, brochures for the Special Olympics and adaptive sports programs were part of the reading material and furnishings. A brief review of rehabilitation catalogs reveals a range of advertised concretuals, primarily recommended and purchased by health providers and paid in full by medical insurance. We mention the rehabilitation catalog specifically as park literature because it apprehends and transforms items for public consumption, such as soap dispensers and bidets, into concretuals that within the park are only conferred after a process of formal assessment and prescription.

Does anyone exit?

The park conceptualized within experience economic theory as a theme park seems to thrive on loyalty, with some themes capturing customers more than others. Once invited into the park, it appears as if customers are not only welcomed back in perpetuity but are taken captive often to their own detriment. Two in particular, psychiatriscapes and developmental disability theme parks, tend to design life-long consumers.

Reviewing research and practice from diverse nations across the globe, Jackson (2005; 2009) decries the increasingly popular practice of prescribing lifelong psychiatric medications which create rather than ameliorate pathology and even lead to dementia and death. Citing methodological inadequacy, Jackson indicts the conceptual, the specialized knowledge held by providers in the psychiatric service park, and evidence-based practice in particular, as vacant, misleading, and the "Perfect Crime" (Jackson, 2009). "By the end of the century, an increasingly large amount of literature has become the psychiatric equivalent of a Big Mac" (Jackson, 2005: 303).

Jackson is not alone in her distress. Williams (2012) renounces the claims about psychosis and other psychiatric diagnostic brands such as schizophrenia as lifelong pathologies. Their work is consistent with the numerous exposures of the profit motive that drives the psychiatriscape (Lane, 2009). We would however, caution against the simplistic view of corporate greed as the impetus behind this park. We see psychiatric counseling professionals as authentic in their work, often using the medium of human relationship to transmit theory and research learned in the academy and further substantiated in continuing education. Given the DSM bible and its evidence-based praxis responses, it follows that these humane providers assign a life-long brand name diagnosis for park eligibility and then conduct their work in this environment without looking further up the longitudinal road.

Now consider the brand, developmental disability. Primarily based on ossified developmental theories from the twentieth century (DePoy and Gilson, 2012), a moniker of developmental disability engages health providers, teachers, and other park employees, and convinces consumers of the need for park habitation.

> Skills such as taking a first step, smiling for the first time, and waving "bye-bye" are called developmental milestones. Children reach milestones in how they play, learn, speak, behave, and move (for example, crawling and walking).
>
> Children develop at their own pace, so it's impossible to tell exactly when a child will learn a given skill. However, the developmental milestones give a general idea of the changes to expect as a child gets older.
>
> As a parent, you know your child best. If your child is not meeting the milestones for his or her age, or if you think there could be a problem with your child's development, talk with your child's doctor or health care provider and share your concerns. Don't wait.
> (Centers for Disease Control and Prevention, 2012)

A third set of brands, independent living and Centers for Independent Living (labeled by those emic to the park with the fond acronym of CILS) forms the design crescendo for the veiled, lifelong disability park.

The history of independent living is characterized as a civil rights movement, emerging in the 1960s alongside deinstitutionalization.

> Independent Living philosophy emphasizes consumer control, the idea that people with disabilities are the best experts on their own needs, having crucial and valuable perspective to contribute and deserving of equal opportunity to decide how to live, work, and take part in their communities, particularly in reference to services that powerfully affect their day-to-day lives and access to independence.

Centers for Independent Living were created to be run by and for people with disabilities, and offer support, advocacy, and information on empowerment in the attainment of independence from a peer viewpoint, a perspective that was hitherto excluded from participation in the discussion and execution of "services for the disabled."

(National Council on Independent Living, 2013)

However, a number of contemporary CILS have morphed into service parks, complete with a bevy of professional services. As the adage goes, a picture is worth a thousand words. Figure 6.5 betrays the hiding place of a Florida CIL in a medical park.

Summary

In this chapter we took on the disability park. Because of its largesse, the full scope of disability design and branding can be visualized in a single book only from a birds-eye perspective, but not from a proximal scope in which details can be ascertained. We posited and illustrated the influence of the experience economy and theme park thinking in the design and branding of disability. Again, we reiterate that this analysis rather than

Figure 6.5 A Florida center for independent living
Source: Photograph by Stephen Gilson

serving as a soured indictment of well-meaning professionals, students, faculty, researchers, and concerned others, is the prelude to social change. Before undesign can occur, one must understand the current status of design and branding, its limitations, motives and values. Only then can areas for redesign be negotiated and potent for advancing equity through-out the full range of humanness.

References

Alexander, J. C., Bartmanski, D., and Giesen, B. (2011) *Iconic Power: Materiality and Meaning in Social Life.* New York: Palgrave MacMillan.

American Psychiatric Association (1968) *Diagnostic and Statistical Manual of Mental Disorders* (2nd ed.). Arlington, VA: American Psychiatric Association Publishing.

American Psychiatric Association (1994) *Diagnostic and Statistical Manual of Mental Disorders* (4th ed.). Arlington, VA: American Psychiatric Publishing.

American Psychiatric Association (2013) *Diagnostic and Statistical Manual of Mental Disorders* (5th ed.). Arlington, VA: American Psychiatric Association Publishing.

Bakhtiari, E. (2013) From HealthLeaders Media '09: Healthcare in the Experience Economy. *Health Leaders Media,* October 16. Available online at www.healthleadersmedia.com/content/240615/topic/WS_HLM2_LED/From-HealthLeaders-Media-09-Healthcare-in-the-Experience-Economy.html## (accessed January 22, 2014).

Ben-Moshe, L., and Powell, J. J. (2007) Sign of our Times? Revis(it)ing the International Symbol of Access. *Disability Studies Quarterly,* 22 (5), 489–505.

Bessant, J., and Maher, L. (2009) Developng Radical Service Innovations in health care: The Role of Design Methods. *International Journal of Innovation Management,* 13 (4), 555–68.

Beverland, M. (2009) *Building Brand Authenticity: Habits of Iconic Brands.* New York: Palgrave MacMillan.

Centers for Disease Control and Prevention (2012) Developmental Disability. Centers for Disease Control and Prevention. Available online at www.cdc.gov/ncbddd/developmentaldisabilities/index.html (accessed January 22, 2014).

Clausen, M. (2012) Binge Eating to have New Diagnosis in DSM-V. Brookhaven Hospital, December 13. Available online at www.brookhavenhospital.com/%E2%80%9Cbinge-eating-to-have-new-diagnosis-in-dsm-v%E2%80%9D (accessed January 22, 2014).

Cornell University (2014) What is Person-Centered Planning? Person Centered Planning Education Site. Cornell University ILR School Employment and Disability Institute. Available online at http://ilr-edi-r1.ilr.cornell.edu/PCP (accessed January 22, 2014).

DePoy, E., and Gilson, S. (2012) *Human Behavior Theory and Applications: A Critical Thinking Approach.* Thousand Oakes, CA: Sage.

DePoy, E., and Gilson, S. (2011) *Studying Disability.* Los Angeles, CA: Sage.

Diament, M. (2012) Steep Cuts To Special Education, Disability Programs Loom. *Disability Scoop,* September 12. Available online at https://www.disabilityscoop.com/2012/09/17/steep-cuts-loom/16463 (accessed January 22, 2014).

Evenson, S. and Dubberly, H. (2010) Designing for Service: Creating an Experience Advantage. *Interactions Magazine*, February 1. Available online at www.dubberly.com/wp-content/uploads/2010/03/ddo_article_designing_service.pdf (accessed January 22, 2014).

Galician, M. (2004) Product Placements in the Mass Media: Unholy Marketing Marriages or Realistic Story-Telling Portrayals, Unethical Advertising Messages or Useful Communication Practices? *Journal of Promotion Management*, 10 (1–2), 1–8.

Gill, C. (1992) Who Gets the Profits. *Mainstream*, 12, 14–17.

Girón, R. (2007) La Antigua Guatemala Without Barrier. Retrieved from *Antigua Daily Photo*, June 24. Available online at http://antiguadailyphoto.com/2007/06/24/la-antigua-guatemala-without-barriers/#.UeMoGlPpais (accessed January 22, 2014).

Imrie, R. (1996) *The Disabling City*. New York: St. Martin's Press.

International Volunteer HQ (n.d.) Volunteer in Guatemala. International Volunteer Headquarters. Available online at www.volunteerhq.org/volunteer-in-guatemala (accessed January 22, 2014).

Jackson, G. (2005) *Rethinking Psychiatric Drugs: A Guide for Informed Consent.* Bloomington, IN: Authorhouse.

Jackson, G. (2009) *Drug-Induced Dementia: A Perfect Crime.* Bloomington, IN: Authorhouse.

Lane, C. (2009) *Shyness: How Normal Behavior Became a Sickness.* New Haven, CN: Yale University Press.

Laurence, B. (n.d.) What Medical Conditions Qualify for Social Security Disability or SSI? *Disability Secrets.com.* Available online at www.disabilitysecrets.com/what-conditions-qualify.html (accessed January 22, 2014).

Leadbetter, C. (2004) *Personalisation Through Participation.* London: Demos.

Licht, A., and O'Rourke, J. (2007) *Sound Art: Beyond Music, Between Categories.* New York: Rizzoli.

McIntyre, A. (2008) *Participatory Action Research.* Thousand Oaks, CA: Sage.

Maryland Department of Mental Hygiene (n.d.) Eligibility for DDA Services. Available online at http://dda.dhmh.maryland.gov/SitePages/eligibility.aspx (accessed January 22, 2014).

MassMatch (n.d.) Assistive Technology Catalogs. MassMatch: Massachusettes Initiative to Maximize Assistive Technology (AT) in Consumer's Hands. Available online at www.massmatch.org/find_at/at_catalogs.php (accessed January 22, 2014).

Mataix-Cols, D., Frost, R. O., Pertusa, A., Clark, L. A., Saxena, S., Leckman, J. F. *et al.* (2010) Hoarding Disorder: A New Diagnosis For DSM-V? *Depression And Anxiety*, 27, 556–72.

Nowak, J. S., and Radelet, F. (2011) Comprehensive Summary of the Final Regulations to the ADA Amendments Act. *National Law Review*, May 9. Available online at www.natlawreview.com/article/comprehensive-summary-final-regulations-to-ada-amendments-act (accessed January 22, 2014).

OCD Center of Los Angeles (1999–2012) Olfactory Reference Syndrome – Symptoms and Treatment. Available online at www.ocdla.com/olfactoryreferencesyndrome.html (accessed February 15, 2014).

Pine, J., and Gilmore, J. (2011) *The Experience Economy.* Cambridge, MA: Harvard Business Review Press.

Rabinowitz, P., and Berkowitz, B. (2013) Participatory Approaches to Planning Community Interventions. Work Group for Community Health and Development. In *Community Tool Box*, chapter 18, section 2. Available online at http://ctb.ku.edu/en/tablecontents/sub_section_main_1143.aspx (accessed January 22, 2014).

Seymour, S. (2008) *Fashionable Technology: The Intersection of Design, Fashion, Science and Technology*. New York: Springer Vienna Architecture.

Summers, D. (2012) Personal Transformation in the Experience Economy: An interview with B. Joseph Pine II. *MWorld*, 11 (3), 17–18.

Titchkosky, T. (2007) *Reading and Writing Disability Differently*. Toronto, ON: University of Toronto Press.

UN General Assembly (2007) *Convention on the Rights of Persons with Disabilities. Resolution Adopted by the General Assembly, 24 January 2007, A/RES/61/106*. New York: United Nations. Available online at www.unhcr.org/refworld/docid/45f973632.html (accessed January 22, 2014).

Washington State Department of Social and health Services (n.d.) Mental Health Frequently Asked Questions. Eligibility for State funded mental health Services. Available online at www.dshs.wa.gov/dbhr/mhfaqs.shtml#dbhr (accessed January 22, 2014).

Williams, P. (2012) *Rethinking Madness*. San Francisco, CA: Sky's Edge.

7 Policy design
Designing disability rights and resources, local through global

> I am not interested in picking up crumbs of compassion thrown from the table of someone who considers himself my master. I want the full menu of rights.
>
> Desmond Tutu

In Chapter 6 we began to address policy as a distant conceptual driver of the disability park. We continue our discussion in this chapter, examining the scope of policy design and its conceptual branding of disability. Before diving into this critical analysis, once again we acknowledge that for the most part, specialized policy design has taken the high ground in attempting to redress historical and even current discrimination and disadvantage. However, while diverse reasoning routes may lead to the same conclusion of opposing such policies, the logic and purposive pathways that justify a conclusive end differ. As example, specialized rights policies have met

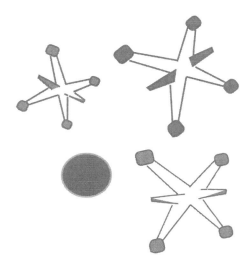

Figure 7.1 The policy game

opposition on fiscal, moral, and praxis grounds, all distinct reasons that become strange outcome bedfellows. So we urge the reader to persevere. Our intent is to both recognize the well-intended work of the past and to retire strategies which we do not believe can inform or accomplish a redesign ideal that eliminates a divided citizenry. We would suggest that undesign and what follows must replace fragments of human rights policies with one universal set of rights which all humans, regardless of bodies and backgrounds own (DePoy and Gilson, 2011).

Taxonomy

There are many ways to carve up and categorize disability policy. One typical organization has been the bifurcation of policy into two primary content arenas: resource distribution and rights policy. More recently, recognizing that policy is not simply its content, scholars have added analytic variables including structure, purpose, process, context, and logical reasoning approaches (Stone, 2001) as elements to guide the dissection and comparison of policy. We would suggest that these divisions only go so far in looking at policy in that they miss more subtle, often inferred, purposes as well as the intricacies of the policy negotiation process. By only considering policies that specifically target disability in their scope, analysis of disability designed into other policies, or even inferred by its absence in policy, is missed. To inform design and branding of human categories in general and disability as our focus, we therefore posit a model of analysis that examines the degree to which disability policy is explicit, embedded, or implicit. Then, to address the full range of policies, we locate policy on a second axis depicting its position as proximal to distal. Table 7.1 depicts the taxonomy that guides our discussion.

Explicit, embedded, and implicit

These three terms refer to the extent to which disability is exclusively, partially, or not mentioned but designed in a given policy. Explicit disability policies are concerned with provision of resources, rights, or other mandates only for individuals who meet diagnostic eligibility criteria of the policy being examined or analyzed. Explicit policies target club members designed as disabled by virtue of their presence within the text of the

Table 7.1 Two-dimensional policy taxonomy

	Explicit	*Embedded*	*Implicit*
Proximal			
Less proximal			
Distal			

policies, as the intended and sole beneficiaries. For us, regardless of how well intentioned, disability-explicit policy narratives ultimately result in creating and maintaining the disability park. Embedded policies are similar group-specific narratives that including disability but design it within broader identity politic policies that create "special" instruments for larger or more diverse population subcategories. These policies build conceptual and concretual parks that design more than one category as the excluded included (Titchkosky, 2007). In the third category, disability-implicit, disability as a named and intentional referent, is absent from formally penned documents but is present by its absence and the meaning for and/or effect of the policy on branded individuals.

Table 7.2 presents an overture for discussion of disability explicit and embedded policy. Because of their difference in mechanisms and thinking from explicit or embedded policy, we hold the analysis of implicit policies until the end of the chapter.

The policy examples in Table 7.2 are organized from proximal to distal, accompanied by their substantive category, ascribed design and branding, and a brief peek at the process through which disability is designed.

With this mini tour in mind, we now turn to the anti-discrimination shibboleth.

Rights policy: Branded by eligibility, designed with unequal rights

In the United States, disability-explicit and embedded anti-discrimination policies purport to create equal opportunity for all ages of branded disability and other park members depending on the scope of the policy. Before delving more into disability-explicit and embedded policy, we first bring your attention to a major design "snafu," at least just under the surface, in all group-explicit rights policies. Although rights policies for disenfranchised groups claim to redress discrimination and disparity for the cluster to which each speaks, once contained in a layer of policy in which typical citizens do not navigate, policy recipients removed from the policy that protects non-park citizenry, are branded as vulnerable, in need of legal protection, and thus lacking in agency (Bickenbach, 2008). Bawer (2012) indicts higher education as the entity which butchered human common good, and then spring loading a pellet gun as the instrument to dissipate the groups crafted by identity politics. Once separated from the bolus of citizenry, the "other" as category becomes ejected from the polis, "We know that when identity is identified categorically, it is catastrophic for the other" (Bawer, 2012). Perhaps because of his passion, Bawer (2012) vilifies multiculturalism without seeing any of its historical benefits, not the least being public awareness. Nevertheless, specialized strategies outlive their usefulness if they exist in perpetuity, as they do not do service in returning the excluded into seamless harmony and equivalence in their political, conceptual and concretual homeland.

Table 7.2 Policy examples, proximal to distal, substantive category, ascribed design and branding, and process through which disability is designed

Proximal to distal policy	Substance	Brand	How designed	What is designed
Access pass – National Park Service	Resource	Permanent physical, mental, or sensory impairment – physician; state or federal agency documentation	Self application. "Phonies" with parking passes are not allowed	Poverty
PCU student disability services	Rights	Learning disability; ADHD/ADD; psychological DX; physical disability or chronic ill health	Self-application: credentials (certification, licensure and/or training) of the diagnosing professional(s)	Students who are provided with inferior rights for the same tuition dollars paid by everyone else
State-specific disability determination services – social security determination	Resource	A person must be unable to do any kind of substantial gainful work because of a physical or mental impairment (or a combination of impairments), which is expected either: to last at least 12 months, or to end in death	Rigorous application for resources	Poverty
State-specific disability determination services – supplemental security income	Resource	Adults: people who are age 65 or older, blind, or disabled and have limited income and impairment must have lasted or be expected to last for a continuous period of at least 12 months or be expected to result in death	Rigorous application for resources	Poverty

Table 7.2 continued

Proximal to distal policy	Substance	Brand	How designed	What is designed
State-specific disability determination services – supplemental security income	Resource	Child: the child may not be working at a job that we consider to be substantial work, a child must have a medically determinable impairment that causes marked and severe functional limitations.	Rigorous application for resources	Poverty Life-long unemployment
Assistive Technology Act of 2004	Resource	The term "individual with a disability" means any individual of any age, race, or ethnicity: (i) who has a disability; and (ii) who is or would be enabled by an assistive technology device or an assistive technology service to minimize deterioration in functioning, to maintain a level of functioning, or to achieve a greater level of functioning in any major life activity	Expands a consumer group so that the assistive technology programs get ongoing public support	Now anyone can be part of the park as long as assistive technology need can be asserted. Designs a service sector park

Table 7.2 continued

Proximal to distal policy	Substance	Brand	How designed	What is designed
IDEA	Rights and resource	The term "child with a disability" means a child with mental retardation, hearing impairments (including deafness), speech or language impairments, visual impairments (including blindness), serious emotional disturbance (referred to in this title as "emotional disturbance"), orthopedic impairments, autism, traumatic brain injury, other health impairments, or specific learning disabilities; and who by reason thereof, needs special education and related services Also to include a child experiencing development delays as defined by the state and measured by appropriate diagnostic instruments and procedures	Specific diagnostic brands are designed as "special"	Delay and resource room fodder
ADA	Rights	(1) Disability The term "disability" means, with respect to an individual, (a) a physical or mental impairment that substantially limits one or more major life activities of such individual; (b) a record of such an impairment; or (c) being regarded as having such an impairment		

Table 7.2 continued

Proximal to distal policy	Substance	Brand	How designed	What is designed
ADAAA	Rights	(1) Disability The term "disability" means, with respect to an individual, (a) a physical or mental impairment that substantially limits one or more major life activities of such individual; (b) a record of such an impairment; or (c) being regarded as having such an impairment		See ADA, now even more people can get diminished rights
United Nations Convention on the Rights of Persons with Disabilities	Rights	Definition of disability: The Convention adopts a social model of disability, and defines disability as including those who have long-term physical, mental, intellectual or sensory impairments which in interaction with various barriers may hinder their full and effective participation in society on an equal basis with others. (*Wikipedia*, 2012)	Internal contradiction – opens opportunity for ICF scrutiny	Vulnerability

Source: (Euthanasia.com, 2013); ADA = Americans with Disabilities Act; ADAAA = Americans with Disabilities Amendments Act; ADHD = attention deficit hyperactivity disorder; IDEA = Individuals with Disabilities Education Act; PCU = Public Contemporary University

From a different stance, one wonders why certain subpopulations have been designed as specialized legislation-worthy (Lehning, 2010) and others exposed to heinous discrimination and even genocide have not. Badinter (2006) and Bawer (2012) provided at least two rationales that resonate with us. In her discussion of gender equality, Badinter suggested that the maintenance of "specialized rights and policies" (in this discussion both disability-explicit and embedded) in essence serve to negate the articulated aims of equality. This insidious process occurs by surreptitious design in which recipients of resources and rights only granted by specialized policies exchange ongoing victimhood for meager benefits. Those who do not want to be branded or are not designed as victims remain under policy that is intended for all citizens. Bawer (2012) supports Badinter's disdain for segregated, layered instruments from an anti-identity politic stance. He suggests that such policies act as polemic simulacra which serve to disembowel informed profound dialog and negotiation. While we agree with that negative or neutral consequences often result from segregated policies, we do not see them as planfully evil.

Disability policy authors building on affirmative action, civil rights, and antidiscrimination initiatives launched by other groups, proceed from the tenet that disability-explicit and embedded policy advances equity, improvements in participation, and supportive services for those who fall under the eligibility criteria (Sander and Taylor, 2012). While such policies claim to create symmetry in opportunity access, wellness, and productivity (Apelmo, 2012; Handley, 2001), we along with Badinter (2006) and critical others would suggest that they do not. Rather, they legalize embodied disability branding through oxymoronic policies that use the strategy of stipulating eligibility criteria, or what is typically recognized as labeling or branding. By oxymoronic policy we refer to policy that contradicts its own narrative by virtue of its outcomes. Applied to disability explicit instruments, although under the protection and availed of the limited benefits of these policies, eligibles join the ranks of those who are labeled as disability category members with their lives and choices designed by others to obtain and maintain benefits.

While we do not naively believe that our globe treats everyone fairly, and as we call for inequity and disparity to be undesigned, we also maintain that legislating "special treatment" for a class of people with atypical bodies is a "Trojan horse" harboring a battalion of negative soldiers. Rather than assuring equality of worth for the same rights, resources, choices, and responsibilities conferred on everyone else (Clarke, 2012), hiding within are inequality and containment. Perhaps most toxic is the ongoing institutionalization of disability in the disability park by partitioning and "logofying" abstract principles and language contained in policy grand narrative. That is to say, qualifying under legislation signifies separation regardless of benefits.

Consider this example. Most proximal and fundamental to individual thriving is the right to live. Yet as early as infancy (not to mention prior to birth), children with medical diagnoses conceptually crafted as disabling are contained in rights policies that propose their excessive burden on their families and beyond. The quote below discusses a case brought to the United States Court of Appeals, 10th Circuit, in which parents of two children diagnosed with myelomeningocele sued a hospital which enrolled their children in a study of this diagnostic category in which supportive care only was provided. Both children died: "The court held that a right to treatment only exists in narrow circumstances, which do not include the category of infants born with myelomeningocele" (Wyszkowski, 2004). This policy decision is only one representative which foregrounds the devalued branding of embodied circumstance in infants such that life itself was "undesigned."

Moving longitudinally forward in life, the Individuals with Disabilities Education Act (IDEA) ostensibly guarantees the right for children in the United States to obtain "free and appropriate education," a right that was denied prior to the passage of PL 94-142. (US Department of Education, n.d.). IDEA also confers resources in the shape of services and products.

As we have stated previously, this analysis does not take a negative position on the necessity for service provision in a standardized educational climate in which the atypical are not well served. In Part 2, we discuss our own vision of design alternatives to "special rights policies." But first analysis of the roles of design and branding of children as they enter the educational wing of the disability park is warranted to illuminate how these strategies wield their power in current contexts and thus can be undesigned and redesigned for substantive change.

Several variables are used in branding all who are named in the eligibility criteria. More specific than more distal policies that we discuss below, these include the child's state of residence, diagnostic crest, professional evaluation, and the extent to which a child's educational attainment is affected by the disabling medical brand name. Here is the short list of brand names meeting the criteria for "special education."

Autism
Deaf-blindness
Deafness
Developmental delay
Emotional disturbance
Hearing impairment
Intellectual disability
Multiple disabilities
Orthopedic impairment
Other health impairment
Specific learning disability
Speech or language impairment

Traumatic brain injury
Visual impairment, including blindness.

(NDCCD, 2012)

For children who are summoned into the disability park with an IDEA invitation, the process and ultimate goals of the policy are broadened beyond academic achievement, choreographing behavioral and "life skills" aims through the Individuals Education Program (IEP) process. Unlike other students whose education is planned and enacted by teachers, legitimate members of the disability education park have a herd of health professionals who sit in consultation with educators to plan and scrutinize progress. Clearly the presence of "related service" personnel, a synonym for health/medical professionals, belies the medicalization model of disability that renders schools bipartite. Further embedded with the IEP process is what Conly (2013) refers to as coercive paternalism, an approach to managing people who are crafted as incapable of autonomous reasoning because of perceived interior deficit. We would see terms such as person-centered planning and self-determination, part of IEPs and other disability-explicit and embedded lexicon, as euphemistic for Conly's phrase which designs people as wards of the "other" who makes plans and decisions "for their own good."

A second assault of disability-explicit policy, unbeknownst to or overlooked by its supporters and implementers, strikes in the form of the diminished rights and conditional resources afforded to the eligibles. We consider disability-explicit policies in a fictitious university campus to illustrate.

The case of disability student services in "public contemporary university"

Two federal disability-explicit policies coalesce to shape disability student services on the Public Contemporary University (PCU) campus; Section 504 of the United States Rehabilitation Act of 1973 and its reauthorizations, and the Americans with Disabilities Act (ADA) of 1990 and the ADA Amendments Act (2008) (now considered as one policy/Act). Both policies are disability-explicit and both claim to protect and promote equality of civil rights.

> Benefits Narrative of Section 504: "No otherwise qualified individual with a disability...shall, solely by reason of her or his disability, be excluded from the participation in, be denied the benefits of, or be subjected to discrimination under any program or activity receiving federal financial assistance."
>
> Eligibility Narrative from Section 504: The Act defines "individual with a disability" as "any person who (i) has a physical or mental impairment which substantially limits one or more of such person's major life activities; (ii) has a record of such an impairment; or (iii) is regarded as having such an impairment.

Benefits Narrative from the ADA: Guided by landmark legislation the civil rights of students with disabilities are asserted and ensured such that they have the same opportunities available as persons without disabilities.

Eligibility Narrative from the ADA: Someone with a physical or mental impairment that substantially limits one or more major life activities of the individual, A record of such impairment, Being regarded as having such an impairment.

Now let us look at PCU's implementation (policy common to most public universities in the United States):

It is the policy and practice of PCU to comply with the Americans with Disabilities Act, Section 504 of the Rehabilitation Act, and the state and local requirements regarding students with disabilities. Under these laws, no qualified individual with a disability shall be denied access to or participation in services, programs, and activities of The University.

In compliance with federal and state regulations, **reasonable accommodations** [emphasis added] are provided to qualified students with disabilities. A qualified individual is a person who, with or without reasonable accommodations, can perform the essential functions of a program or course requirements. The essential requirements of an academic course or program need not be modified to accommodate an individual with a disability.

The University has a designated Disability Support Office located in its own, accessible building, as the office that coordinates services for students with disabilities, as part of the continuing effort to make the campus accessible.

Final responsibility for selection of the most appropriate accommodation rests with the University and is determined on a case-by-case basis.

Students are encouraged to meet with the director to develop a plan for their academic accommodations. A request for accommodation is deemed reasonable if it:

- Is based on documented individual needs; in all cases of non-apparent disability;
- Allows the most integrated experience possible

and

- Does not compromise essential requirements of a course or program;
- Does not pose a threat to personal or public safety;
- Does not impose undue financial or administrative burden;
- Is not of a personal nature.

In order to obtain benefits students must:

- Self identify as having a disability to faculty or staff
- Provide, at the student's expense, current appropriate documentation of disability and accommodation need from a qualified medical or other licensed professional
- Follow the PUC published procedures for requesting a specific accommodation or service. Note: It is the student's responsibility to meet the timelines and procedural requirements established by The University scheduling exams, requesting assistance, requesting alternate formats texts etc. If the student fails to provide adequate notice of the need for space and/or assistance he/she is still entitled to the accommodation, but there is no guarantee that it can be provided in the fullest measure
- Give letters requesting accommodations to faculty when appropriate
- Meet essential standards for courses and programs; maintaining status as a student who is otherwise qualified, with or without accommodations.
- Request and receive current, relevant documentation that supports requests for accommodations, academic adjustments and/or auxiliary aids and services
- Determine eligibility for accommodations based on a review of appropriate documentation
- Determine the appropriate accommodations for each student based on the individual's need
- Establish essential functions, abilities, skills, knowledge and standards for courses, programs, services, jobs and activities or facilities and to evaluate students on this basis
- Determine the appropriate standards in developing, constructing, remodeling and maintaining facilities
- Have appropriate staff discuss students and their disabilities in order to implement requested accommodations (particularly instructional accommodations)
- Deny a request for accommodations, academic adjustments or auxiliary aids and services, and/or barrier removal in facilities if the documentation does not demonstrate that the request is warranted, or if the individual fails to provide appropriate documentation
- Select among equally effective accommodations, academic adjustments and/or auxiliary aids and services
- Refuse unreasonable accommodations, academic adjustments or auxiliary aids and services, and/or facility-related barrier removal requests that impose a fundamental alteration on a program or activity of the university.

Analyzing this policy narrative highlights the requisite designing of the atypical student as needy on the basis of a legitimated medical brand name. Yet, who is considered "protected" and who is not is a moving target, owing to the vagueness of the policy text. Dissimilar to other PCU students who have academic faculty advisors, disability-park students are remanded to a geographically isolated location for their advising which takes a village, primarily of non-academic staff. Once invited into the park, students requesting any assistance from academic faculty must divulge personal information that no other student is required to share. And yet, even the presence of abrogation of privacy rights, while not desirable, is not as intolerable as the practices branded by two worn phrases: "reasonable accommodation," and "undue financial or administrative burden."

What is reasonable?

While often interpreted as fairness and equality, reasonable accommodation is just another synonym for diminished benefit, despite PCU charging identical tuition. Note that the term "reasonable" precedes the benefit of accommodation. We address accommodation in just a moment but stay with reasonable for now. At PCU, legitimated students requesting assistance from the disability park staff may receive alternative options that avail them of academic access. But reasonable is in the eyes of the beholder. Take the example of Dr. Popular and Dr. Obtuse, both of whom teach sections of the same course. Because Dr. Popular's classroom is located on the second floor of a building without an elevator, his section, although superior in learning opportunity to Dr. Obtuse's section, is not an option for the non-stair walkers.

Or consider another exemplar from the University of Maine. We interviewed Joshua, whose natural hearing does not receive the amplitude sufficient to access oral interchange in most on-site university classroom environments as they are currently designed. In his recent disability studies seminar, he was provided with a frequency-modulated loop system that only had one microphone for a single lecturer. Because this course was not structured as a lecture monolog, his device not only truncated his access to in-class discussion and activity, but also served to breach Joshua's brand confidentiality and provoke an "egalitarian utilitarian" structural change that decreased dialog for all students.

Accommodation refers to adjustment to a standardized world on a case-by-case basis. Although accommodations can often be useful and productive they also risk the obverse. Joshua's accommodation foregrounds the potential for failure of accommodation for the atypical body. But a larger scope of concern opens with accommodation in the form of product, environmental and/or programmatic responses to specific bodies. This strategy is dual purpose as it reifies embodied disability as a brand name while insidiously preserving the status quo. Healing rift between body and context through dealing a single card to a single player sustains the gaming within the disability park while the standard world continues to cater to ±2 standard deviations from the mean on the bell curve (DePoy and Gilson, 2007).

Taking undue financial or administrative burden to task

We often wonder what other group protected by rights policies would accept rights being trumped by the claim of economic scarcity. Yet, undue burden is inscribed front and center in the ADA and its Amendment Act cousins and Section 504 and its cousins despite the claim that disability is omnipresent throughout the longitudinal scope of human life, albeit more weighty on the upper end of years. Yet, in case after case, the economic challenge is upheld in the US "justice" or perhaps "unjustice" system. A point to consider here is the interconnectedness and thus foible of legislating human rights as an individualized response. This approach begets the utilitarian argument and to some extent deserves it. Given the impenetrable black holes in the ADA (and its amendment cousins) and similar policies which prescribe rights as affordable accommodations, it becomes hard to counter the utilitarian claim that expensive responses to a minuscule few deprive the majority. Still, the economic hierarchy violates humanitarian reasoning, and does even more intellectual work awaiting praxis as the undue burden clause raises the awareness for needed fundamental redesign of rights for a full range of humans, to be accomplished as discussed in Part 2.

Before more extensive travel, one more point needs to be visited in the ADA (and its updates), its enforcement. Responsibility for raising the ADA and the ADAAA lies with the park residents. The narrative below illustrates this design in the workplace:

> If your reasonable accommodation request is denied...
> - If your reasonable accommodation request is denied, you will receive a written notice explaining the specific reasons for the denial and your appeal rights.
> - You can ask the Executive Director to assign an impartial mediator from outside the agency to assist in resolving the matter informally. Requesting mediation is voluntary on your part. If you are not satisfied with the mediation process, you can file an equal employment opportunity (EEO) complaint.
> - To initiate an EEO complaint, you must contact an EEO counselor within 45 days of receipt of the written notice denying your reasonable accommodation request. If you request mediation, you must still contact an EEO counselor within 45 day of receiving the denial notice. The Bureau of the Public Debt in the Department of Treasury processes EEO complaints for the Access Board. To contact an EEO counselor, call Bureau of the Public Debt, 304-480-6527.

Note the officious tone and even the absence of a toll free telephone number. If feeling vulnerable already, how likely is it that an individual would buck a system, even if legal resources advertise their wares on television commercials?

Global rights: The UN Convention on the Rights of Persons with Disabilities

Ostensibly, the UN Convention defines disability through the lens of the social model (DePoy and Gilson, 2011). Yet the lexicon defaults to embodied deficit as the causal agent and the context as secondary: "those who have long-term physical, mental, intellectual or sensory impairments which in interaction with various barriers may hinder their full and effective participation in society on an equal basis with others."

Corporeal design invites the bearer into the global amorphous disability park, one which articulates rights but in actuality, positions atypical bodies for surveillance in large part with a similarly contradictory tool, the International Classification of Functioning (ICF). Developers and proponents of this taxonomy claim its progressive conceptual foundation as one which defines disability as interaction between body and context.

- Body functions
- Body structures
- Activities and participation: what people do from a menu of desired activities (e.g., learning, communication, mobility, self care, etc.)
- Environment: human and non-human support effects on function.

Yet, magnifying its parts and processes renders this claim false as only body functions and structures are operationalized in the World Health Organization instrument, the Word Health Organization Disability Assessment Scale (WHODAS).

> WHODAS 2.0 does not currently assess environmental factors. Assessment of a respondent's functioning includes enquiries about the current environment of the respondent, but coding is based on functioning and disability, not on the environment.
> (Üstün, Kostanjsek, Chatterji, and Rehm, 2010: 33)

How then is environment captured if it is missing in action from the assessment tool? The UN Convention on the Rights of Persons with Disabilities, while theoretically enacted to raise awareness and reduce discrimination and disadvantage experienced by populations identified or identifying as disabled, is often persuasive in the abstract but lacks substantive content, enforcement, and thus is policy simulacra as well. Many terms that are at the heart of the policy are often undefined. Even more extreme, the mechanisms for enforcement are absent, designing a grand narrative at the global level. The branding mechanism of the UN Convention, the WHODAS 2.0, further reifies the deficient body as the locus of disability throughout the globe.

Designing resource allocation and poverty

Resource distribution policies guide the provisions of designer disability services and resources assigning benefits to legitimate disability park frequenters based on the hierarchy of worth that we referred to as pedigree in previous chapters. Unfortunately, these policies design disability as poverty as well even in its absence.

The Access Pass (US Geological Survey, 2013) is a free ticket to those who qualify. Interestingly, parking placards for disability parking are not considered as legitimate evidence of eligibility, perhaps because they confer "phony" disability status to so many who desire privileged parking real estate. Regardless of income or personal wealth, the stamp of a physician certifying permanent physical, mental, or sensory impairment qualifies an individual for free use of national park resources. Named "disability privilege" by Stone (2001), the provision of resources even if they are not needed implicitly brands disability as poverty and thus confuses responses to each through conflation.

The Social Security Disability Insurance Act (SSDI) (established by the Social Security Amendments of 1956, in the United States) is more direct in designing disability as poverty. It provides safety net public support to individuals who acquired embodied conditions and were invited into the disability club through a meritorious portal.

> To qualify for Social Security disability benefits, you must first have worked in jobs covered by Social Security. Then you must have a medical condition that meets Social Security's definition of disability. In general, we pay monthly cash benefits to people who are unable to work for a year or more because of a disability.

Yet, subsistence support only is received. Considering the serious disparity in employment opportunity between park inhabitants and their distant neighbors beyond the park ramparts, we question the wisdom or ethics of designing poverty through the provision of meager benefits. While safety net support, in our opinion, is a moral imperative, we would suggest that it should be both temporary and humane, until opportunity can be redesigned as equivalent for all.

Although there have been some changes in law, further designing poverty are the penalties of earning minimum or close to minimum wages when an individual does obtain gainful employment. Health insurance benefits may be lost even if not provided by the employer. Such policies are not major incentives to leave disability park poverty for equivalent or even more extreme poverty outside of its perimeter.

> While the SSDI program is a central component of the US social safety net, it suffers from two substantial ailments that limit its effectiveness and threaten its long-term viability. First, the program is ineffective in assisting the vast majority of workers with less severe disabilities to reach their employment potential or to earn their own way. In fact, the program provides strong incentives to applicants and beneficiaries to remain out of the labor force permanently, and it provides no incentive to employers to implement cost-effective accommodations that would enable disabled employees to remain on the job. Consequently, large numbers of work-capable individuals voluntarily exit the labor force, apply for, and ultimately receive SSDI annually. In 2010, fully 2 percent of the SSDI-insured population – 2.9 million workers – applied for SSDI benefits. Somewhere between 50 and 60 percent of applicants will eventually receive an award. But even those who are ultimately denied benefits will spend substantial time – typically one to three years – out of the labor force before they have exhausted all appeals. At that point, their reemployment prospects may be substantially worse than they were at the time of initial application.
>
> (Salam, 2012)

A major argument against increasing the public support benefits for those who are excluded from employment is the potential for fraud. Yet this discussion does not seem to make its entrance into academic analyses and policy reform think tanks in any useful manner.

> One of the inevitable dangers of talking about SSDI reform is that it is easy to seem as though you're accusing all SSDI beneficiaries of being dishonest layabouts. The truth is very different. A large number of beneficiaries really are profoundly disabled, and many more are emotionally distressed and socially isolated. Indeed, a lack of attachment to the working world can in some cases exacerbate these problems.
>
> (Salam, 2012)

The quote above is curious in that it foregrounds the medicalization of unemployment. Note that we are not taking a position about employment or unemployment as central to human worth. However, we are suggesting that designed poverty is unacceptable and needs to be dismantled such that all people have basic human rights and dignity. This point brings us to a related economic issue, the design and branding by charity which we introduced but now discuss in more detail.

Designing and branding by charity

The origins of designing the atypical body as the object of charity can be located in the Middle Ages. It was not unusual to find members of the clergy in the Christian religions, Islamic societies (Plattner, 2011), and Buddhist monks in the Far East (Nakamura, 2006) providing treatment to those who were considered ill. Faith as a healer also has its roots in the Middle Ages. People who could not see or think as most others did, among other human differences, were often the objects of faith healing, a practice that provided concrete evidence of God's love, presence, and power (Finucane, 1995). Charity in the form of service and almsgiving exonerated the giver in the eyes of God, designing purpose for the extremes of human difference. Through the work of St. Francis of Assisi, the suffering of the poor and sick (particularly individuals identified with leprosy) gave a moral role to the recipients of care, as well as to those providing care. Faith-based care for those who approximated the low end of worth was born and now serves as the archetype of contemporary secular charities and institutions (DePoy and Gilson, 2004) mostly branded with the logo of "non-profit." Investigating the meaning of this brand name however, reveals multiple and unexpected understandings: "the nonprofit sector suffers from the distinction of being the only sector whose name begins with a negative, as Harvard Business School Professor Allen Grossman has noted. It apologizes for itself before it begins" (Pallotta, 2008: 4).

Within formal tax law, the following narrative defines the scope and primary aim of non-profit corporations: "Nonprofit corporations, by definition, exist not to make money but to fulfill one of the purposes recognized by federal law: charitable, educational, scientific, or literary" (Nolo, 2014). This broad designation locates much of the disability park within the abstract realm of charity, obfuscating its fiscal face. However, consider the following analysis:

> The real driver is the group-think influenced by adoption of the Orwellian "non-profit" label. Distinguishing between "non-profit" and "for-profit" is misleading. For any venture to stay afloat, revenues must meet or exceed expenses. The excess of revenues over expenditures is profit, whether earned by a private or public company. The only significant difference between "for-profit" and "non-profit" is that the former pays taxes on the excess of revenues over expenditures, while the latter doesn't. To be accurate, ventures should be called "taxed" or "untaxed." The labels imply good versus bad, or altruistic versus selfish. But a venture, taxed or untaxed, is neither one nor the other.
>
> (Kilbourne, 2012)

The two brief quotes above do much intellectual work. First, the name "nonprofit" is simply a tax structure that legally invites deductible donation.

So, contrary to its explicit message of charity, the brand does not mean that services are being provided at no cost or that park employees are working out of the goodness of their hearts so to speak. Rather, this corporate designation, names the charitable industrial complex by Buffett (2013) is profitable for a very few on the backs of too many. Buffett is compelling in his argument:

> As more lives and communities are destroyed by the system that creates vast amounts of wealth for the few, the more heroic it sounds to "give back." It's what I would call "conscience laundering" – feeling better about accumulating more than any one person could possibly need to live on by sprinkling a little around as an act of charity.
> But this just keeps the existing structure of inequality in place. The rich sleep better at night, while others get just enough to keep the pot from boiling over. Nearly every time someone feels better by doing good, on the other side of the world (or street), someone else is further locked into a system that will not allow the true flourishing of his or her nature or the opportunity to live a joyful and fulfilled life.
>
> (Buffett, 2013)

However, Palotta (2008) raises other major "snafus" that are too often swept under the proverbial rug in the logic, or illogic" of the not-for-profit system. Similar to our thinking, he queries "Where before we thought of opening a homeless shelter, we need now to ask what it would take to end homelessness in our city" (Palotta, 2008: 184).

Palotta then criticizes the structural and legal limitations that devitalize non-profit entities, detailing the rules under which these "second-class" capitalist segments must operate in exchange for tax exemptions, and illuminating how such constraints serve the for-profit sector, albeit surreptitiously. The expectation that desire for high income and altruism cannot or should not co-exist within the same human relegates non-profit "do-gooders" to disproportionately low salaries when compared to their for-profit counterparts, sending talent heading for the profit hills.

Similarly, disallowing equivalent investment potential in for-profit and non-profit business deflects capital to the profit arena, rendering non-profit agencies as poor stepchildren in a constant struggle for survival, which in itself siphons off the fiscal potency of the scant non-profit bank account necessary to meet human need: "What if a system that frowns on self-interest turns out to be an inferior way of serving the interests of others?" (Palotta, 2008).

Most fundamental are the questions of why expectations that park services are or should be branded as charitable, be exonerated from paying tax, or be segregated and prohibited from using the success strategies of the profit sector to do good work. The non-profit brand is just another simulacrum for designing disability as poverty and creating a class of non-citizens who serve as altruistic testing grounds. History persists.

Disability-implicit policy

We have not yet engaged with disability-implicit policy, but do so now. As defined above, disability implicit policies do not name disability within the policy but design it by its absence or desired absence. Consider, for example, health insurance policy which allows medical insurance firms to screen for preexisting conditions and weight.

> Gone are the days of just signing up for health insurance and hoping you don't have to use it. Now, more employees are being asked to roll up their sleeves for medical tests – and to exercise, participate in disease-management programs and quit smoking to qualify for hundreds, even thousands of dollars' worth of premium or deductible discounts.
>
> (Appleby, 2012)

Given the cost of medical insurance and the escalating costs for medical service in general, the intent of these types of policies seems to be both fiscally sound and productive for individual health.

> Proponents say that such plans offer people a financial incentive to make healthier choices and manage chronic conditions such as obesity, high blood pressure and diabetes, which are driving up health care costs in the USA. Even so, studies of the effect of such policies on lifestyle changes are inconclusive.
>
> (Appleby, 2012)

While not specific to embodied disablement design, these policies tell a story of a profit incentive dressed up as concern for humans. Moreover, the responsibility for embodied condition is placed on the individual without regard for the ability of many to control weight or related corporeal phenomena. Consider for example, individuals whose providers prescribe medications that produce weight gain even with careful diet and exercise. It seems to us that the design of disablement lies in fiscal, tobacco, alcohol, and pharmaceutical camps and even more insidiously in the food and beauty industries, both which have much to say about "healthy" weight. We are not excusing people from responsibility for their own health. Rather, we are urging a post-postmodern examination of disability-implicit policies, particularly with regard to how they design and brand the value of bodies, populations, and behaviors and then hang valued outcomes on these policy doorposts that may have nothing to do with individual choice.

Summary and query: Branding and designing morality?

We close this chapter with some queries about the efficacy of current policy in designing disparity reduction and thus morality. Just to recap, three types of disability policies, explicit, embedded, and implicit, all have a role in using narrative to design and brand disability. Explicit and embedded policies, despite some which claim to design disability as a phenomenon beyond the body, by their eligibility criteria all locate disability within the body. Disability-implicit policy, by suggesting what "should not be" accomplishes this same aim, branding bodies as responsible for what may be beyond their control. While the policies may create some benefits for the owners of these bodies, the design and branding of disability remains pejorative, often riddled with essentialism, negative stereotype, and the perpetuation of the normal/abnormal binary (Bickenbach, 2008). Moreover, focus on bodies excuses action from a broader scope.

As revealed above, policy is much more complex than its explicit verbiage and articulated desired outcomes. Policy skepticism seems not only warranted but essential to the promotion of informed change. As noted by Kymlica (2007) in his analysis of multiculturalism, and Davis (2006) in his discussion of justice, global human rights policy is plagued by two overarching problems. The first is the failure of current categorical frameworks to do viable work in carving up humanity into useful categories. Kymlica's assertion provides one of the foundational pillars of our view, as we question the legitimacy of so many diverse and vague narratives for disability despite the commonality of all designed as embodied deficit. It is difficult to see how "rights" policies which target and isolate populations for inferior benefits such as reasonable accommodation are useful for achieving the asserted purposes of full participation.

A related issue identified by Kymlica (2007) is the time sequence of designing and implementing targeted and generic policy. Applied to disability, we suggest that targeted distributive and protective legislation designs disability as disjuncture. Consider social security disability insurance that one enters through the body deficiency portico and then expands disability as disjuncture through coerced poverty. Or ponder the disabling brands of vulnerable, in need of specialized assistance, at risk, and object of charity that are conferred in the disability park that provides tax exempt economic opportunities and advantage to providers and disability designers in exchange for relinquishing the best tools of the market trades. Analysis of disability explicit and embedded policy reveals it as a grand narrative, a brand of designed identity policy that on the surface speaks of resources and equity for eligible bodies but in essence, disables the recipient through abstract, obfuscated means (Smith, 2007).

Both nationally and internationally, we recognize the aim of these policies for redressing discrimination and exclusion, particularly in a standard, corporatized world context in which population specific policies and resources are the predominant distributive model. However, through a post-postmodern lens, the apprehensible intent of disability explicit and embedded policy is open for interrogation and analysis and necessary if movement away from oxymoronic policy to population-wide equality and justice is to occur.

Part 2 awaits.

References

Apelmo, E. (2012) (Dis)Abled Bodies, Gender, and Citizenship in the Swedish Sports Movement. *Disability and Society*, 27 (4), 563–74.
Appleby, J. (2012) More U.S. Employers Tie Health Insurance to Medical Tests. *USA Today*, April 2. Available online at http://usatoday30.usatoday.com/money/industries/health/story/2012-04-01/employee-health-incentives/53932628/1 (accessed January 23, 2014).
Badinter, É. (2006) *Dead End Feminism*, trans. J. Borossa. Cambridge: Polity.
Bawer, B. (2012) *The Victim's Revolution*. New York: Random House.
Bickenbach, J. (2008) Disability, Non-Talent and Distributive Justice. In K. Kristiansen, S. Vehmas, and T. Shakespeare, *Arguing About Disability: Philosophical Perspectives*. London, UK: Routledge, pp. 105–23.
Buffett, P. (2013) The Charitable-Industrial Complex. *New York Times*, July 26. Available online at www.nytimes.com/2013/07/27/opinion/the-charitable-industrial-complex.html?_r=0 (accessed January 23, 2014).
Clarke, S. R. (2012) *Foundations of Freedom: Welfare-Based Arguments Against Paternalism*. New York: Routledge.
Conly, S. (2013) *Against Autonomy: Justifying Coersive Paternalism*. Cambridge: Cambridge University Press.
Davis, L. (2006) Life, Death, and Biocultural Literacy. *Chronicle of Higher Education*, 52 (18), B9–10.
DePoy, E., and Gilson, S. (2004) *Rethinking Disability: Principles for Professional and Social Change*. Pacific Grove, CA: Wadsworth.
DePoy, E., and Gilson, S. (2007) The Bell Shaped Curve: Alive and Well and Living in Diversity Rhetoric. *International Journal of Organisations, Communities and Nations*, 7 (3), 253–60.
DePoy, E., and Gilson, S. (2011) *Studying Disability*. Los Angeles, CA: Sage.
Finucane, R. C. (1995) *Miracles and Pilgrims*. New York: Macmillan.
Handley, P. (2001) 'Caught Between a Rock and a Hard Place': Anti-discrimination Legislation in the Liberal State and the Fate of the Australian Disability Discrimination Act. *Australian Journal of Political Science*, November, 515–29.
Kilbourn, P. (2012) For- and Non-Profit Are Misleading Labels. *Wall Street Journal*, December 23. Available online at http://online.wsj.com/article/SB10001424127887323723104578187503700917488.html (accessed January 23, 2014).
Kymlicka, W. (2007) Multicultural Odysseys: *Navigating the New International Politics of Diversity*. New York: Oxford University Press.
Lehning, A. J. (2010) Local Government Adoption of Aging-Friendly Policies and Programs: A Mixed Methods Approach. Doctoral Dissertation, University of California, Berkeley. Available online at http://escholarship.org/uc/item/1jh9q6wr (UMI 3413420)
Nakamura, K. (2006) *Deaf in Japan*. Ithaca, NY: Cornell University Press.
NDCCD (2012) Categories of Disability Under IDEA. NICHCY National

Dissemmination Center for Children with Disabilities. Available online at http://nichcy.org/disability/categories#deafness (accessed January 23, 2014).

Nolo (2014) Tax Concerns When Your Nonprofit Corporation Earns Money. Retrieved from NOLO Law for All. Available online at www.nolo.com/legal-encyclopedia/taxes-nonprofit-corporation-earnings-30284.html (accessed January 23, 2014).

Palotta, D. (2008) *Uncharitable*. Medford, MA: Tufts University Press.

Plattner, M. (2011) Disability in the Eyes of Religion. *MyHandicap*. Available online at www.myhandicap.com/disability-religion-islam-buddhism-christianity-jewish.html (accessed February 13, 2014).

Salam, R. (2012) David Autor on Disability. The Agenda. *National Review Online*, May 2. Available online at www.nationalreview.com/agenda/298741/david-autor-disability-reihan-salam (accessed January 23, 2014).

Sander, R., and Taylor, S. (2012) *Mismatch: How Affirmative Action Hurts Students It's Intended to Help, and Why Universities Won't Admit It*. New York: Basic Books.

Smith, S. (2007) *Applying Theory to Policy and Practice*. Newport: Ashgate.

Stone, D. (2001) *Policy Paradox: The Art of Political Decision Making, Revised Edition*. New York: Norton.

Titchkosky, T. (2007) *Reading and Writing Disability Differently*. Toronto, ON: University of Toronto Press.

Üstün, T. B., Kostanjsek, N., Chatterji, S., and Rehm, J. (2010) *Measuring Health and Disability: Manual for WHO Disability Assessment Schedule (WHODAS 2.0)*. Geneva: World Health Organization.

US Department of Education (n.d.) Building the Legacy: IDEA 2004. US Department of Education. Available online at http://idea.ed.gov (accessed January 23, 2014).

US Geological Survey (2013) Overview of the Access Pass. USGS: Science for A Changing World, January 9. Available online at http://store.usgs.gov/pass/access.html (accessed January 23, 2014).

US Social Security Administration (n.d.) Social Security. Disability Planner: How You Qualify For Social Security Disability Benefits. Available online at www.ssa.gov/dibplan/dqualify.htm (accessed January 23, 2014).

Wyszkowski, J. (2004) Legal Rights of Disabled Infants to Receive Life-Sustaining Medical Treatment. *Connecticut Public Interest Law Journal*, 4 (1), 181–209.

8 Designing disability
Beyond the limits of humanness

> For many persons with a disability, the greatest struggle is to have others accept them as human.
>
> The common institutional practice at state hospitals of burying the dead without name or date indicated the extreme of this loss of individuality.
>
> Bertha Flaten (1875–1905) was institutionalized because she had seizures. When she died, a cast-concrete marker with the number 7 was placed on her grave. There are many thousands of such graves around the United States.
>
> (Smithsoniam, n.d)

In this chapter, we enter the dark abyss of designing the legitimacy of the atypical body for membership, quasi-membership, or exclusion from the category of human. Geneticized, branded and designed as not normal, undesirable, and in need of change (DePoy and Gilson, 2011; Gedge, 2010), embodied disablement can provide an important but often circumvented analysis of the explicit and implicit design of the legitimate human body, its symbolism, and responses, including institutionally sanctioned violence (Iadacola and Schupe, 2013) that such bodies elicit from diverse local through global social and cultural entities. Beyond simply theorizing, this dialogue begins to exhume substantive potent examination of the design and branding of humanness, a critical topic of negotiation too frequently interred.

Consistent with the legitimacy approach that organizes much of the thinking work in this book, humanness, in this chapter, and then throughout the remainder of the book, is lexically characterized as the set of attributes that endows an individual with legitimate membership in the category of human and thus endows that individual with equivalent rights and opportunities, at least ostensibly, that are afforded to other category members. Fuentes (2012) reminds us, however, that humanness is complex, pluralistic and difficult to conceptually capture. Thus, the attributes envisioned as human are changeable within context and beckon for the eschewal of simplistic myths about categorical similarities in favor of precision. Consistent with Fuentes' pronouncements, albeit through alternative spectacles, Smith (2010) urges the examination of humanness and personhood as the basis for making the world a better place for all beings.

Woven into the legitimacy framework, post-postmodernist thinking helps us undertake Fuentes' (2012) and Smith's (2010) charges by bringing multiple sources to bear on this colloquy about humanness. Countering postmodernism, post-postmodern thought takes aim at irony, skepticism, and gossameriness of its predecessor, with the intent of returning a body of palpable, but innovative and reshuffled substance to the realm of knowledge. Because post-postmodern work both engages and reorganizes multiple theoretical, spiritual, aesthetic, and disciplinary actors on its interactive stage, this contemporary thought has great potency in furthering and deepening both the formulations of and answers to complex questions such as the major ones in this chapter, "who belongs to the category of humanness," "who does not," and what is the nature of the design and branding continua of humanness?

Within this synthetic approach, a curious matrix of theory and experience provoked our thinking about the role of the embodied atypical in designing the perimeter of humanness beyond which diverse levels of acceptance through non-acceptance are crafted. So, before excavating evidence, we decided to share with you the thinking and experiential processes that gave shape to querying the role that disability designed as embodied takes in the conferral or removal of humanness.

How did we arrive here?

Several years ago, we had the opportunity to hear a conference paper on wrongful life and wrongful birth policies inscribed in court decisions in Israeli policy (Mor, 2014). Although a number of theorists had already written in this area (Feldman, 2009), Mor's powerful discussion actually kick-started our own thinking and reading about the interstices between atypical bodies and humanness. Through discussion and reading, more fundamental questions about the meaning of "human" in human rights policies began to make their way to the physical and virtual shelves of our library. In the previous chapter, the term "human rights" was used without specificity in defining "human" and its obverse, "not human." Of course, everyone knows the characteristics of human and humanness, right? But when does humanity begin, how is it designed through prenatal screening, allowed to be born and once born verified or falsified with the atypical body as reflection? In this chapter, these questions are broached through continuing a discussion of policy and enlisting the assistance of the atypical body as a designer of humanness boundaries and what lies beyond.

A second area that joins policy and further amplifies thinking about humanness is technology. We only mention it here to trace the multiple paths that informed the agenda about humanness and then revisit technology in detail in Chapter 11. Our own recent work in two areas of technology research and development and related teaching, movement-inspired robotic devices and avatar communication, were particularly influential in that they led to the literature on cyborg studies and post-humanism (Haraway, 1991; Kurtzweil, 2006; Wolfe, 2010). This literature queries the acceptable boundaries of the human corpus and engages in heated debates about the extent to which exogenous paraphernalia diminish or augment humanness (Weyand, Bundle, and McGowan, 2009). As an example, Case (2010) suggests that all people in the contemporary world are both cyborgs and more human as result of digital networking and devices, while Kelly (2009) vehemently opposes technological reinvention of atypical bodies.

Learning from students is particularly robust. Each year in our course on introduction to disability studies, we discuss historical practices aimed at embodied difference. Each year, the entrée into disability histories, although revisionist, as looking back through contemporary eyes cannot be avoided, contains documentation of embodied difference as a regular curiosity. As reflected in the disability studies literature, students encounter the atypical body as context dependent, and although not always the case, marginalized through elimination with those at the extremes, engendering the most severe consequences of being denied humanness. But, until the students in the class grapple with an analysis of current disavowal of humanness, they bristle at historical practices such as leaving atypical infants to die, institutionalizing those with unacceptable behavior, and showcasing children with mobility impairments on telethons.

We learn from them that it is necessary for both students and their faculty to clarify that these areas of study do not and should not begin with arguments for ethical or moral correctness. Rather, ethical debate awaits a full grasp of the complexity that inheres in any discussion of human categorization. As example and reflected in our discussion of selective abortion below, we are always reminded that we need to emphasize to students the critical importance of parsing issues such that each can be fully analyzed without leakage that distills and obfuscates the focus of analysis. Not all abortion discussion is about the right to choose versus the right to life. Distinguishing the right to choose from the role of selective prenatal screening and pregnancy termination policies and practices is seminal in understanding the design and branding of the humanness boundaries that are offended by embodied disablement. Once dissected for the students, a current form of legitimating entry into the universe of humanness diminishes disdain for previous civilizations. We thus continue to learn from our students that the removal of obfuscating moral sediment and flotsam is in order to render the focus of analysis crystal clear.

Perusing virtual and onsite museum exhibitions and the emerging literature about disability art, aesthetics and installations has been another fertile field for seeding thought about the work done by the embodied atypical in setting the parameters which welcome or disinvite individuals and groups from the category of acceptable humanness (Siebers, 2010).

Finally informing the humanness agenda is the death of our beloved aunt, Louise, whose later life reflects an archetypal intersection of disability designed as embodied and humanness. As her condition, diagnosed as Huntington's disease, became more noticeable, family members moved from descriptive terms of pity to denial of her humanity. Loving relatives whispered, " She would be better off dead," she is no longer herself," and so forth. When she died last year, common euphemisms such as "now she is at peace," or "her suffering is over" were spoken, despite anyone having conversed with her about the peace or suffering that she may or may not have experienced during her life without and then with Huntington's disease. More profoundly illustrative of dismantling her humanness, any celebration of Louise's life felt absent at her own funeral, as the few in attendance prattled on about their daily lives, not noticing that the purpose of the family gathering was to acknowledge the life lived and the death of a once beloved family member.

Given the huge scope of imagery, narrative, belief, and intentionality that shape and reflect acceptable humanness, this chapter is primarily a contemplation on policies that target embodied acceptance through institutional violence and elimination. We only devote one chapter in this book to design and branding humanness delimited by policy analysis while we continue to read, think and develop this work for the future.

Navigating the humanness field

We now enter and explore the intersection of embodied diversity and humanness through four conceptual but intimate subdivisions within the residential property of policy. Table 8.1 depicts the conceptual organization through which policy and its meanings for assigning humanness to bodies are analyzed.

The taxonomy below further parses and sharpens what has been referenced in recent literature as "disqualification" from humanity (Siebers, 2010). Violating humanness is the gateway through which one must pass to challenge humanness. Atypical embodied condition, ascertainable through observation or report, catches the watchful eye of the humanness police so to speak and begins the interrogation of legitimacy of any offending body as human.

Once illegitimacy as human is established, the remaining three divisions in the taxonomy move from the least to most severe design responses. Revising the illegitimate offender activates the disability park through behavioral interventions, practicing "normalcy" or similar body modification. More severe is reinvention, which speaks to the augmented redesign of deficient bodies with the use of non-organic parts and processes. Denial

Table 8.1 Four conceptual subdivisions

Concept	Definition
Violating humanness	Legitimating the atypical body – what embodied criteria of "humanness" are lost, never obtained or otherwise not present?
Revising the illegitimate	In order to instil or restore humanness, what elements of atypical embodiment are changed and how?
Reinventing embodied humanness	How have bodies been reworked, redesigned to expand/contract the range of humanness (prosthesis, robotic enhancements, cyborg, avatar)?
Denying humanness	When embodied revision or reinvention cannot occur, what historical and contemporary methods are used to eliminate the violating body (selective abortion, terminating life)?

of humanness designs the offender out of humanity through preventing, denying, or dismissing the worth of life.

In this chapter, as noted above, we focus the remainder of our discussion on selected policies which design and brand violations through denial of humanness. This work serves as the basis for subsequent discussions and thought about revision and reinvention through undesign and redesign not only of disability but more broadly of humanness and humane coexistence in which diversity is not merely simulacrum but a substantive and defining constant of our vision for fair and just global environments. Four major policy arenas are interrogated as they expose the role of design and branding in crafting desirable humanness and its most distal boundaries.

Selective abortion

Medical rhetoric is perhaps the most ostentatious in the parade of values subsumed in and reflected by the normal body, the desirable, and the body legitimately branded as disabled. Even before birth, policy guiding prenatal testing is designed to identify, capture and distinguish the normal from the abnormal, and thus can take the position of defining the attributes of humanness that are branded as never obtained by the abnormal (Mills and Erzikova, 2012; Parry, 2013). These "abnormals," if allowed to join the living, are assumed to suffer or struggle more than others who are typical or cause such distress for proximal to distal normals from parents through taxpayers (Wasserman and Asche, 2006). Thus, the prevention of such births is seen as caring and compassionate by some, such as Garrison (2012): "I believe that abortion of a disabled fetus can be a compassionate choice made for morally sound reasons, and does not at all conflict with the respect due to disabled people."

Potential sufferers can be saved through the benevolence of prenatal testing policies specifically naming Down syndrome, other intellectual genetic markers of intellectual impairment, and neural tube defects among others as violating conditions. However, it is doubtful that selective abortion for any other group would be supported as a humane gesture on the basis of scientific data. According to Hubbard:

> Scientists and physicians in this and other countries are once more engaged in developing the means to decide what lives are worth living and who should and should not inhabit the world.... Except that now they provide only the tools, while pregnant women themselves have to make the decisions, euphemistically called choices.
>
> (Hubbard, 2013: 82)

Support for Hubbard's position is not simple. Teasing out prevention from devaluation of living beings is often invoked to counter vilification of selective abortion (Raz, 2004). Yet, Glover's (2006), and Wasserman's and Ashe's (2006) words resonate with Hubbard's thinking:

> What does it do to your sense of being a valued member of society to realize that there are people who go to great lengths to avoid the birth of someone like you?
>
> (Glover, 2006: 5)

> The justification for enabling a woman to decide whether to have a child is stronger than the justification for enabling her to decide what kind of child she will have. Pregnancy makes massive demands on a woman's body; parenthood involves an enormous, open-ended commitment. To treat the difference between having a disabled and a nondisabled child as being of a similar magnitude as the difference between having and not having a child greatly exaggerates the burden of disability and ignores the source of so much of that burden.
>
> (Wasserman's and Ashe, 2006: 54)

Similar to Hubbard's viewpoint, we do not take a position on the right to choose to have a child. Moreover, in concert with Raz (2004), the distinction among preventing life and supporting the living is an important one to visit and analyze. Having done so, it is clear to us that policies supporting prenatal testing and selective abortion are made by the living who are reflecting on the living, and illuminate and distinguish the design of violating bodies that squeeze through the scientific turnstiles erected to prevent their existence.

Furthermore, comparisons of the reasons for preventing the birth of a violating body reveal the disavowal of gendercide and racial genocide, but not for eliminating bodies that do not meet functional standards. To the

contrary, even the argument below made against racialized abortions fully
affirms abortion for functional limitations.

> Whatever the intent of the abortion industry may be by functional stan-
> dards, abortion is a racist institution. In the United States, black
> children are aborted at 5 times the rate as white children and Hispanic
> children don't fare much better.
>
> (Abort73.com, 2013)

Now consider Dollar's comparative analysis of gendercide and disability:

> I don't think such decisions are at all the same as decisions to abort a
> baby girl because her father's family wants a son to carry on the family
> name, or to abort a baby boy because a mother says that her sons
> haven't completely fulfilled her desires as a parent. Arguing that they
> are the same belittles the suffering that people with many types of
> disabilities experience – not because of how other people treat or
> perceive us (although that can cause a different kind of pain), but
> because these disabilities cause real damage to body, mind, and spirit.
>
> (Dollar, 2012)

Entered in evidence of the design of an undesirable or violating life are
both the title and content of Douglas' (2008) book, *Freedom, Healing for
Parents of Disabled Children*. This memoir begins with chapter 1, The Storm,
and proceeds with the first narrative sentences, "Something was wrong. I
sensed it moments after her birth" (p. 1).

Douglas then proposes prayer as the pathway necessary to overcome
grief and proceed to more positive configurations of a family living with
disappointment and despair. This viewpoint reflects an historical trend of
the twentieth century for which Olshansky (1962) was perhaps best known.
Olshansky's approach designed the embodied atypical as a violating condition to be grieved, and thus posited a developmental grieving sequence
enacted immediately upon the birth a "defective baby."

Throughout the longitudinal process of a life, atypical functioning,
appearance and/or experience perceived as resulting from the corpus is
branded as disability (DePoy and Gilson, 2011). Thus, designing a body as
legitimately disabled in essence requires that the criteria for desirable and
typical development and function not be met.

Of particular note is the sanctioned prenatal elimination of bodies
violating the "intelligence criterion." We quote Kolbrener below, as her pen
scribed a poignantly distressing article about the plight of babies with
Down syndrome in the ultra-Orthodox Jewish community in Israel.

> When Shmuel, my sixth child, arrived with Down syndrome, I cried
> bitterly as I imagined myself dead and him homeless; I played hostess

to numerous other fantasies, my own and those of other women, who came to cry by my childbed.

It is by now a pretty widely held truth that nobody, but nobody, wants to give birth to a child with Down syndrome. Now there are at least two ways in Israel for a woman to rid herself of so untoward a burden. She can, as my more secular-minded cousin did, abort early. Or she can do what my ultra-Orthodox neighbor did and "abort" late by unloading her cargo at the nearest hospital and fleeing.

I have heard many stories over the years of women in ultra-Orthodox communities who have availed themselves of the latter option. Here is how the system works in my Jerusalem neighborhood:

After a mother leaves the hospital, her first stop before returning home – strangely empty-handed – is the ultra-Orthodox "family planner," a well-known figure who is a pillar of trust and discernment in such a matter. The mother leaves her newborn's details with her.

Then, the family planner will put an ad in the local Orthodox paper, Yated Ne'eman, ("Wanted: Mother") to find a home for the child since the hospital extends its hospitality to healthy newborns for just one month. The placement is easier than one would think. True, there's a stigma attached to birthing and raising a Down syndrome child of one's own. But paradoxically, a family who shelters such a child is seen as doing an immense mitzvah; there are plenty of eager mothers willing to raise the baby, until it becomes too much of a burden and is passed to another home. And so, with the ease and simplicity by which one might get rid of an unwanted kitten, an unwanted baby is cast out into the world.

(Kolbrener, 2013)

Goodey (2011) provides an alternative explanation in his compelling work and one which we see as potentially restorative of humanness. Rather than positioning intellectual impairment as an entity in itself, one that begets suffering, and thus should be compassionately eliminated before individual pain begins, Goodey characterizes intelligence and its relative diminishment as contextual rather than neurological, exposing the design of cognitive capacity as constructed for the purpose of ascribing social status. He supports his claim with evidence showing the fickle nature of intelligence quotient testing, which surrenders to social pressures in both its lexical and operational definitions. Thus, using Goodey's framework, annihilating cognitive violation is a social control design, not a fundamental altruistic function as claimed by Dollar and her and contemporaries. "Culture is itself the root of intelligence. It is not simply a lens through which we are seeing refracted some otherwise stable component of human nature" (Goodey, 2011: 283).

Rights and delays

Now, moving longitudinally forward we revisit the definition of disability posited by two penultimate rights policies, the Americans with Disabilities Act of 1990 (ADA), the ADA Amendments Act of 2008 (ADAAA), and the Disability and Equality Act of 2010 in the United Kingdom:

ADA and ADAAA definition:
(1) has a physical or mental impairment that substantially limits one or more major life activities; OR (2) has a record of such an impairment; OR (3) is regarded as having such an impairment.

A *physical impairment* is defined by ADA as "any physiological disorder or condition, cosmetic disfigurement, or anatomical loss affecting one or more of the following body systems: neurological, musculoskeletal, special sense organs, respiratory (including speech organs), cardiovascular, reproductive, digestive, genitourinary, hemic and lymphatic, skin, and endocrine."

Equality Act of 2010:
A person has a disability if:
• they have a physical or mental impairment
• the impairment has a substantial and long-term adverse effect on their ability to perform normal day-to-day activities.

Developmental theories and policies that enshrine them structure educational progress, social role, functional, emotive, and other expectations for acceptable human procession from before birth through the end of life. As we discussed previously, based on nomothetic methods of inquiry, these theories seek to paint and then semantically define the normal human according to what is most frequently observed at a particular age and then take an axiological and tautological turn, assigning value to commonality. As elucidated in previous chapters, this curvilinear design is a champion in extracting what "should be" from what is most frequent. Using this scheme, "what should be" orbits around the average to set as the minimum standards for human growth and development on the basis of age (DePoy and Gilson, 2012).

The Developmental Disabilities Act (DDA) in the United States contains further rhetoric on the role of developmentally or age-normed policy in undesigning humanness. According to the Act, delay is designed as:

a severe, chronic disability of an individual 5 years of age or older that:
1   Is attributable to a mental or physical impairment or combination of mental and physical impairments;
2   Is manifested before the individual attains age 22;
3   Is likely to continue indefinitely;

4 Results in substantial functional limitations in three or more of the following areas of major life activity:
  i. Self-care;
  ii. Receptive and expressive language;
  iii. Learning;
  iv. Mobility;
  v. Self-direction;
  vi. Capacity for independent living; and
  vii. Economic self-sufficiency.
Reflects the individual's need for a combination and sequence of special, interdisciplinary, or generic services, supports, or other assistance that is of lifelong or extended duration and is individually planned and coordinated, except that such term, when applied to infants and young children means individuals from birth to age 5, inclusive, who have substantial developmental delay or specific congenital or acquired conditions with a high probability of resulting in developmental disabilities if services are not provided.

This characterization both divulges violations to humanness and moves us to a discussion of the exclusion of the offender through containment.

Before we begin this analysis, we once again invoke the learning derived from our students and thus clarify this discussion exclusively as questioning about revising illegitimate bodies rather than a proclamation of the value or lack thereof of any services or professional activity. We assert that, in order to be precise in posing and pondering labyrinthine queries, complexity needs to be parsed and reduced such that the object of analysis is clearly bounded, demarcated, absent of moral debris, and logically approached, without which focused dialog cannot occur. So, without being interspersed with related but tangential remains this discussion analyzes the display of and response to humanness violations, not the value of service provision. Our intent is not to prescribe action, but rather to focus on querying the body as microcosm of designed and branded meaning to inform thought and innovation leading to dignity for all involved.

Item #5 in the DDA provides a story that designs those with the brand of developmental violations as lifelong members of the disability park. This design denies legitimate humanness by eviscerating human agency despite self-determination rhetoric (DePoy and Gilson, 2011). In a recent presentation given by graduates of an early intervention master's degree program, well-intended students reflected the DDA policy mandates, essentially capturing and institutionalizing the violation of children in a service system in perpetuity. It was even more curious to note that comments from the audience affirmed the need for policy supporting such exclusion, espousing the grand narrative of the inhumanity of the disabled bodies, many referring to their own children with violating brands. In the presentation context, terms such as "typically developing" and "atypically developing" masquerade as euphemistic emblems for normal and illegitimate child growth and development respectively. Legitimated membership in these service systems designs neediness and eschews the potential for human agency.

As lightly grazed but not substantively addressed above, genetic counseling is the method used to facilitate decisions about participation in selective abortion, particularly for known offenders who are thinking of their own offspring or for mothers whose age is associated with a high incidence of producing a violating infant. From the outset, the offending chromosomes are problematized and scripted as severely distressing: "The central concern of most people seeking genetic counseling is the fear of having a child who might have a physical, intellectual or severe social handicap" (Gardner, Sutherland, and Shaffer, 2011: 9).

Selective genetic and surgical manipulation of impaired fetuses and bodies further shines the spotlight on measures taken to reinvent bodies towards the norm.

Among the many policies and related praxis revealing desired revisions for violating adult bodies are vocational rehabilitation, plastic surgery, and assistive technology. We take up these measures in other chapters of this book.

Contesting life

As mentioned above, wrongful birth and wrongful life policies were most powerful in provoking our thinking about humanness. Unpacking such controversial policy and practice juxtaposes humanness, economics, jurisprudence, and more profoundly axiology and ontology to raise questions about the perimeters of humanity and who guards them, violates them, and then is responsible for the emotive and fiscal costs of living as a denied human. Reuter (2007) refers to both wrongful birth and life policies as internally contradictory.

In the presence of genetic testing, individuals are both held responsible for obtaining information about their genetic composition in order to eliminate future corporeal design flaws and rhetorically claimed to have agency regarding their decisions. Yet, embedded within the context of the designer baby and social views of quality of life, Reuter claims the "responsibilization" to perpetuate human evolutionary advancement becomes an "unfreedom."

Both wrongful birth and life policies assert that the life of a "defective" child is so heinous that he/she should not be alive (Rimon-Zarfaty and Rax, 2012). Note here that the primary focus of this analysis is on the label "wrongful" as it betrays the denial of humanness and futility of living for children branded as disabled. We do not take on embodied harm caused by active medical intervention in utero or postnatally, nor are we discussing these policies as malpractice issues.

The distinction between birth and life policies lies in who brings the legal claim against whom. In wrongful birth, the parent initiates action against the physician for providing insufficient information necessary for parents to make an informed decision based on predicted quality or designed a priori as lack thereof of human life, while in wrongful life, the child or child advocate is the plaintiff (Wolbring, n.d.).

Labeling both policies as wrongful rather than malpractice illustrates the denial of life. As articulated by Kato and Hyoron (2005): "its [the policy's] negativity is thorough in the sense that it denies the meaning of life completely" (p. 298). So, while the subjects of these actions are alive, the formal, legal disavowal of their humanness is inscribed in titles and texts of the policies that allow for punitive action and recovery of monetary damages for failing to prevent a contested life from occurring.

An argument supporting wrongful actions is provided by Marzano-Parisoli, in the discussion of Harris's work.

> To put someone in a harmed condition means to augment suffering in the world and not to avoid avoidable pain. And to augment suffering in the world is morally unacceptable. This is why the conclusion is that to bring a child into being who will live in a disabling condition is, for Harris, morally wrong.
>
> (Marzano-Parisoli, 2001: 644–5)

Together with Marzano-Parisoli (2001), we do take a position here, as we find Harris' and others' claims that support these policies as indefensible on proximal to distal fronts. First and foremost is the title denoting denial of humanness of the individual who was wrongfully born on the basis of a standard of quality of life that is mythic. The claim that dependence is lifelong for offending rings hollow as we are not aware of anyone who does not depend on others for his/her very existence. Thus, autonomy, defined as independent functioning, is simply simulacrum with no foundation unless called upon for political or parkesque euphemistic work. What we mean by euphemistic work is the function of invoking the absence of autonomy as rationale for park services at best and denial of life at worst.

Moving distally, that the potential to lob wrongful birth and life at offending bodies does not exist for any other human brand label designs an axiological story that is hard to renounce once legally dubbed as "wrongful" and "damaged." Legal damages are varied in type and application, but common to all are monetary sums awarded when the plaintiff is deemed to be harmed or to be named as the subject of loss. Unlike malpractice suits, where the title confers responsibility on the provider, wrongful birth and life choose living itself as the locus of both harm and loss. So, together with others, we claim that designing the embodied atypical as a life not worth living jettisons the offender from humanness.

Actually, it seems rather difficult to affirm that there exists a fixed and immutable model of normality and health that can really make it possible to distinguish between normal and healthy people whose life is worth living and abnormal and disabled people whose life is, on the contrary, wrongful and not worth living. Moreover, once we accept "that life is not always in the nature of a blessing"...as was indeed recognized and emphasized in ancient times by Job and by some of the early Greek poets such as Hesiod, Theognis, and Bacchylides – one might seek damages "for being born of a certain color, another because of race"....The direct consequence would be the recognition of a duty to refrain from procreating disabled children only because they are "different" and because, as such, they are subject to discrimination.

(Marzano-Parisoli, 2001: 642)

Of course, to enact a wrongful birth or life suit, the interloper must be alive. But, when living becomes a violation of humanness, it can be lawfully terminated with professional assistance.

Ending life

This section refers not to suicide by one's own hand, but rather by legalized professional assistance to kill. In this chapter, we refer to the four types of euthanasia defined in Wolbring's classic work:

Assisted suicide: I kill myself but someone else gives me the tool.
Voluntary euthanasia: Someone else kills me with my consent.
Non-voluntary euthanasia: Someone kills me when I am unable to give my consent (i.e., a person in a persistent vegetative state).
Involuntary euthanasia: Someone kills me without asking me; therefore without my consent.

(Wolbring, 1998)

Physician-assisted suicide is designed as altruistic for the offending body, as well as for those who are considered family, as the goal of its practice is ostensibly to preserve human dignity for people branded as terminally ill or incurably disabled (Procon.org, 2012). Thus, hastening death in the style of *They Shoot Horses Don't They?* is deemed as kindness through preventing suffering of the subject slated for termination as well as for his/her loving onlookers. (Ganzini, Goy, Dobscha, and Prigerson, 2009).

We conclude this chapter with physician-assisted suicide specific to the designed members of the disability club, once again not taking a position on the right to die, but rather for the purpose of unlading this practice to illuminate the role of the embodied atypical in establishing the boundaries beyond which humanness is denied. As eloquently stated by Davis, euthanasia is a practice only deemed appropriate for those:

People with disabling or degenerative conditions, or with terminal illnesses [who] fall into this category ["right to die"] while others, who may be equally suicidal, but have no obvious illness or disability, are considered "wrong to want to die" and are helped to live. We even have suicide prevention strategies and teams to help those who are suicidal to survive.

(Davis, 2004)

Moreover, unlike prenatal testing and wrongful birth issues, debate regarding physician-assisted suicide removes the variable of incompetence to make sound decisions about one's own life because of immaturity of age or "mental incapacity" from the ethical fray. By doing so, the cultural stories told by proponents of assisted suicide arguments for atypical embodiment purify the view and thus create a rich illustration of how the violating body which is determined to be beyond revision or reinvention captures contextual values and conflicts and joins the ranks of *Homo sacer* (Davis, 2006b).

In a recent graduate course on theories of humans, students read an overview of disability theory (DePoy and Gilson, 2012) and then watched the film, *Million Dollar Baby*. Not one student expressed consternation or even questioned that, once paralyzed, Maggie perceived her life as not worth living, or that in time this perspective could change. We were struck by this acceptance on the part of thoughtful and well-intended students that paralysis was an offending embodied characteristic disemboweling the value of a life and thus "of course" served up for extermination. Once again, we are not taking a position but rather pointing out a prevalent world view that eschews the offending body from humanness and thus, in this circumstance, being alive.

For some scholars, singling out violating bodies for such assistance has been analogized to genocide (Coleman, 2010). For others, such as Davis (2006a), physician-assisted suicide provides the freedom to escape from invasive, painful medical intervention that would prolong life. He argues that in the absence of one's physical capacity to terminate life, assistance is the exercise of individual choice and agency.

Euthanasia has a long history in multiple geographies and is currently a multi-faceted entity with too many faces to examine in this short chapter section. Subject to scrutiny are fiscal, professional, religious, technological, medical, professional responsibility, insurance and future soothsaying, among many other variables. So we do not approach these variables in this work, but narrow our analysis to inform the design and branding of humanness as it relates to the embodied atypical.

Even with the wide girth of variables thrown into the argument stew, underpinning the acceptance or rejection of these practices seems in large part to boil down to the valuation placed on both the meaning of the construct of human life in itself and individual lives meeting the criteria for human worth and dignity (Bérubé, 2011). The other concerns mentioned above seem to swirl around the juxtaposition of the meaning of life and dollars, responsibility, technology, and future prediction. So the acceptability of voluntary death or sanctioned killing, aided or unaided, peeks into the axiological soul of a culture, allowing leakage of values and ethics regarding the nature of life into the public.

Prior to the ascendency of contemporary medical intervention, the controversy about assisted suicide was silent, as it did not involve public scrutiny or opinion. Legalizing medical practices contradictory to the Hippocratic oath with the tools of this asserted life-preserving trade uncloseted and thus opened for debate practices which had been intimate. For example, the classic 1915 case in which Haiselden, a physician, chose not to operate on a neonate with a severe "deformity" created an ethical maelstrom by raising the duty of professional withholding, as well as direct administration of a lethal agent as a means to end life.

Look at the following argument against the viability of assisted suicide and related voluntary death practices:

> Fear, bias, and prejudice against disability play a significant role in assisted suicide. Who ends up using assisted suicide? Supporters advocate its legalization by suggesting that it is needed for unrelievable pain and discomfort at the end of life. But the overwhelming majority of the people in Oregon who have reportedly used that state's assisted suicide law wanted to die not because of pain, but for reasons associated with disability, including the loss of autonomy (89.9 percent), the loss of the ability to engage in activities that make life enjoyable (87.4 percent), the loss of dignity (83.8 percent), and the loss of control of bodily functions (58.7 percent). Furthermore, in the Netherlands, more than half the physicians surveyed say the main reason given by patients for seeking death is "loss of dignity.
>
> (Disability Rights Education and Defense Fund, n.d)

Just to provide a thumbnail of the complexity involved in debates about physician-assisted suicide or mercy killing, we provide a quotation of "pros and cons" in Table 8.2.

A particularly poignant argument illuminating the role of the atypical corpus in denial of humanness is the "slippery slope" position. Opponents fear that once unleashed, mercy killing will move to genocide for bodies designed as undesirable (Miller, 1997).

Reiterating our reluctance to take a position on euthanasia, the literature and debates in favor of or opposing this chimera are presented to illuminate the design of embodied worth and refuse.

Summary

In this chapter, we introduced the notion of the atypical body as refracting

Table 8.2 Pros and cons concerning physician-assisted suicide

Pros	Cons
Tremendous pain and suffering of patients can be saved.	It would violate doctors' Hippocratic oath.
The right to die should be a fundamental freedom of each person.	It demeans the value of human life.
Patients can die with dignity rather than have the illness reduce them to a shell of their former selves.	It could open the floodgates to non-critical patient suicides and other abuses.
Healthcare costs can be reduced, which would save estates and lower insurance premiums.	Many religions prohibit suicide and the intentional killing of others.
Nurse and doctor time can be freed up to work on savable patients.	Doctors and families may be prompted to give up on recovery much too early.
Prevention of suicide is a violation of religious freedom.	Government and insurance companies may put undue pressure on doctors to avoid heroic measures or recommend the assisted-suicide procedure.
Pain and anguish of the patient's family and friends can be lessened, and they can say their final goodbyes.	Miracle cures or recoveries can occur.
Reasonable laws can be constructed which prevent abuse and still protect the value of human life.	Doctors are given too much power, and can be wrong or unethical.
Vital organs can be saved, allowing doctors to save the lives of others.	
Without physician assistance, people may commit suicide in a messy, horrifying, and traumatic way.	

cultural conceptuals of humanness and beyond. Because of the colossal magnitude of this agenda, the chapter narrowed its focus to selected policy exemplars, each which betrayed a different layer of response to the violating body. As is evident in the discussions above, the relationship between atypical embodiment branded as disabled and legitimacy of humanness provides a scholarly multiplex awaiting further mining. The policies in this chapter are not simply about atypical bodies and disability design, but rather about views of humanness and the non-examples mirrored by such bodies. What constitutes humanness is a complex set of questions and responses which can be visualized in large part through examining what is slated for prevention, change, or execution.

We would suggest that analysis of the atypical body as microcosm for humanness continues to be concealed in an under-explored intellectual mausoleum. If continued, this dormancy allows brand names such as human rights, citizenship, human responsibility, triage, disability, and even health to remain vague and unjustly distributed. The atypical embodied can be potent in lighting pathways such that the clarity necessary for the undesign and redesign of human worthiness are traversed. Thus this chapter while addressing who has a ticket to wear the brand of disability, now has expanded the scope of park analysis to the design of the undesirable human as the basis for undesign and redesign. Having broadened the scope of designing and branding disability to designing humanness, we now move to the craft, the tools of the trade so to speak.

References

Abort73.com (2013) Abortion and Race. *Abort73.com*, March 28. Available online at www.abort73.com/abortion/abortion_and_race (accessed January 26, 2014).

Bérubé, M. (2013) Humans, Disabilities, and the Humanities? National Humanities Center. *On the Human*, January 17. http://onthehuman.org/2011/01/humans-disabilities-humanities/

Case, A. (2010) We Are All Cyborgs Now. *TED Women*, January. Available online at http://new.ted.com/talks/amber_case_we_are_all_cyborgs_now (accessed January 26, 2014).

Coleman, D. (2010) Assisted Suicide Laws Create Discriminatory Double Standard for Who Gets Suicide Prevention and Who Gets Suicide Assistance: Not Dead Yet Responds to Autonomy, Inc. *Disability and Health Journal*, 20, 39–50.

Davis, A. (2004) A Disabled Person's Perspective on Euthanasia. *Disability Studies Quarterly*, 24 (3). Available online at http://dsq-sds.org/article/view/512/689 (accessed January 26, 2014).

Davis, L. J. (2006a) Assisted Suicide and the Rights of the Disabled. NPR, September 27. Available online at www.npr.org/templates/story/story.php?storyId=4866181 (accessed January 26, 2014).

Davis, L. J. (2006b) Life, Death, and Biocultural Literacy. *Chronicle of Higher Education*, 52 (18), B9–10.

DePoy, E., and Gilson, S. (2011) *Studying Disability*. Los Angeles, CA: Sage.

DePoy, E., and Gilson, S. (2012) Disability as Microcosm. Queries about the Boundaries of Humanness. *Societies*, 2 (4), 302–16.

Disability Rights Education and Defense Fund (n.d) Why Assisted Suicide Must not be Legalized. Available online at www.dredf.org/assisted_suicide/97-DREDF-website-version.html (accessed January 26, 2014).

Dollar, E. P. (2012) Why Prenatal Screening for Gender and Disability Are Not The Same. *Patheos*, January 25. Available online at www.patheos.com/blogs/ellenpainterdollar/2012/01/why-prenatal-screening-for-gender-and-for-disabilities-are-not-the-same (accessed January 26, 2014).

Douglas, N. (2008) *Freedom: Healing for Parents of Disabled Children*. Olive Leaf Ministries.

Euthanasia.com (2013) Euthanasia Pros and Cons. Available online at www.euthanasia.com/proscons.html (accessed January 26, 2014).

Feldman, D. (2009) Human Rights of Children with Disabilities in Israel: The Vision and the Reality. *Disability Studies Quarterly*, 29 (1). Available online at http://dsq-sds.org/article/view/172/172 (accessed January 26, 2014).

Fuentes, A. (2012) *Race, Monogamy, and Other Lies They Told You: Busting Myths About Human Nature*. Los Angeles, CA: University of California Press.

Ganzini, L., Goy, E. R., Dobscha, S. K., and Prigerson, H. (2009) Mental Health Outcomes of Family Members of Oregonians Who Request Physician Aid in Dying. *Journal of Pain and Symptom Management*, 38 (6), 807–15.

Gardner, R., Sutherland, G. R., and Shaffer, L. G. (2011) *Chromosome Abnormalities and Genetic Counseling*. New York: Oxford University Press.

Garrison, V. (2012) Disability, Prenatal Testing and the Case for a Moral, Compassionate Abortion. *RH Reality Check*, August 16. Available online at http://rhrealitycheck.org/article/2012/08/16/disability-prenatal-testing-and-case-moral-compassionate-abortion (accessed January 26, 2014).

Gedge, E. (2010) Genetics, Disability and Symbolic Harm. In I. Lange, and Z. Norridge, *Illness, Bodies and Contexts: Interdisciplinary Perspectives*. Witney: Interdisciplinary Press.

Glover, J. (2006) *Choosing Children: Genes, Disability, and Design*. Uehiro Series in Practical Ethics. New York: Oxford University Press.

Goodey, C. (2011) *A History of Intelligence and "Intellectual Disability": The Shaping of Psychology in Early Modern Europe*. Farnham, MA: Ashgate.

Haraway, D. (1991) *Situated Knowledges in Simians, Cyborgs, and Women*. New York: Routledge.

Hubbard, R. (2013) Abortion and Disability: Who Should and Should Not Inhabit the World? In L. J. Davis (ed.), *Disability Studies Reader*. New York: Routledge, pp. 74–86.

Iadicola, P., and Shupe, A. (2013) *Violence, Inequality, and Human Freedom* (3rd ed.). Lanham, MD: Rowman and Littlefield.

Kato, S., and Hyoron, S. (2005) On the Idea that I Should Not Have Been Born at All: Wrongful Life and the Limits of Bioethics. *Japanese Sociological Review*, 55 (3), 298–313.

Kelly, K. (2009) 4 Arguments Against Technology. *Harvard Business Review HBR Blog Network*, April 17. Available online at http://blogs.hbr.org/2009/04/4-arguments-against-technology (accessed January 26, 2014).

Kolbrener, L. (2013) Mothers of Down Syndrome Babies Have Options in Ultra-Orthodox Jerusalem. *Jewish Daily Forward*, July 18. Available online at http://forward.com/articles/180308/mothers-of-down-syndrome-babies-have-options-in-ul/?p=1 (accessed January 26, 2014).

Kurtzweil, R. (2006) *The Singularity is Near*. New York: Penguin.

Marzano-Parisoli, M. M. (2001) Disability, Wrongful-Life Lawsuits, and Human Difference: An Exercise in Ethical Perplexity. *Social Theory and Practice*, 27 (4), 637–59.

Miller, T. (1997) Should physician-assisted suicide be legalized? No. *Before I Die: Medical Care And Personal Choices*, April 22. Available online at www.wnet.org/bid/vp-assisted.html (accessed January 26, 2014).

Mills, C. B., and Erzikova, E. (2012) Prenatal Testing, Disability, and Termination: An Examination of Newspaper Framing. *Disability Studies Quarterly*, 32 (3). Available online at http://dsq-sds.org/article/view/1767 (accessed January 26, 2014).

Mor, S. (2014) The Dialectics of Wrongful Life and Wrongful Birth Claims in Israel: A Disability Critique, in A. Sarat (ed.) *Studies in Law, Politics, and Society*, 63: 113–46.

Olshansky, S. (1962) Chronic Sorrow: A Response to Having a Mentally Defective

Child. *Journal of Social Casework*, 43, 190–3.

Parry, W. (2013) Designing Life: Should Babies Be Genetically Engineered? *Live Science*, February 18. Available online at www.livescience.com/27206-genetic-engineering-babies-debate.html (accessed January 26, 2014).

ProCon.org (2012) Euthanasia. Top 10 Pros and Cons: Should Euthanasia or Physician-Assisted Suicide be Legal? Retrieved from *Procon.org*, May 8. Available online at http://euthanasia.procon.org/view.resource.php?resourceID=000126 (accessed January 26, 2014).

Raz, A. (2004) Important to Test, Important to Support: Attitudes Toward Disability Rights And Prenatal Diagnosis Among Leaders of Support Groups for Genetic Disorders in Israel. *Social Science and Medicine*, 59 (9), 1857–66.

Reuter, S. (2007) The politics of "wrongful life" itself: discursive (mal)practices and Tay-Sachs disease. *Economy and Society*, 36 (2), 236–62.

Rimon-Zarfaty, N., and Rax, A. (2012) Abortion Committees as Agents of Eugenics: Medical and Public Views on Selective Abortion Following Mild or Likely Fetal Pathology. In G. Kin, *Community: Reproductive Technologies Among Jewish Israelis*. New York: Berghahn Books, pp. 220–5.

Siebers, T. (2010) *Disability Aesthetics*. Ann Arbor, MI: University of Michigan Press.

Smith, C. (2010) *What is a Person*. Chicago, OH: University of Chicago Press.

Smithsonian (n.d) Identity. Smithsonian National Museum of American History, *EveryBody: An Artifact History of Disability in America*. Available online at http://everybody.si.edu/place/identity (accessed January 26, 2014).

Wasserman, D., and Asche, A. (2006) The Uncertain Rationale for Prenatal Disability Screening. *Virtual Mentor*, 8 (1), 53–6.

Weyand, P., Bundle, M., and McGowan, C. (2009) The fastest runner on artificial legs: Different limbs, similar function? *Journal of Applied Physiology*, 107, 903–11.

Wolbring, G. (1998) Why Disability Rights Movements Do Not Support Euthanasia: Safeguards Broken Beyond Repair. Independent Living Institute. Available online at www.independentliving.org/docs5/Wolbringeuthanasia.html (accessed January 26, 2014).

Wolbring, G. (n.d.) Wrongful Birth/Life Suits. International Center for Bioethics and Disability. Available online at www.bioethicsanddisability.org/wrongfulbirth.html (accessed January 26, 2014).

Wolfe, C. (2010) *What is Posthumanism*. Minneapolis, MI: University of Minnesota.

9   Designing and branding disability through concept and politically correct labeling

The scope of conceptuals was introduced in Chapter 2. In this chapter, we enter and more closely rub elbows with the craft of designer disability through engaging with omnipotent words, text, and imagery. These arti-facts of human production, reception, and interaction are the primary communicators and locus for inviting interpretation (Varnum and Gibbons, 2001). All three influence and, to some extent, converge to imply meaning, manipulate behavior, persuade, reflect, and assign value. Words, text, and image have provided a rich sea of inscription and form in which disability theories do their axiological, theoretical, and proclamation work. We therefore consolidate our attention on these human crafts to further analyze how each and then all together design and brand disability.

Defining and differentiating each craft of text, word, and image is no longer simple in a universe in which these symbolic entities intermingle. Consider definitions for each below:

Text
- the original words and form of a written or printed work
- an edited or emended copy of an original work
- the principal part of a book exclusive of front and back matter
- the printed score of a musical composition
- any segment of written or printed discourse ordinarily appearing between spaces or between a space and a punctuation mark
- a number of bytes processed as a unit and conveying a quantum of information in communication and computer work.

Word
A unit of language, consisting of one or more spoken sounds or their written representation, that functions as a principal carrier of meaning.

Image
- a mental picture or impression of something
- a mental conception held in common by members of a group and symbolic of a basic attitude and orientation
- idea, concept.

(Merriam-Webster, 2014)

From the lexical definitions above, both word and text fit within the genre of the spoken or articulated representation, while image seems to be distinguished by its visual, pictorial nature. Yet, each definition includes parts of the others. As example, letters and words are written as symbols, logo typically denoting image is contained in the definition of text, all hold or imply the symbolic nature open to interpretation and curiosity and, all reside in the cephalic penthouse adjacent to design.

To further obfuscate the distinctions among these three constructs, consider Lee's work:

> This project started nearly twenty years ago as an assignment in my typography class at art school. Students were encouraged to see letters beyond their dull, practical functionality.
>
> The challenge is to visualize the meaning of a word, using only the graphic elements of the letters forming the word, without adding any outside parts. The challenge was very hard, but the reward of "cracking" a word felt great. So this became a lifelong project for me.
>
> (Lee, 2011)

In reading for this chapter in particular, we therefore aimed at understanding the craft of text, word, and image, though consulting the thinking productions of others. Several trends were relevant and insightful in cradling design and branding of humanity in general, and disability specifically. First, we looked at the contemporary rethinking of the historical container of text, word and image, the book, as this material structure has been not only a repository of concept and meaning, but also a respected transmitter, albeit on a hierarchy of book types and publishers. Past, present, and future printed pages are being transformed into other media, with screens now dominating much of the intellectual and narrative universe (Institute for the Future of the Book, n.d.). The virtual representation of print has in essence transformed text into image and spoken word, leading us to query the extent to which distinction among text, word, and image is even possible, useful or important.

Consider the PDF (portable document format) file, for example. It is an image, often of text and words. Given its visible and intentional division between the image, conversation, and the thought of the characters, we turned to comics for craft guidance. Situated within a semiotic framework (Chandler and Munday, 2011), analysis of the interstices of textual and visual belies the power of sign and signifier. "The balance of power between words and images which after the printing press shifted in favor of words seems now in favor of shifting in image" (Varnum and Gibbons, 2001: ix).

From a semiotic eye, however, words and images are equivalent to one another in their communicative power in that they are all produced, decoded, and assigned meaning (Chandler and Munday, 2011; Radcliffe, 2012). Both are accessed through visual means primarily, but both can also be accessed directly or indirectly through oral verbatim and/or oral interpretive means.

Synthesized with semiotics, work on the current and future book and on the purposive structural coexistence of imagery and text in comics brought us to the theme of "reading" rather than attempting to erect fences between pictorial and lexical conceptual crafts of designing and branding meaning. In its usage here, reading refers not only to words and text but also more broadly to the interpretation of material and virtual universe that supplies the fodder for crafting meaning (Chandler and Munday, 2011).

As Smith (2011) reminds us in her encounter with horror film, however, reading, whether engaging with image, word, or story occurs at multiple depths from patina to profundity. Thus, the reading of the conceptuals, often despite the creator's intent, can undermine itself. We now turn to "reading" design and branding of disability in diverse words, texts and images.

The craft of designing humans as developing normals

Building on Chapter 4, in this section we wrestle with the language and image of developmental theory, a framework which organizes a trilogy of narratives, anatomy, psychology, and physiology (DePoy and Gilson, 2011), designing humanity into two categories, normal and not normal. Synonyms in an online dictionary for the term "development" include expansion, elaboration, growth, evolution, unfolding, opening, maturing, maturation, maturity. Reading meaning inherent in this passel of similar words we find unidirectional movement or growth from diminutive to grand, immature to mature, naïve to wise, unripened to succulent. These theories, whether on a minuscule proximal or a grand systemic scope can be read at multiple levels from prediction of, and thus guidance for what one should be and do at specific ages, to what one should not be and not do. Since significant theoretical ground has been reified and implanted in the cultural and praxis lexicon depicting the desirable human, not much surface needs to be excavated to reveal the chronological design of disability attached to the atypical corpus both linguistically and pictorially (Dudley-Marling and Alex, 2010).

Inspecting deeper, however, developmental theory moves beyond meaning about normalcy to craft the hierarchical design of the disability park and the knowledge which drives it. Both elite status of professionals and the knowledge generated and held by those who travel in such circles is crafted as "scientific." Moreover, because its of its systematic and logical nature scientific knowledge is depicted as authorative and superior to other thinking (Hoyningen-Huene, 2013).

Locating science at the apex of epistemic and ontologic merit nourishes the medicalization model of disability, despite the inability of its favored child, logical positivism, to support its own claim of being the methodological owner of monistic truth (Keupink and Shieh, 2010). Yet, the

Cochrane Collaboration is perhaps one of the most powerful authenticators of professional "evidence" to guide health care. Most legitimate and considered the gold standard for generating evidence is the true experiment, in which research is structured according to the tenets of logical positivism (DePoy and Gitlin, 2011), which can only verify or falsify theory, and thus cannot sit on the proof throne despite its reputation for being able to do so. Words such as randomization, manipulation, and control craft the design of a lexicon of elite literature, which seeks to verify group characteristics and distinguish them from non-group features. Theoretically and methodologically restricting the focus of inquiry to precise nomothetic aims and structures designs the ontology of within group similarities and between group differences as the basis for reading the normal and the not normal.

Look at the definition of research adopted by the Cochrane Collaboration (2013):

> The term research means different things to different people, but is essentially about finding out new knowledge that could lead to changes to treatments, policies or care. The definition used by the Department of Health is: "The attempt to derive generalisable new knowledge by addressing clearly defined questions with systematic and rigorous methods."
>
> (Cochrane Collaboration, 2013)

Even a surface reading of this text reveals its elitism in that profound meaning can be accessed only if one knows the craft of investigatory "rigor," a set of systematic research practices (Hoyningen-Huene, 2013) known to relatively few.

We provide just a few more basic words and their definitions from the Cochrane Collaboration to illustrate how meanings are read and designed in the world of knowledge production specific to developmental theory (CASRC, 2011) and its translation into normal and not normal.

Variable
A factor that differs among and between groups of people. Variables include patient characteristics such as age, sex, and smoking, or measurements such as blood pressure or depression score. There can also be **treatment** or condition variables, e.g. in a childbirth study, the length of time someone was in labour, and outcome variables. The set of values of a variable in a **population** or sample is known as a **distribution**.

Validity
The degree to which a result (of a measurement or study) is likely to be true and free of **bias** (systematic errors). Validity has several other

meanings, usually accompanied by a qualifying word or phrase; for example, in the context of measurement, expressions such as 'construct validity', 'content validity' and 'criterion validity' are used. See also: External validity, Internal validity

Normal distribution
A statistical distribution with known properties commonly used as the basis of models to analyze **continuous data**. Key assumptions in such analyses are that the data are symmetrically distributed about a **mean** value, and the shape of the distribution can be described using the **mean** and **standard deviation**.

(Cochrane Collaboration, 2013)

The last term, normal distribution, is the linchpin of developmental theory. Reading this concept and its elegant imagery once again presented in this chapter, Figure 9.1 reveals its craft as it hitches life-influential terms, normal and not normal, to a statistical gambling artifact first discovered by De Moivre (Bellhouse, 2011), as we discussed in Chapter 3. Table 9.1 show-cases just some of the words and text that emerge from developmental theory and serve as craft for designing and branding disability as age-related embodied deviance (CASRC, 2011).

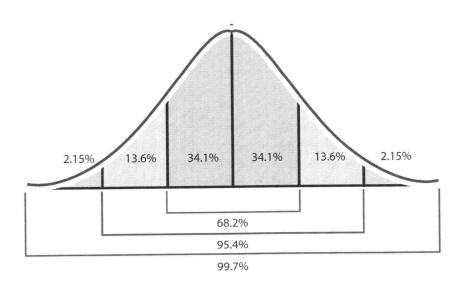

Figure 9.1 The bell curve

Table 9.1 Words and text that have emerged from developmental theory

Words	Text	Source
Developmental milestones	Skills such as taking a first step, smiling for the first time, and waving "bye bye" are called developmental milestones. Children reach milestones in how they play, learn, speak, behave, and move (crawling, walking, etc.)	Centers for Disease Control and Prevention, 2012
Developmental delay	Refers to the process in which children go through changes in skill development during predictable time periods, called developmental milestones. Occurs when children have not reached these milestones by the expected time period. For example, if the normal range for learning to walk is between 9 and 15 months, and a 20-month-old child has still not begun walking, this would be considered a developmental delay	CASRC, 2011
Underachiever	A person (as a student) who fails to achieve his or her potential or does not do as well as expected	Dictionary.com, 2013
Memory decline	Normal aging is associated with a decline in various memory abilities in many cognitive tasks; the phenomenon is known as age-related memory impairment or age-associated memory impairment	Wikipedia, 2013

Now examine the crafting of normal, its non-example, and the medicalization of not normal in the images in Figures 9.2 to 9.4. The images presented frolic with Figure 9.1 to craft powerful disability design. Figure 9.2 can be read on the surface as a set of questions organized as a legitimate instrument to test a child's attainment of normalcy. The box on the right identifies the deeper level of meaning, the risks for which a parent must seek evaluation for an invitation for their children and themselves into the disability park.

Figure 9.3 colors abnormality within the scanned lines of what used to be within the privacy of an individual skull but is now is rendered as beautiful imagery displaying the spectrum of light. The visual can be read as science, pathology, or painting. If read as science, the authority contained in such images is so compelling that even in the presence of empirical or clinical support to the contrary (Uttal, 2013), the collage of iridescence

Your Baby at 2 Months

Child's Name   Child's Age   Today's Date

How your child plays, learns, speaks and acts offers important clues about your child's development. Developmental milestones are things most children can do by a certain age.

Check the milestones your child has reached by the end of 2 months. Take this with you and talk with your child's doctor at every visit about the milestones your child has reached and what to expect next.

What most babies do at this age:

Social/Emotional
- ☐ Begins to smile at people
- ☐ Can briefly calm himself (may bring hands to mouth and suck on hand)
- ☐ Tries to look at parent

Language/Communication
- ☐ Coos, makes gurgling sounds
- ☐ Turns head toward sounds

Cognitive (learning, thinking, problem-solving)
- ☐ Pays attention to faces
- ☐ Begins to follow things with eyes and recognize people at a distance
- ☐ Begins to act bored (cries, fussy) if activity doesn't change

Movement/Physical Development
- ☐ Can hold head up and begins to push up when lying on tummy
- ☐ Makes smoother movements with arms and legs

Act early by talking to your child's doctor if your child:
- ☐ Doesn't respond to loud sounds
- ☐ Doesn't watch things as they move
- ☐ Doesn't smile at people
- ☐ Doesn't bring things to mouth
- ☐ Can't hold head up when pushing up when on tummy

Tell your child's doctor or nurse if you notice any of these signs of possible developmental delay for this age, and talk with someone in your community who is familiar with services for young children in your area, such as your state's public early intervention program. For more information, go to www.cdc.gov/concerned or call 1-800-CDC-INFO

Figure 9.2 Developmental milestone survey
Source: Adapted from "Your Baby at 2 Months"
ww.cdc.gov/ncbddd/actearly/pdf/checklists/Checklists_2mo.pdf

and color patterns can assign a person to the current park or intervention, care, and/or ongoing scrutiny.

In Figure 9.4, graphs are used to provide a convincing scientific picture, telling a comparative story of normal and its obverse the impaired "dip" in hearing acuity resulting from typical aging. We remind you again that we are not opposing surveillance, brain imaging, or audio testing, but rather we are reading the multiple meanings crafted by design and branding normal and not normal emerging from the narrative of developmental theory. Figure 9.2 uses words and authoritative structure, while Figure 9.3 employs an artist's palette as its tool. Figure 9.4 juxtaposes linear images to

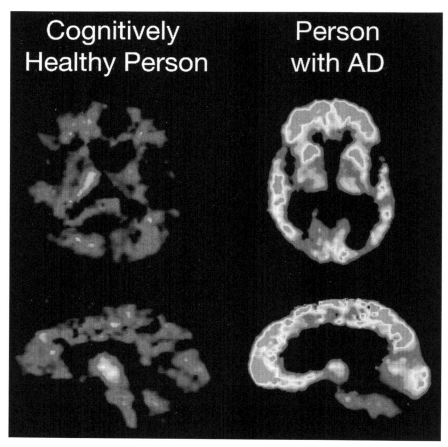

Figure 9.3 Brain scan of normal (left) and abnormal (right) aging brain
Source: National Institute on Aging, US National Institutes of Health

chronicle age normed level of hearing with related change branded as impairment. All three craft compelling, credible, and legitimately disabling design status within a medicalized context, identifying the underprivileged body even when age related change is expected and typical.

Following on the heels of developmental theory and its foundation triumvirate of anatomy, physiology and psychology, naming the type of the atypical body is a dynamic craft as we introduced in Chapter 4. It is curious to note that even when attempting to craft non-medicalized models of disability, vernacular such as cognitive impairment, physical disability, motor limitation, are used and thus have no way to deny their reading as medical even when pleading the contrary. Scan the titles from the *Disability Studies Quarterly*, a scholarly journal that in large part designs the cannon

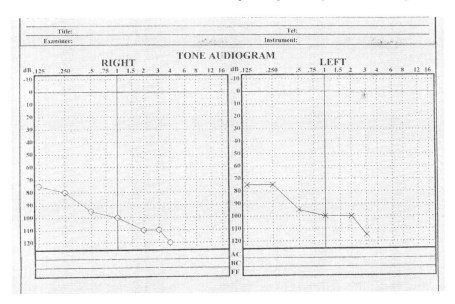

Figure 9.4 Audiogram
Source: Shutterstock

of disability studies knowledge, in Box 9.1, for examples. Despite the assertion of disability as a social construction made by the authors of these
articles, their titles are read as medicalized shorthand, using broad embodied categories occupying the non-normal reaches of the bell curve as
descriptive. Later in this chapter, we read the conceptuals of disability studies in more detail, but for now we remain in the park, and languish a bit
longer in text.

Box 9.1 Selected titles from *Disability Studies Quarterly*

- Communication Mediated by a Powered Wheelchair: People with
  Profound Cognitive Disabilities
- Men's Short-term Experience of Acquired Physical Disabilities in
  Japan
- Accidents Happen: An Art Autopathography on Mental Disability
- Next to Normal and the Persistence of Pathology in
  Performances of Psychosocial Disability

Conceptuals beyond person-branding

The disability park uses unique jargon to refer to what outside of the park would engender a different lexicon. While there are many such terms and narratives, reading of even three (supports, para, and "respectful" language), can be extrapolated to broader understanding of the jargon craft.

To sample the term "support," examine the text below.

> Supported Employment is a way to move people from dependence on a service delivery system to independence via competitive employment. Supported Employment provides a vehicle to enable eligible individuals to enter into competitive employment where they would otherwise, due to the impact of their disabling conditions, be unable to do so. Recent studies indicate that the provision of on-going support services for people with severe disabilities significantly increases their rates for employment retention. Supported Employment encourages people to work within their communities and encourages working, social interaction, and integrations with their non-disabled peers.
>
> (NYSED, 2012)

It does not take much depth of reading to find the internal contradictions in the narrative above, such as the assertion of independence just above the need for on-going "support," a euphemism for services and dependency. Moreover, in the last sentence, the oxymoronic inclusion rhetoric (Titchovsky, 2007) is tucked into this cornucopia of circumlocutions.

A second word part in the form of prefix used to distinguish the park is "para." Prefixes are placed at the beginning of a word to alter its meaning (Merriam-Webster, 2014). According to Dictionary.com (2013), para is

> most often attached to verbs and verbal derivatives, with the meanings "at or to one side of, beside, side by side" (parabola; paragraph; parallel; paralysis), "beyond, past, by" (paradox; paragogue); by extension from these senses, this prefix came to designate objects or activities auxiliary to or derivative of that denoted by the base word (parody; paronomasia), and hence abnormal or defective (paranoia), a sense now common in modern scientific coinages (parageusia; paralexia). As an English prefix, para-, may have any of these senses; it is also productive in the naming of occupational roles considered ancillary or subsidiary to roles requiring more training, or of a higher status, on such models as paramedical, and paraprofessional:, paralegal; paralibrarian; parapolice.
>
> (Dictionary.com, 2013)

Perpetuating the park, the prefix para in referring to disability phenomena can be read as both demeaning and segregating, as in Paralympics, para-transit and so forth. Similarly, we read "respectful disability language" (Mobility International USA, 2006) as park linguistics that serve to sustain the park by redirecting action into debates about proper parlance.

Although present throughout the history of language, political correctness (PC) entered its heyday in the 1980s through the gates of academia (Hughes, 2010). There is no dearth of heated exchange on the value of language policing. According to Hughes, political correctness is complex in that "it is liberal in its aims but illiberal in its practices" (Hughes, 2010). Hughes further elucidates the extremes of the PC debate with the following questions:

> Has political correctness succeeded in redefining morality by the introduction of the new concept of "ethical living"? Has it succeeded in eliminating prejudice? Or has it enabled some to be quicker to "take offense" where none was intended, forcing others into elaborate stratagems to avoid "giving offense"?
>
> (Hughes, 2011: x)

Mobility International USA (2006), while no longer insisting on the use of person-first language, uses the euphemism "respectful disability language" as one of its design and branding crafts. Look below at the text on their website.

General guidelines for talking about disability

- Refer to a person's disability only when it is related to what you are talking about. For example, don't ask "What's wrong with you?" Don't refer to people in general or generic terms such as "the girl in the wheelchair."
- When talking about places with accommodations for people with disabilities, use the term "accessible" rather than "disabled" or "handicapped." For example, refer to an "accessible" parking space rather than a "disabled" or "handicapped" parking space or "an accessible bathroom stall" rather than "a handicapped bathroom stall."
- Use the term "disability," and take the following terms out of your vocabulary when talking about or talking to people with disabilities. Don't use the terms "handicapped," "differently-abled," "cripple," "crippled," "victim," "retarded," "stricken," "poor," "unfortunate," or "special needs."
- Just because someone has a disability, it doesn't mean he/she is "courageous," "brave," "special," or "superhuman." People with disabilities are the same as everyone else. It is not unusual for someone with a disability to have talents, skills, and abilities.
- It is okay to use words or phrases such as "disabled," "disability," or "people with disabilities" when talking about disability issues. Ask

the people you are with which term they prefer if they have a disability.

- When talking about people without disabilities, it is okay to say "people without disabilities." But do not refer to them as "normal" or "healthy." These terms can make people with disabilities feel as though there is something wrong with them and that they are "abnormal."
- When in doubt, call a person with a disability by his/her name.

Once again, reading the internal contradictions is obvious. If "people with disabilities are the same as everyone else," why are these semantic commandments barked at all? Social interaction in the park even has its own etiquette manual (United Spinal Association, 2013), using words, text, and image in the form of a comic book.

Even the Associated Press legislates (censors perhaps) disability reference.

> In a first, the "journalist's bible" will include guidance for reporters on how to write about mental illness and conditions like autism.
>
> Officials behind the influential Associated Press Stylebook say they've added a new entry for "mental illness." The addition to the guide – which is relied upon by reporters at news outlets nationwide – advises journalists not to mention a diagnosis of autism, bipolar disorder, schizophrenia or other mental disorders unless it is germane to the story and properly sourced.
>
> (Diament, 2013)

It is remarkable that so much time and energy is devoted to crafting the correct disability monikers with vehement proponents weighing in on what words are acceptable. Yet new words and text continue to supplant what is in style at the time, and those who were ardent supporters of one lexicon move fickly to the next linguistic fad when it emerges. This type of ongoing branding talk certainly is a powerful and sustainable park design craft as it refracts much of spotlight away from alternative, progressive social change, keeping debate at the twaddle level.

Before departing the disability park words and text, we draw your attention to one more reading, negative textual space, or what is not articulated or imaged. Language is not simply restricted to what is apparent, explicit, and spoken, but also has the potential to wield its power in its vacant spaces or what we have previously referred to as the tyranny of the opposite, or what is not said (DePoy and Gilson, 2011). The words, phrases, and sequencing that comprise respectful disability language are cobbled by committee (so to speak) for the purpose of political correctness. Modifiers that are part of human experience (such as crippled), rather than being reconceptualized as human diversity, remain visible in the flesh and its activation, but unspoken. Social devaluation of those with the silenced conditions bleeds through the shrouds of linguistic finagling.

While we agree with Hughes (2010) regarding the unacceptability of oppression, we part ways on language policing as the means to redress this inequity. As asserted above, focus and refocus on simulacra are just that and no more, siphoning off energy from social change to trap it within the unproductive boundaries of verbal jousting. Note Hughes' implied approval for ethnic but not for disability language.

> Political correctness is a serious matter, grounded in suffering, preju-dice, and difference, and has certainly made everyone consider the plight of others, giving a new emphasis to respect. But it has also provoked a great deal of satire, irony, and humor, which have their place in a study of this kind. Some of it is unexpected: we have become used to Jews and blacks telling jokes about themselves and reclaiming ethnic slurs; but now we have jokes being told about cripples, by crip-ples who insist on using that designation.
>
> (Hughes, 2010: x)

Perhaps Hughes is a captive in the park as well.

Outside the park

Included in reading disability conceptuals outside the park are the words, text, and imagery that range in purpose, structure, content, and outcome. Our particular concern in this chapter is in one area of reading; disability studies language.

Reading the language of disability studies is a logical segue from the park to the rhetorical intent of disability studies scholarship to dismantle the containment of disability within a medicalized perspective and related envi-ronment. At the outset of this discussion, we confess our perspective that the current words, texts, and images of disability studies are recognizable, jargonesque, and unintentionally maintain the park albeit in an opposi-tional tone.

Taking a mini-step back in time to the 1980s, consistent with other popu-lation studies, disability studies in large part emerged as a rebellious child so to speak. Opposing the portrayal and imagery of disability as embodied deviance, limited function, and exclusion from opportunity, disability stud-ies espoused a non-medical counterculture (Bolaki and Gair, 2012; Cheyney, 2011; Siebers, 2010). Reimagining the Victorian definition of disability as environmental unpreparedness to accept and respond to the range of atypical bodies, scholar-activists such as Finklestein (1980) proposed an alternative reading of disability as, "the outcome of an oppres-sive relationship between people with impairments and the rest of society" (p. 47). Within the nascent field, the word disability, defined as embodied condition was replaced with a new brand, impairment. It is curious, however, that impairment carries meanings similar to disability. Look at the parcel of synonyms in one online dictionary:

> accident, adulteration, adversity, affliction, bane, blemish, blow, break-age, bruise, casualty, catastrophe, cave-in, contamination, corruption, debasement, depreciation, deprivation, destruction, deterioration, detriment, devastation, disservice, disturbance, evil, hardship, harm, hurt, illness, impairment, infliction, knockout, marring, mischief, mishap, mutilation, outrage, pollution, ravage, reverse, ruin, ruining, spoilage, stroke, suffering, waste, wound, wreckage, wrecking, wrong.
>
> (Dictionary.com, 2013)

Impairment as an alternative to the word disability remains an accepted and well-used moniker for the embodied atypical, admitting in evidence the defective body as central to disability even if discrimination is held as the disabling factor. While the emphasis shifts to a different syllable, the impaired body remains central to disability studies, in essence perpetuating the binary status quo, albeit sporting the contemporary brand of impairment.

The language of disability studies does not remain restricted to the body, however. A short while ago, a former student of ours sent a draft paper that she had written in a graduate disability studies class. It became obvious upon reading the first few paragraphs that postmodernism muscled the linguistic as well as theoretical skeleton of her good ideas. Although postmodernism has been an important trend for vacuuming out cobwebs of the medicalization model of disability from the literature, retaining it as a disability studies cannon is riddled with several problems. First, disability studies is not exempt from characteristic criticisms of postmodernism. That is to say, while exposing language and symbol as simulacra, postmodernists have not replaced the void with substance. So if disability studies is presented as "trope" it lacks the theoretical substance that its scholars seek.

Second, Foucault (1980) and Derrida (1997) have been important thinkers, rendering socially situated meaning transparent in arenas in which meaning is obscured by other narratives (e.g., science). Continuing to repeatedly double back to these two thinkers does little, however, to advance the field to more substantive theory and praxis, now possible with the emergence and potency of post-postmodernism.

Third, while oppression and discrimination are essential to read and expose, getting stuck in this muddle continues to sustain the "us and them" binary without much ado to heal the disjuncture. The linguistic and theoretical crafts of disability studies steeped in postmodernism suffocate new ideas. In essence, the cannon of disability studies reflects the postmodern criticism of deconstruction. Through its own linguistic style, vocabulary and reiteration of philosophy that has outlived its usefulness, too much of the disability studies language achieves what it claims to oppose, the identification and thus segregation of atypical bodies from human diversity.

Crafting disability design through image

In Chapter 6, a short discussion of how the international symbol of access (ISA) introduced imagery for disability. In this chapter, we more explicitly read imagery as craft. Each year, we find that expanding student reading and understanding of access beyond wheelchairs, low vision, and hearing limitation is a major project. Even with carefully structured assignments requiring an enlarged reading and analysis of accessibility, students struggle to stretch their world view. It is not surprising, given the popular media practice pictured in Figure 9.5, and reading the cartoons in Figure 9.6.

Figure 9.5 is a typical set-up screen for audio preferences on a home-entertainment DVD. With recent legislation, subtitling on DVDs is contained in most films mastered for home entertainment. As depicted in Figure 9.5, films in which English is the primary language provide two types of subtitles, one parkesque "for them" and the others for the rest of us. For "us" translation subtitles are provided for dialogue only, while English subtitles are solely designated for "them," viewers who are deaf or hard of

Figure 9.5 Subtitles

Figure 9.6 Iconic disability brands

hearing. Reading the meaning implies disability designs. The first message tells of the differential need or preferences in subtitle style related to hearing capacity. Second, creating different schemes for linguistically distinct audiences assumes that each viewer needs or wants only one type of subtitle. We were under the impression that people in all linguistic cultures exhibit diversity of hearing capacity. Third is the presumption that English language speakers would only access subtitles if these film consumers were branded with impaired hearing. Finally, segregated captioning has acquired an acronym, SDH (subtitles for deaf and hard of hearing) elevating it to an iconic brand, advertising the park in the privacy of one's home.

The SDH strategy conducts its branding craft so well that revising the design scope is a complicated process. SDH as an icon succeeded closed captioning, although both are still used. Different from closed captioning available to only those invited into the hard of hearing park, SDH is ubiquitous on home entertainment DVDs. Digital technology provided the method to alter the intrusive appearance of closed captioning. So, while similar in appearance to language translation-only subtitles, SDH keeps its branding both on the set-up screen and through its content (SELCO Cataloging, 2007). We wonder why all subtitles are not equivalent and seamless, given the possibility that non-English language speakers might also need or prefer more the expansive subtitling provided by the SDH brand.

Until 2011, although some limited responses to bodies with other atypical characteristics have been part of the twentieth and twenty-first centuries, a synthetic reading of visual culture (Candlin and Guins, 2009; Miller, 2010) exposes the power of these iconic brands in crafting only limited conditions as the penultimate symbols of disability and thus those marked worthy of access features institutionalized in legislation. More recently, the cartoon in Figure 9.7 entered the iconic branding scene.

Although we have not seen this icon displayed beyond the screen, it is an up and coming actor in the political economic disability park. We are not at all baffled by the creation of the image nor will its future proliferation be an astonishment, given the ascendency of autistic spectrum disorder as linguistic moniker in the disability park.

Figure 9.7 The autism brain

Finally, New York City announced its adoption of the new and improved ISA (Basken, 2013) shown in Figure 9.8. While the Gordon College students who designed this symbol meant to animate the body branded by the ISA, and to suggest forward thinking so to speak, the cartoon does nothing to move beyond the perpetuation of the disability park wheelchair as iconic brand for the diversity of human bodies and experiences.

What remains troubling is the power of these iconic global images to craft disability and even park responses to such limited embodied human experiences. Reading this restraint assures that a significant part of environmental response is devoted to the erection of built environment features that allow access only for some. Reading these images at a more profound level divulges what images are missing, the tyranny of the opposite discussed in regard to language but present in imagery as well. This reading highlights truncated accessibility responses, getting the world off the hook, so to speak, for designing environments to meet and welcome the full spectrum of human diversity.

The craft of imagery does not stop with accessibility cartoons. As we have discussed in previous chapters, film, art, literature, television, music, and virtual visuals all can be read as crafting the design of disability as the embodiment "other" club that few would choose to join (Halifax, 2009; Hall, 2011). We would suggest that the word "disability" itself should be read as a designer moniker, one that is born out of political correctness, exercising its craft to derail humane innovation, and one that is first in line for undesign and redesign.

Figure 9.8 New York City's new and improved ISA

Summary

This chapter began an in-depth exploration of the crafts of disability design and branding. Here, the focus centered on text, word, and image. The three, although distinct on their surface, overlap as screen-mediated interaction and art have increasingly smudged the boundaries among the three. We demonstrated how each and then all three together pack power through their craft both within the disability park and outside it.

References

Basken, P. (2013) A Team of Academics Redesigns an Icon. *Chronicle of Higher Education*, May 20. Available online at http://chronicle.com/article/New-York-City-Embraces-a/139355 (accessed January 29, 2014).

Bellhouse, D. (2011) *Abraham De Moivre: Setting the Stage for Classical Probability and Its Applications.* Boca Raton, FL: CRC Press.

Bolaki, S., and Gair, C. (2012) CFP: Disability and the American Counterculture. Retrieved from *Disability Studies, Temple University*, September 17. Available online at http://disstud.blogspot.com/2012/09/cfp-disability-and-american.html (accessed January 29, 2014).

Candlin, F., and Guins, R. (2009) *The Object Reader.* London: Routledge.

CASRC (2011) What is Developmental Delay and What Services are Available if I Think My Child Might be Delayed? *How Kids Develop.* Child and Adolescent Services Research Center. Available online at www.howkidsdevelop.com/developDevDelay.html (accessed January 29, 2014).

Centers for Disease Control and Prevention (2012) Learn the Signs. Act Early. Developmental Milestones. Centers for Disease Control and Prevention, July 5. Available online at www.cdc.gov/ncbddd/actearly/milestones/index.html (accessed January 29, 2014).

Chandler, D., and Munday, R. (2011) *A Dictionary of Media and Communication.* Oxford: Oxford University Press.

Cheyney, J. (2011) The Rhetoric of Ableism. *Disability Studies Quarterly*, 31 (3). Available online at http://dsq-sds.org/article/view/1665/1606 (accessed January 29, 2014).

Cochrane Collaboration (2014) About Us. Cochrane Collaboration. Available online at www.cochrane.org/about-us (accessed January 29, 2014).

Cochrane Collaboration (2014) Glossary. Cochrane Collaboration. Available online at www.cochrane.org/glossary/5#letterr (accessed January 29, 2014).

DePoy, E., and Gilson, S. (2011) *Studying Disability.* Los Angeles, CA: Sage.

DePoy, E. and Gitlin, L (2011) *Introduction to Research: Multiple Strategies for Health and Human Services* (4th ed.). St. Louis, MO: Mosby.

Derrida, J. (1997) *Of Grammatology.* trans. G. Spivak. Baltimore, MD: Johns Hopkins University Press.

Diament, M. (2013) Reporters Get New Guidance On Disability Lingo. *Disability Scoop*, March 12. Available online at www.disabilityscoop.com/2013/03/12/reporters-disability-lingo/17473 (accessed January 29, 2014).

Dudley-Marling, C., and Gurn, A. (2010) *The Myth of the Normal Curve.* New York: Peter Lang.

Finkelstein, V. (1980) *Attitudes and Disabled People: Issues for Discussion.* International Exchange of Information in Rehabilitation Monograph 5. New York: World Rehabilitation Fund.

Foucault, M. (1980) *Power/Knowledge: Selected Interviews and Other Writings, 1972–1977.* New York: Knopf Doubleday.

Halifax, N. V. (2009) *Disability and Illness in Arts-Informed Research: Moving Toward Arts Informed Research.* Amherst, NY: Cambria Press.

Hall, A. (2011) *Disability and Modern Fiction: Faulkner, Morrison, Coetzee and the Nobel Prize for Literature.* New York: Palgrave MacMillan.

Hoyningen-Huene, P. (2013) *Systematicity: The Nature of Science.* Oxford: Oxford University Press.

Hughes, G. (2010) *Political Correctness: A History of Semantics and Culture.* Chichester: Wiley-Blackwell.

Institute for the Future of the Book (n.d.) The Institute for the Future of the Book. Available online at Mission: www.futureofthebook.org/mission.html (accessed January 29, 2014).

Keupink, A., and Shieh, S. (2010) *The Limits of Logical Empiricism: Selected Papers of Arthur Pap.* Dordecht: Springer.

Lee, J. (2011) *Word As Image.* New York: Penguin.

Merriam-Webster (2014) text. *Merriam-Webster Dictionary.* Available online at www.merriam-webster.com/dictionary/text?show=0andt=1362674122 (accessed January 29, 2014).

Merriam-Webster (2014) word. *Merriam-Webster Dictionary.* Available online at www.merriam-webster.com/dictionary/word (accessed January 29, 2014).

Miller, D. (2010) *Stuff.* Malden, MA: Polity.

Mobility International USA (2006) Respectful Disability Language. Mobility International USA. Available online at www.miusa.org/ncde/tools/respect (accessed January 29, 2014).

NYSED. (2012, October 15) Access VR. Supported Employment. New York State Education Department, September 23. Available online at www.acces.nysed.gov/vr/supportedemployment (accessed January 29, 2014).

Radcliff, T. (2012) Essay: A Universal Language of Images. *Facebook Stories,* October 1. Available online at www.facebookstories.com/stories/1937/essay-a-universal-language-of-images (accessed January 29, 2014).

SELCO Cataloging (2007) Cataloging Bulletin – Subtitles for the Deaf and Hard of Hearing. *SELCO Cataloging,* October 30. Available online at http://smartinvesting.selco.info/download/attachments/33882113/Subtitles+for+the+Deaf+and+hard+of+Hearing+.pdf?version=1andmodificationDate=1272475199070 (accessed January 29, 2014).

Siebers, T. (2010) *Disability Aesthetics.* Ann Arbor, MI: University of Michigan Press.

Smith, A. M. (2011) *Hideous Progeny: Disability, Eugenics, and Classic Horror.* New York: Columbia University Press.

Titchkosky, T. (2007) *Reading and Writing Disability Differently.* Toronto, ON: University of Toronto Press.

United Spinal Association (2013) *Disability Etiquette: Tips on Interacting with People with Disabilities.* Jackson Heights, NY: United Spinal Association.

Uttal, W. (2013) *Reliability in Cognitive Neuroscience: A Meta-Meta-Analysis.* Cambridge, MA: MIT Press.

Varnum, R., and Gibbons, C. T. (2001) *The Language of Comics: Word and Image.* Jackson, MI: University of Mississippi Press.

10 Craft of policy in design and branding

In previous chapters, we have introduced and begun a more substantive examination of the scope of disability policy in three major categories, disability explicit, embedded, and implicit. Much policy territory was covered. Although we do believe that specialized policy was crafted as a vehicle to redress historical disadvantage, we would suggest that its perpetuation and expansion is not useful at best and harmful at worst in the twenty-first-century context. In this chapter we therefore analyze how the policy craft is designer and branding mechanism for disability as segregated, dependent on park expertise, and at the extreme, elimination from humanness. Examining its craft in the twenty-first century both descriptively and critically, provides a sound basis for informing policy undesign and redesign to move closer to the ideal of equality of rights and opportunity.

Scholarship concerned with the process of policy initiation to policy implementation travels in many academic and theoretical countries. Given that policy is only one actor in designing and branding disability, in this chapter, we find that a sharp focus is key in order not to get lost in the vast policy landscape. Therefore, we use a delimited set of boundaries and sequences to answer specific questions about the crafting mechanisms through which disability in the United States in particular, and recently in other countries following suit, have and continue to design, implement, and sustain disability-explicit and -embedded policies, both of which have served, perhaps inadvertently, to perpetuate negative stigma and segregation attributes of the disability park.

As introduced previously, we assert that while explicit and embedded disability policy may design well-intended response to need, in essence and most feasibly unplanned, these policies are fraudulent in their claims to improve conditions and opportunity for individuals and groups who qualify and thus are branded as disabled in the twenty-first century. While masquerading as safety nets, protections, and services, policy verbiage along with other subpopulation specific policy neglects instrumental and institutional segregation, dependence, and exchange of meager resources for a life of poverty. "Beneficiaries" are thus designed and branded as burdensome and needy by their eligibility, as well as their acceptance of the gifts proffered by these policies, while the instruments absolve institutions, commerce and community from providing full and equivalent access to resources and opportunities afforded to non-qualifying others.

Perhaps the term beneficiary is a misnomer given its definition "as to derive benefit or advantage; profit; make improvement" (Dictionary.com, 2013). We would suggest that the individuals and groups meeting the eligibility criteria for coverage or protection under such policies are not necessarily the primary beneficiaries of disability explicit, embedded, and to some extent implicit policies. Thus, designing policies seems to enact the art of disguise not only in what is gained through a policy, but by whom, how, and why.

Just as a minuscule detour, we harken back to the Middle Ages to remind you of the belief that atypical bodies were placed on Earth not for their own benefit, but for others who ministered to them. By showing their altruism and worth as caregivers, typical people entered the pearly gates on the stepping stones of the embodied atypical. Back to the present, it seems as if the policy world adopted this chicanery. So now we begin a progressive reading so to speak of policy narrative as well as practice, assimilating diverse but relevant views that often nurture relationships among strange bedfellows, as we see in the discussion below.

Pre-policy: Who speaks first?

By pre-policy, we refer to the thinking, action, and communication processes that precede the articulation and development of policy. How does a need for a formal policy response even emerge, who articulates it, verifies it, why, and then how are the legitimate spokespersons recognized and sanctioned to march on?

The first dilemma is to determine how human need is crafted as the basis for policy response. Once again, where one takes a stand on this complex question depends on where one is conceptually, morally, and socially seated.

The rational school of policy analysis, introduced as bounded rationality by Simon in 1957 is now referred to with more contemporary jargon such as evidence-based, post-positivist, or problem solving (Fischer, 2003). Common to these logico-deductive approaches are the identification and verification of social problems to which policy needs to respond as an empirically informed and logically developed enterprise. Box 10.1 presents the steps of a ubiquitous form of rational policy development, the infamous logic model: "A logic model is a conceptual tool for planning and evaluation which displays the sequence of actions that describes what the science-based program is and will do" (National Institute of Food and Agriculture, 2009).

This "reasoned" process is used for both planning and evaluation of policy and programmatic outcomes and their surveillance. However,

---

Box 10.1 Deductive pre-policy logic model

Inputs (what we invest)
Outputs:
    Activities (the actual tasks we do)
    Participation (who we serve; customers and stakeholders)
Outcomes/impacts:
    Short term (learning: awareness, knowledge, skills, motivations)
    Medium term (action: behavior, practice, decisions, policies)
    Long term (consequences: social, economic, environmental etc.)

---

exfoliating the rhetorical integument of such models, one can see the influence of two ruling classes, cost and interest group, on subsequent sequential thinking and action. This point is affirmed by Bardach (2009), who explicates public policy as primarily concerned with resource distribution and then queries it through a market lens: "What private troubles warrant definitions as public problems and thereby legitimately raise claims for public resources? It is usually helpful to view the situation through the Market failure lens" (p. 2–3)

By market failure, Bardach is referring to the principle born in economic theory which exposes the impaired, ill conceived and insufficients market strategy to meet the level of demand. When such an economic debacle occurs, it is not uncommon for the government to intervene. It is therefore not surprising to Bardach that market failure tips the balance of expense and service or goods production to the unprofitable side such that public policy moves to rescue the market.

In essence, the formal part of logic models conform to Bardach's (2009) perspective as the model begins with costs, further divulging the fiscal organs of policy development. Preceding the measured elements forming the major corpus of concern, logic models do however, contain one step (listed in Box 10.1) or what we have referred to as pre-policy. In deductive logic models, pre-policy involves the specification of "situation and priorities" where situation includes a statement of needs, symptoms, and stakeholder engagement, followed by priorities which set the action agenda and *a priori* list of desired outcomes within the identified resources and constraints.

Along with numerous others (Baumgartner and Jones, 2009; Elkind, 2011; Fischer, 2003; Greenhalgh and Russell, 2009; Hajer and Wagenaar, 2003), we are critical of deductive policy development schemes for several reasons. First, and most fundamental, is the acceptance of an uncomfortable epistemic foundation for policy crafting. What we mean here is that the same scientific narrative that tells developmental and medicalization stories of disability results in constraining thought about human need and response. As detailed by Stone (2011) and Hajer and Wagenaar, (2003), policy is a human enterprise and thus is sloppy, influenced by unanticipated events and phenomena, and can move in diverse directions depending on who is in the lead at any one time, albeit within a limited scope of change. So, on this epistemological front, we are in agreement with the postmodernists, who see narrative as local, and logico-deductive scientific thinking as one of the grandest narratives of them all, particularly in the policy arena.

Second, despite the proclaimed intent of policy to solve and/or respond to social problems, somehow the problem has gone missing from the full equation of policy narrative. In typical logic models such as the one presented in Table 10.1, political correctness moves problems into the situation room, sequestering them behind closed doors, only allowing the elite to deliberate on their substance and define criteria for their resolution, and then of course, rebranding them for more public acceptance. Without a clear problem statement, what is being "solved" by policy and for whom are obfuscated.

Even if the concept "problem" is regarded, we would suggest that the discussion leaves problem statements in the realm of vagary, implied, rarely articulated as issues to be solved, and when identified, stated in terms of a preferred solution or disguised as a need statement (DePoy and Gilson, 2009). Once again, who is the speaker, what the problem is, and to whom are veiled.

Consider this simple example to make the distinction among the three.

- **Preferred solution statement**: There is an insufficient number of access features in built environments.
- **Disguised need**: The problem is that we need more access features in built environments.
- **Problem statement**: The built environment has many barriers to full access.

While, on the surface, each of the three texts seems to be addressing the problem of inequality of access, a more precise examination of the symbolic (in this case words and syntax) ignites understanding.

The first statement proposes a scenario that can only be successfully resolved by one outcome – more built features. The second statement designs need as the problem itself, conflating the two. An actual problem statement begs for more analysis, liberating the problem from a single need or preferred solution, and thus leaving it open for analysis and innovation that can only occur when the problem is expanded to look at direct as well as tangential influential factors. In the third statement, the undesirable circumstance of limited built-environment access awaits solutions from multiple thinkers. So moving beyond the preferred solution in the first statement and the articulated need in the second, an adequate problem statement "sticks to the knitting," so to speak, by positing the unacceptable condition to which multiple solutions can be linked. For example, barriers, even if left intact, an option sanctioned by the undue burden clause hitched to reasonable accommodation, can be circumvented by other creative means (e.g., the use of technology or humans to equalize access). But problem statement #1 (calling for the option of more features) summons disability-park experts to the job. As example of a resolution to problem statement #3, consider the public library staff who could not make changes to their historical building within their budget and expertise. So they closed stacks to all visitors and brought materials to them in human hands as the basis for equal access. We see this solution as one that resides in creative equal justice thinking outside of the park. This solution considered using humans to meet the full range of human need and usability in the context of the library.

Now, before any further discussion, consider a formal definition of problem:

a: A question raised for inquiry, consideration, or solution.
b: An intricate unsettled question.
c: A source of perplexity, distress, or vexation.
d: Difficulty in understanding or accepting, I have a problem with your saying that (Merriam-Webster, 2013).
e: What is wrong (Winter, 2003).

Note that, in the lexicon above, there is no mention of empirical support, implied solution or need, and of course these omissions are not surprising, given that problems are value statements about what is not acceptable (Fischer, 2003). Moreover, what is a problem to one is not a problem to all. According to Dwyer (2011) and DePoy and Gilson (2009), a problem is simply an undesirable circumstance, clearly implying or even shouting value. As example, the individual who previously had full access to the library with open stacks, and thus had no problem with this arrangement, may now have a problem with the need to request materials. Or consider the large literature arguing with itself about the problem of being "overweight." For those who choose to eat because they love food, enjoyment trumps body weight and thus measured body poundage is not a problem. Yet to the physicians who care for those individuals, as well as for those who perceive the high cost of medical care as a function of poor health behavior, choices to exceed desirable medical weight are clearly problematic and undesirable. For the pharmaceutical firm that manufactures diet pills, the problem of weight, although advertised as one for individuals in the target market, may not be a problem at all, as it produces profit through the actions of medicine development and sales.

As we noted above, Bardach (2009) makes a point about market failure moving a private to pubic problem as the government steps in purportedly to maintain fiscal stability. However, his claim is challenged here, as the lines between government and commerce are perforated. The complexity of disability park problems and public policy solutions often move in both directions, public to private and visa versa. As example, consider underemployment of individuals branded as disabled with mental health diagnoses. Despite the claimed social problem of lack of opportunity along with policy responses to ostensibly prevent discrimination, underemployment continues, often indicting the individual with a diagnosis as the locus of the problem. We do not take on the argument that everyone is employable or should even be employed. The point here is to illustrate the complexity of problem statements and often ineffectual one-way routes to their analysis and proposed resolution through the policy craft.

Moreover, for the penultimate market goal of profit, an identified problem for some can be transmogrified into opportunity. As you will read in the material on undesign and redesign of disability, this point endorses not only critical analysis but can instigate innovative action.

Amplifying complexity, now consider the definition of social problem. Given the broad and diverse coverage of definitions and conditions comprising social problems, we selected Mahoney's (2008) definition and its caveats as the basis for discussion but also critique. As we see in clarifiers below, even to Mahoney, social problems originally cast in empirical roles lose their credibility as deductive actors. Mahoney first notes an objective condition or one that exists and can be verified from the corpus of a problem, but then even he proceeds to eviscerate his own definition.

According to Mahoney, all social problems are defined by four essential elements:

1. The objective condition must be perceived to be a social problem publicly. That is, there must be some public outcry. People must become actively involved in discussing the problem. Public attention becomes directed toward that social condition.
2. The condition must involve a gap between social ideals and social reality. That is, the condition must run counter to the values of the larger society. At the beginning of the 20th century alcohol abuse was perceived to be a very serious social problem, responsible for family breakdown, abandonment of children, accidental death at work, and violence in society. A "Temperance Movement" emerged that further consolidated public opinion to a point that people wanted to do something about it.
3. A significant proportion of the population must be involved in defining the problem. (A large proportion of the population must be concerned about the condition...It must have national attention. If only a small segment of the population gets involved you have an interest group pushing for the general public to do something about the condition – not a social problem).

4. The condition must be capable of solution through collective action by people. If no solution is perceived possible, people will resign themselves to their fate. A good example is government bureaucracy: If everyone takes the attitude that "you can't fight city hall," government bureaucracy doesn't emerge as a social problem. Rather, it is a part of life that everyone must live with.

The caveats
If people affected by a condition are influential, or powerful, the condition is more likely to be considered a social problem than if those affected are not influential.

A condition affecting a relatively small segment of the population is less likely to be considered a social problem than if it has adverse effects on a much larger segment of society.

A rapid increase in the number of people affected by a social condition is also important – perhaps even as important as the number of people affected!

The mass media also play an important role in the selection and definition of social problems... The liberal press will highlight certain issues while the conservative press will select others.

Finally, ideology plays an important role in determining which conditions are singled out as social problems. Ideology also determines how a social problem is defined. Conservatives and liberals agree that America has a poverty problem – but they do not agree on a specific definition of the problem, nor do they agree on how the problem should be solved.

(Mahoney, 2008)

Thus, despite the definition of problem as an empirical animal, its core organs are ideology, influence, and perceived or experienced undesirable consequences. As simply stated by Bardach (2009), a social problem is characterized as follows "something is wrong with the world but note that wrong is a very debatable term" (p. 2). Yet, social policy is branded as the great problem solver. Look at how Wikipedia, a popular media site, names and describes the craft of social policy: "Social policy often deals with wicked problems. Social policy is defined as actions that affect the well-being of members of a society through shaping the distribution of and access to goods and resources in that society."

Given the aim of social policy to enact solutions to social problems, the pre-policy journey to identify the problems to which disability explicit and embedded policies are directed is a rugged set of convoluted passages. In many policies, it is difficult to navigate to the central "problem" at all. As example, in the Americans with Disabilities Act (ADA), the word problem was found only once in the original text: "historically, society has tended to isolate and segregate individuals with disabilities, and, despite some improvements, such forms of discrimination against individuals with disabilities continue to be a serious and pervasive social problem."

Winter (2003) expands this problem statement to medical model devaluation and thus oppression and marginalization of disabled persons. Yet, the US Department of Justice Civil Rights Division interprets this same "problem" as an unrealized goal, camouflaging a preferred solution.

> In the years since the Supreme Court's decision in Olmstead v. L.C., 527 U.S. 581 (1999), the goal of the integration mandate in title II of the Americans with Disabilities Act – to provide individuals with disabilities opportunities to live their lives like individuals without disabilities – has yet to be fully realized.
>
> (US Department of Justice Civil Rights Division, 2011)

We are not isolated in our incredulity regarding a critical reading of this narrative. The "problem statement" above, even with its explicit claim to promote equality does so in a manner that posits the preferred solution of continuing to design and brand "not disability" as both existing and aggrandized through its claims to the contrary.

Searching disability legislation in the United States and beyond, unearthed even more craft of grand narrative, thereby licensing policy interpreters to ascribe meaning and worth in the name of science.

> Whereas empiricism treats language and meaning as an ornament of social behaviour, a discursive approach makes clear that discourse and social meaning are internal to the very social systems we seek to research. Without them, the institutional practices of a society cannot be understood; indeed, they would not even function, if they could exist at all.
>
> (Fischer, 2003: viii)

In evidentiary support, we enter the grand dam of disability rights legislation (the ADA) as well as its technological servant (the Assistive Technology Act). Both begin with asserted pre-policy "findings," a linguistic symbol that implies a systematic, empirical rationale for the generation of truths to which policy then is directed. Yet, to the contrary, the vague nature of the words in the policy are resplendent as illustrated so aptly by the interpretation by the Justice Department; we want to and can be like the mythic able-bodied. From this short reading of problem statements or their proxies contained in policy, axiological and connotative uncertainty and plurality are made transparent.

Despite a critical eye, we do not wake up in the morning thinking that policy makers and the pre-policy process intend to dupe the public. Rather, the craft of policy-making in itself provides the incubator for multiple motives, power jockeying, and influence to be brought to bear on how disability design and branding are crafted: "Whereas empiricism bases causal explanation on the metaphors of either the mechanism or the organism, the narrative mode of knowing is geared to the metaphor of contextualism" (Fischer, 2003).

Following Fischer beyond the myth of empirical objectivity itself and its employability as the most rigorous epistemology for policy activation therefore can be much more exacting and precise than scientism in comprehending the craft of design embedded within context, prodding undesign and reconstituting policy for redesign. The questions to be asked and answered about pre-policy process by the post-empiricist analyst include:

- Who is speaking the value text of the problem?
- How are these speakers branded with legitimacy?
- What are the speakers' motives in asserting the problem status of an issue?
- How does the problem catch and engage the broader legislative eye and corpus respectively?
- How does the pre-policy narrative and its presentation influence public perception?
- When do issues become branded as public issues and how?
- In designing a problem and its articulation, what is lost, gained, and by whom?
- Who are dissenters and how are they met with response?

Baumgartner, Berry, Hojnacki, Leech, and Kimball (2009), have one set of answers to these questions. They assert that protection of the status quo is the ultimate crafter of the pre-policy industry. Thus, crafting issues as problems is done in such a manner as to preserve the resources, influence, and power of those who already hold it. The curiosity here then is how to discover the "man behind the curtain" as the basis for recrafting problem narratives in service of efficacious policy for asserted beneficiaries. In first reading the work of Baumgartner *et al.* (2009), one might disagree with their analysis on the grounds that social change occurs and is contained in policy rhetoric. But further thought raises curiosity about the role and even the potential of pre-policy stories to prompt social revision. In searching for causes of social change, policy itself was rarely mentioned. As stated by Weinstein who reincarnates the perspective of Durkheim,

> Whereas sociocultural processes generally operate to maintain order and preserve the status quo, movements and technological innovation are specifically designed to change the balance in ways great or small.
> (Weinstein, 2010: 131)

Making more frequent appearances, particularly in the literature of sociology of change, are technology and innovation, discovery, collective movements creating dissonance and conflict, demography, climate, modernization, and ideas (Openstax College, 2012; Weinstein, 2010). And then, of course, Bardach's (2009) market orientation enters the fray. Given the role of policy in maintaining institutional sameness and fiscal prudence, it is feasible now to envision how current pre-policy stories craft the status quo albeit in veiled ways.

Once again, we turn the spotlight on the ADA and its cousin the ADA Amendments Act (ADAAA), which tells a story of inequity and meets it with the same. From a narrative analytic perspective, the story may be partially articulated, spawning beliefs that change will occur, while in essence serving to siphon off explosive tension that could potentially lead to profound social movement, change, and rebalancing resource distribution.

Moving beyond the pre-policy storyboard: The craft of policy

There is a large literature containing stories about how policy is crafted once the pre-policy phase is complete. In this section of the chapter, we do not engage the full scope of the policy process, but rather critically visit and thus highlight parts which are both problematic and promising for evocative undesign and redesign.

Recent news media have heightened concern for bipartisanship haggling, showcasing on screen, the failure of the Executive and Legislative branches of the US government and other similar national entities throughout the globe to act civilly and get down to the business of protecting the public and meeting public need. Yet, the official patriotic story inscribed on electronic flash cards (presented below) and other such materials for all to view (and in particular for indoctrinating secondary school students with national propaganda) reads policy as a smooth collaboration between the public and the government as a set of five sequential steps.

> Flash cards: One for each of five policy steps
> 1   Setting and clarifying the national agenda.
> 2   Formulation of a policy response.
> 3   Adoption or passage of laws to meet the targeted element of national agenda.
> 4   Implementation through creating rules and procedures for implementing the policy narrative.
> 5   Evaluation-judgment from diverse groups about the efficacy of the policy.
>
> (Sparknotes, 2013)

The pre-policy "setting the national agenda" phase has tied with evaluation (Step 5) for the winner of the most political spin award. Peruse this narrative below with our questions about the meaning of lexical and conceptual symbol embedded (emboldened).

Box 10.2 Questioning lexical and conceptual symbols

When something (**what is the scope of this word?**) becomes a concern (**what is meant by concern and for whom?**) for a significant (**how many of whom are enough?**) number of people, that concern becomes part of the national agenda, the list of things that the public (**who are the public and are they an essential group?**) wants (**what does wanting entail and how is wanting made known to whom?**) the government to address. An issue becomes part of the national agenda for any of the following reasons:

- **As part of a larger trend**: Some trends, like the rise in violent crime in the 1980s and early 1990s, lead people to demand (**Really? What people? What does demand mean and then what follows?**) government action, especially for stronger federal law enforcement.
- **After a major event**: Sometimes, a single event forces an issue onto the agenda (**Do we hear Deborah Stone's (2011) voice here?**). The September 11th attacks, for example, led many Americans to demand an increase in national security (**Who translated desire for security to undressing in the airport**). Likewise, the Exxon Valdez oil spill in 1989 prompted many to call for environmental protection.
- **Through an interest group**: An interest group or members of a social movement work to raise public awareness of an issue. If enough people get involved, the issue can get put on the national agenda (**Who is legitimate to speak as an interest group?**).
- **Speeches**: Prominent politicians attempt to put an issue on the agenda through speeches. The president is particularly able to do this due to the amount of media coverage of the White House. (**Now we are getting to the core of policy, political spin lulls listeners into an allusion of understanding. We see political speeches as part of the entertainment industry**).

The skeleton of the asserted national agenda development illustrates the power of words in spawning beliefs that a process is transparent and palpable by those who attend to it. Similarly, #5, the evaluation flash card, is riddled with spin and myth, implying that evaluation is a public enterprise, in which those outside of government and paying interest groups may actually have a say in the efficacy of a policy and its outcomes. Yet, given the interpretive linguistic relativity challenge that Hajer and Wagenaar (2003) pose as a function of the networked global society, the meanings of the words used in media, text and narrative, and political speech are not unitary and thus elicit contrasting, context-embedded understandings. The semantic muddle, unbeknownst to too many listeners, provides both obfuscation and opportunity for actors in the policy process, but certainly does not lend itself to the inclusive fiction implied in this linear waltz scripted above.

Policy finagling related to the recent sequestration in the United States submits a prime example repudiating any story of rational, empirical policy process. We offer this example not only for critique but as noted throughout, for design guidance. Elucidating the human interactive policy *modi operandi* can illuminate the convoluted crafts necessary to undesign and redesign disability.

Crafting entry into the policy narrative begins with its title, sequestration. Just consider the word sequestration itself as defined and expanded in Thesaurus.com (2013):

> Definition: Seclusion
> Synonyms: aloneness, aloofness, beleaguerment, blockade, concealment, desolation, detachment, hiding, isolation, privacy, privateness, quarantine, reclusion, reclusiveness, remoteness, retirement, retreat, seclusiveness, separateness, separation, shelter, solitude, withdrawal.

In opposition to the inclusive story of policy told to students above, the title slide, sequestration itself, comes with a full set of semiotic baggage, implying secrecy about jockeying dollars. Then, similar to many other policy narratives, the public wallet is sculpted into a horror story as Congress decreases fiscal resources behind its locked deliberation doors, without significantly up-ending the status quo of the disability park among other institutional structures. Look at the monster in this narrative.

Bottom line
> The sequester would place tens of thousands of Americans with disabilities at greater risk for hunger and homelessness, endanger the education of millions of children with disabilities and delay employment services and disability benefits for scores of people with disabilities – including disabled veterans – who are, on average, already at greater risk of poverty.
> (National Council on Disability, 2013)

The fiscal story then is translated into doom. While we are not disputing the potential of budget cuts to decrease park services, we would suggest (as we discuss in detail in subsequent chapters) that headlines designed to elicit fear, pity, and other negative emotions serve to rally groups to reinstate "what was" rather than move to what could and should be.

A second craft is termed the "christmas tree bill." This type of bill is one which is passed because of the unrelated ornamentation hung on its fundamental branches. Consider as example the classic "highway bill" debated in

Congress in 2005 (Boaz, 2005). In addition to earmarking almost US$2,000,000 for museums, pork barrel support for over 4000 special projects adorned this bill. Unbeknownst or not easily ascertainable by those outside of the Congressional walls, practices such as christmas tree bills and related legislative collages such as the Budget Control Act of 2011 conceal special interest initiatives within legislation narrative for political advantage.

Advocacy is the substance of the third policy design craft. While broad in its praxis, scope, and actor guild, advocacy can generally be defined as "the act or process of advocating or supporting a cause or proposal" (Merriam-Webster, 2013). The actors' guild in this genre of political influence ranges from individuals, to grass roots groups, to highly trained and paid lobbyists.

Teles and Schmitt (2011) suggest that social change does not occur without advocacy. They then proceed to characterize advocacy as an incremental and even *sub rosa* ongoing non-linear craft in which knowing who to approach and how to nurture the elite are the tools for success. Volunteer and local advocacy is privy to public hearings and spaces. Yet, according to Mullen (2012), decisions about resources are not within their purview: "Budget bills in particular are subject to last-minute changes behind closed doors even though those negotiations may have been preceded by extensive public hearings."

Outcome evaluation of advocacy is thus difficult, given that change through this craft is often specific to non-fiscal issues and lethargic until an event awakens lawmakers. Thus, without sustained attention and activity, policy languishes and bathes in its own past (Teles and Schmitt, 2011). One might suspect that wealth has a large role in inciting change. Thus, advocacy in the form of corporate lobbying is an ongoing, robust, and often headlined craft.

Mathur (2011) even suggests that lobbying is analogous to bribery, in that goods and services are traded among lobbyists and legislators in order to gain political advantage. Given that in 2012, 12,389 lobbyists and US$3.3 billion were devoted to lobbying efforts, one would expect that this action is highly influential in the policy process. (Mathur, 2011). Yet, according to Baumgartner *et al.* (2009), the grand narrative of lobbying for change is devoid of evidence.

> If what they [lobbyists] are supposed to be doing is producing change, interest groups are a surprisingly ineffectual lot. A focus by the media and many academics on explaining political change or sensational examples of lobbying success obscures the fact that lobbyists often toil with little success in gaining attention to their causes or they meet such opposition to their efforts that the resulting battle leads to a stalemate. Of course, many lobbyists are active because their organizations benefit from the status quo and they want to make sure that it stays in place. We will show that one of the best single predictors of success in the lobbying game is not how much money an organization has on its side,

but simply whether it is attempting to protect the policy that is already in place.

(Baumgartner et al. 2009: 6)

Synthesizing the crafts of local advocacy and big money lobbying, we would agree with Baumgartner *et al.* (2009), who claim that advocacy supports the aim of policy to maintain the status quo unless it is more profitable not to do so. While, this realization derails the use of advocacy for expedient change, it makes room for exposing and activating the efficacious change agent to be used for undesign and redesign. Once again the market reigns.

Advertising is one market strategy that has met with significant success in manipulating people and thus causing change. It is therefore part and parcel of politics and policy change as can be seen with the preeminence of visual culture acting as political leadership. Although we try to keep up with media renditions of politics, elections, political parties, and the policy process, it is difficult to dig behind its theatrical façade and scripted dialog. Visual culture parades in front of the closed doors of policy decision makers and to a large extent renders an understanding of the policy process impenetrable by the layperson. We often remark about the "Hollywoodesque" quality of politics, as our leaders emerge from film and speak words authored by spin doctors and advertisers. Slogans, logos and person branding are crafted as authentic democracy, but what democracy means and how it is operationalized are obscured until such events as bank failures and corporate bailouts grace the media headlines (Spiller and Bergner (2011).

It is therefore not unexpected that disability policy is designed not only to maintain the status quo but to fatten it. As example, the ADAAA retains the inequitable clauses of reasonable accommodation and undue hardship, but now applies these caveats, "not as good but branded as good enough for the alters," to an ever-expanding population of eligible persons who believe in this legislation as the rights equalizer. While the ADAAA may be seen as improving access for some, its expansive girth creates torpor for more fundamental change. Advocates therefore seek more of the sameness in place of alternatives that demand equality of rights.

The academy as false-jacketer

Before leaving the policy process we discuss one more group, the academy, as false-jacketer. We first encountered the term "false-jacketer" in the classic endogenous study conducted by Maruyama (1981). Used to refer to bogusly branding another person, we have found it richly descriptive for many contexts. Here, we look to the academy for two major crafts: 1) its use of politically correct dialog to name and thus substitute for thoughtful and critical policy analysis, and 2) promoting the science narrative as the basis for pre-policy need statements and post-policy outcome evaluation.

To illustrate the first false-jacketing phenomenon we turn to our own university. Each semester, in our university, students in policy classes are shuttled to the state capital to provide testimony advocating for welfare reform as continued coverage for recipients. Thus, welfare reform is simply euphemistic for more of the same, truncating opportunity for students to engage in progressive discussion, debate and challenge necessary to induce social change. Perhaps unknowingly, faculty false-jacket welfare policy as a problem solver when in essence, it maintains poverty, segregation, and dependence while students are fed a meal of policy rhetoric garnished with the branding discussed by Spiller and Bergner (2011).

This point brings us to the second post-policy craft, promoting the logico-deductive narrative as the basis for policy promulgation and outcome assessment. This epistemic theme seems ubiquitous as we have discussed its presence in so many contexts. As example, the evidence that students were required to present to the legislature for their policy testimony assignment discussed above, consisted of the narrative of poverty surveillance, counting the numbers of adults and children who live below the poverty line, but never explicating cause or refracting policy failure back to legislators. Reflecting the traditions seen in the ADA and its 2008 amendments, "not as good but good enough" tossed with legislated gratitude from safety net recipients, students urge legislators to do more of the same, continue policies for subsistence rather than undesign inadequacy.

We do not need to revisit the points here regarding the limitations of empirical or logic models of policy need and response. But we see the university as in large part responsible for failing, unintentionally, to educate students in the epistemic diversity that can and should inform substantive policy analysis and praxis. Just a simple perusal of the titles and abstracts in a recent issue of the *Disability and Health Journal* reveals the quantitative preferences for publication of articles focusing on health and disability policies, not to mention the conflation of the two constructs and the medicalized model implications for disability crafted in this tangle. Moreover, despite the title asserting its concern with health, all of the articles are about illness, another unintentional false-jacket. We reiterate that this criticism is not an attack but an opportunity for the academy as we discuss in the next section.

The post-policy craft: Outcome evaluation

Revisit the logic model or empirical model of policy analysis to view the finale, the empirical measurement of outcome. Several of the authors already cited (DePoy and Gilson, 2009; Fischer, 2003; Hajer and Wagenaar, 2003; Spiller and Bergner, 2011) have illuminated the dereliction of duty innovation resulting from logico-deductive methods of evaluation, beginning with the omission of an adequate problem statement and concluding with measurement delimited only to specified outcomes at the expense of a broader examination of policy results.

Disability implicit policy provides an exemplar. A recent article in the *New York Times* reported about embodied devastation caused by working with a chemical, n-propyl bromide, or nPB, used in cushions and other products. As eloquently stated:

> [This story] it is a parable about the law of unintended consequences. It shows how an Environmental Protection Agency program meant to prevent the use of harmful chemicals fostered the proliferation of one, and how a hard-fought victory by OSHA in controlling one source of deadly fumes led workers to be exposed to something worse – a phenomenon familiar enough to be lamented in government parlance as "regrettable substitution … "
>
> OSHA devotes most of its budget and attention to responding to here-and-now dangers rather than preventing the silent, slow killers that, in the end, take far more lives. Over the past four decades, the agency has written new standards with exposure limits for 16 of the most deadly workplace hazards, including lead, asbestos and arsenic. But for the tens of thousands of other dangerous substances American workers handle each day, employers are largely left to decide what exposure level is safe.
>
> (Urbina, 2013)

Two failures in both pre- and post-policy are relevant and illustrative here. First, implicit in the short paragraphs above is the limited scope crafted by the Occupational Safety and Health Administration (OSHA) of the pre-policy "problem," immediate harm caused by workplace hazards. Also contained in the journalistic narrative is the role of cost in delimiting the problem only to threats perceived in the present. Flowing from a deficient problem statement is inadequate policy driving praxis that does not serve a cumulative lifetime of workplace hazard, despite its omnipotent danger.

Second, the reliance on measurement of outcome variables specified in an undeveloped problem statement does not capture the adequacy of the policy to meet human need. Rather, OSHA examines its own belly button, hoping that no lint is unturned that reveals unaccomplished tasks. Thus, this formative approach leaves policy outcomes at the starting gate without scrutinizing policy adequacy even for purported aims. It is clear from this article that the policy itself is ill-conceived for its rhetorical aim of protection of workers, bringing us to query the plausibility that it serves another master or masters, some concrete and some conceptual.

We would suggest that disability explicit and embedded policies suffer from many of the same foibles discussed in the disability-implicit OSHA policy above. We have already discussed the craft of putative narrative. As we noted, disability rights policies such as the ADA, Section 504 of the Rehabilitation Act, the Individuals with Disabilities Education Act, and so forth, assert their design for promoting equality of opportunity for disability branded eligibles who have been the objects of discrimination and exclusion. Although problem statements for which these policy were crafted are absent or shriveled, implied in each is at least an increase in representation of individuals with atypical bodies in work and educational settings. Coming face-to-face with the Harris Poll Gap Survey results (National Organization on Disability, Kessler Institute; Harris Interactive, 2010), however, continues to reveal the serious underemployment and disproportionately poor high school and college completion rates of the respondents, with only twenty-one percent employed in comparison to fifty-nine percent of typical individuals. Given these data, we are left with unanswered questions about the actual problems articulated in the secretive chambers of the policy elite. On the other hand, if these policies were crafted to promote equality of opportunity and representation and even these outcomes are not being met, it seems logical to conclude that the policy instruments are not doing their jobs and perhaps should be fired from service. Instead, the ADA is expanded to cover more people, appearing to us as if it is intended to do more of the same, fail to achieve its implied aims for an even greater number of unsuspecting eligibles.

A second amazement prompts us to search for reasons that these policies are condoned by the alleged but unrequited beneficiaries. As example, in a recent study examining how university architecture and spatial policy shape who can study and thus produce knowledge, many students who used wheeled mobility were not only satisfied but protective and defensive of the small and inferior segregated space that they could access on a large state university campus (Gilson and DePoy, 2011). They were satisfied to have any space at all and did not think about the meaning of space and spatial policy not only in crafting second-class citizenry, but in perpetuating this containment praxis for future students. Such gratitude for something that "is not as good as what all others have" remains querulous for us as policy and diversity rhetoric mimic one another, gaining fans from their own captives. This last point brings us to our final conversation in this chapter, the craft of services as designers.

The service craft

According to Mann and Stapleton (2012), "America's disability policies are failing both taxpayers and the working-age population with disabilities. Even as program expenditures have risen, the economic status of this population has fallen even farther behind that of its non disabled peers." Turkewitz and Linderman write:

> The very program that is supposed to be their safety net is actually the source of the problem, experts say. S.S.I. traps many disabled people by limiting their income to levels just above the poverty line, and taking

away their cash benefits if they achieve any level of security.
(Turkewitz and Linderman, 2013)

Similarly, numerous authors bemoan the failure of policy and the multiple services they establish and fund as failing to achieve goals for their purported beneficiaries (The Arc, n.d.; National Council on Disability, 2013). The Arc lists major unmet needs for individuals with qualifying embodied conditions, including civil rights, employment, safety net support, and long term care among others as in need of policy and programmatic revision. But the revisionists typically propose more of the same. Along with authors who discuss the entropy inhernet in disabiity policy and the service park, we continue to wonder why more of what does not produce desired outcomes and even worse, results in harm, is summoned by committed and well meaning people. While the sinister perspective might look exclusively at who benefits from the status quo, we do not see a world in which the intentional aim of inadequate policies and services is failure. There are multiple narratives to consider and then peel away to observe the policy service crafts at work. In this last section, we take on the synthesis of the disability industry with professional socialization, a mine, once understood, to be most productive for undesign and redesign. Because the disability park and its commercial foundation are built on the tenets of specialized knowledge and skill as necessary to help invited guests with embodied conditions function in a standard world, the craft of acculturating employees is an important industry in itself and an entry point for redesign as we discuss in more detail in subsequent chapters. Here, we provide the analytic rationale for this direction.

First, consider the industry. As early as 1992, Gill and Albrecht exposed the disability industry as a means of providing economic gain to all except those who received good and services. It was not until the second half of the following decade that Riley (2006) reintroduced this perspective into the disability literature hitching it to the opportunity star. According to him, disability and business should recognize a yet unfulfilled relationship. We agree that disability and business need one another in transparent and change producing ways, but unlike Riley, we assert that despite rhetoric to the contrary, disability and business have been and are intimately engaged, albeit in an often opaque manner. Cultivation of the design and branding of the broad category of disability locating its members as needy and thus dependent on specialized disability services for their very survival is accomplished in large part by the craft of acculturation. However, because the call to altruism is often presented in opposition to market and economic principles, the role of the economy in crafting policy and services remains contained to reimbursement schemes but goes no farther. We would suggest that undesign and redesign must recognize and make public the load bearing market timbers supporting the weight of disability policy and services in order for undesign and redesign to succeed. Helping and profit can occupy the same sentence without coming to fisticuffs. Yet, from recruitment simulacra throughout academic professional socialization, it is only just nascent to find business and helping professional students rubbing elbows in the same classes.

Building on a lifetime of socialization, the academy recruits genuine gems, the professional students who enter the park with the expressed desire to help others. We do not critique these well-intentioned students and the professionals into which they grow, but rather look at the fundamentals of the tapestries which indoctrinate them, capture them and their clientele, and maintain the grand narrative of the necessity of keeping the park intact, well fed, inscribed in policy, and expanding without speaking about the disability industry.

As evidence of the business element of helping banished from the lexicon of helping world, look at the descriptions of social work and occupational therapy, two of the helping professions that frequent the park:

> Help mends. In thousands of ways, social workers help people help themselves. People of every age. From every background. In every corner of the country – wherever we're needed – starting here and now. Welcome to your source for professional advice, inspiring stories – even a social worker directory. Social workers. Help starts here.
>
> (National Association of Social Workers, 2013)

> In its simplest terms, occupational therapists and occupational therapy assistants help people across the lifespan participate in the things they want and need to do through the therapeutic use of everyday activities (occupations). Common occupational therapy interventions include helping children with disabilities to participate fully in school and social situations, helping people recovering from injury to regain skills, and providing supports for older adults experiencing physical and cognitive changes.
>
> (American Occupational Therapy Association, 1993–2013)

Once the recruit is legitimated, he/she begins the process of professional socialization. The literature on professional and organizational socialization reveals the roles of the academy and the workplace in assuring indoctrination. Professional socialization refers to the transmission of knowledge, skills, values, attitudes, behaviors and even fashion to novitiates such that they espouse and display their professional feathers and maintain the integrity and survival of their fields. Interestingly, Kasar and Clarke (2000) begin their work on professionalism in occupational therapy with the following list of professional behaviors: "Dependability, professional presentation, initiative, empathy, cooperation, organization, clinical reasoning, supervisory process, verbal communication, and written communication" (p. 3). They then follow with context: "Consumer aware-ness, rapid changes in technology and far reaching advances in the monetary reimbursement system have created the need for change" (p. 3).

The texts therefore identify desired behaviors within a reimbursable context, affirming the design of professional helping as an economic entity delimited to payment for services, but neglecting the larger economic motives of the park. We would suggest that a full discussion and analysis of the disability park including its economic vitality is critical for prompting change and that this informed, critical dialog needs to begin within the academy. According to Salutin (2013), "Higher education should expand students' awareness and teach them to think critically, not turn them into social cogs."

Without such education, novices enter the service park steeped in the knowledge, skill, and jargon of their service park professions, including the politically correct lexicon of the day designing and branding service recip-ients. As students transition to agencies and organizations they encounter another set of acculturation hurdles, branded organizational socialization in the large and growing literature on the normative park. Socialization into the park comprises a powerful set of messages, rituals and linguistic signifiers of belonging that can only be challenged through critical debate.

Sullivan (2005) reminds us that the professions so critical to human flourishing in a specialized advanced technological society have lost legiti-macy as they become enmeshed with profit. Look at what Smith and Routel (2010) have to say about the transition park, and by extension the full scope of the disability park:

> Like other social service and educational industry processes, the tran-sition from special education services to supports received in community settings has been commodified and reified, controlled by educational and human service professionals, meeting the needs of the industries that they represent and capitalism in general, and serving to keep people with disabilities and their families segregated and isolated.
>
> (Smith and Routel, 2010)

It is not surprising that given his assertion of professional value, Sullivan (2005) beseeches members of professional groups to undesign and redesign their duties, ethics and functions. In the chapters on undesign and redesign, we agree and suggest how park professionals can join in this effort, one that must begin early and become solidified in the academy with a full discussion of the role of the market economy within the policy and park contexts.

Summary

In this chapter, the crafts of policy and the professional helping accultura-tion of the disability park have been discussed and analyzed. Proceeding through the policy process, we illustrated the grand narrative of empirical policy and the inadequacy of this model for informed and textured policy scrutiny necessary for undersign. Clearly, the dismal outcomes for the asserted beneficiaries, the eligibles of disability explicit, embedded, and even implicit policy beg for profound dialog and thought, with transparency and redesign of market strategies for social and public "good" at the desirable outcome helm.

Following on the heels of policy are services and providers comprising the park. A brief glance at professional socialization places the spotlight on other relatives ripe for redesign, the craft of professional education both before and during tenure at the academy.

References

Albrecht, G. (1992) *The Disability Business: Rehabilitation in America.* Newbury Park, CA: Sage.

American Occupational Therapy Association. (1993–2013) About Occupational Therapy. Available online at www.aota.org/en/About-Occupational-Therapy.aspx (accessed February 5, 2014).

Bardach, E. (2009) *A Practical Guide for Policy Analysis.* Washington, DC: CQ Press.

Baumgartner, F. R., Berry, J. M., Hojnacki, M., Leech, B. L., and Kimball, D. C. (2009) *Lobbying and Policy Change: Who Wins, Who Loses, and Why.* Chicago, IL: University of Chicago Press.

Baumgartner, F., and Jones, B. (2009) *Agendas and Instability in American Politics* (2nd ed.). Chicago, IL: University of Chicago Press.

Boaz, D. (2005) Congress's Latest Christmas Tree Bill. Cato Institute commentary, May 13. Available online at www.cato.org/publications/commentary/congresss-latest-christmas-tree-bill (accessed February 5, 2014).

DePoy, E., and Gilson, S. (2009) *Evaluation Practice.* New York: Routledge.

Dwyer, C. (2011) Penn Professor Charles Dwyer: "How to Get Anyone to Do Anything You Want." YouTube, May 20. Available online at www.youtube.com/watch?v=UCBH7aaw5hs (accessed February 5, 2014).

Elkind, S. (2011) *How Local Politics Shape Federal Policy; Business, Power, and the Environment in Twentieth-Century Los Angeles.* Chapel Hill, NC: University of North Carolina Press.

Fischer, F. (2003) *Reframing Public Policy: Discursive Politics and Deliberative Practices.* Oxford: Oxford University Press.

Gill, C. (1992) Who Gets the Profits. *Mainstream,* 12, 14–17.

Gilson, S., and DePoy, E. (2011) The Student Body: The Intersection of Spatial Design, Architecture, and Cultural Policy in University Communities. In A. C. Carey, and R. K. Scotch, *Research in Social Science and Disability, Volume 6: Disability and Community.* Bingley: Emerald, pp. 27–47.

Greenhalgh, T., and Russell, J. (2009) Evidence-Based Policymaking: A Critique. *Perspectives in Biology and Medicine,* 52 (2), 304–18.

Hajer, M., and Wagenaar, H. (2003) *Deliberative Policy Analysis.* Cambridge: Cambridge University Press.

Kasar, J., and Clarke, N. (2000) *Developing Professional Behaviors.* Throfare, NJ: Slack.

Kessler Foundation, National Organization on Disability, and Harris Interactive

(2010) Kessler Foundation/NOD Survey of Americans with Disabilities Survey of Americans with Disabilities, July 26, 2010. Available online at www.2010disabilitysurveys.org/indexold.html (accessed February 5, 2014).

Mahoney, J. S. (2008) Sociology 302 (Section 002) Contemporary Social Problems, Fall, 2008 (Syllabus/Contract). Defining Social Problems. Available online at www.people.vcu.edu/~jmahoney/define.htm (accessed February 5, 2014).

Mann, D., and Stapleton, D. (2012) A Roadmap to a 21st-Century Disability Policy. *Mathematica Issue Brief*, 12 (1), 1–4. Available online at www.mathematica-mpr.com/Publications/PDFs/disability/roadmap_ib.pdf (accessed February 5, 2014).

Maryuma, M. (1981) Endogenous Research: Rationale. In P. Reason, and J. Rowan, *Human Inquiry: A Sourcebook of New Paradigm Research*. New York: John Wiley and Sons.

Mathur, V. K. (2011) Is Lobbying to Buy Political Influence Bribery? *Standard-Examiner*, March 18. Available online at www.standard.net/topics/opinion/2011/03/18/lobbying-buy-political-influence-bribery (accessed February 5, 2014).

Mullen, M. (2012) Closed-Door Dealmaking Undermines the Legislative Process. *State Integrity Investigation*, August 7. Available online at www.stateintegrity.org/closed_door_dealmaking_undermine_the_legislative_process (accessed February 5, 2014).

National Association of Social Workers (2013) Help Mends. Available online at www.helpstartshere.org (accessed February 5, 2014).

National Council on Disability (2013) What Will Sequestration Mean for People with Disabilities? Available online at www.ncd.gov/newsroom/022813 (accessed February 5, 2014).

National Institute of Food and Agriculture (2009) Logic Models. US Department of Agriculture. Available online at www.csrees.usda.gov/about/strat_plan_logic_models.html (accessed February 5, 2014).

Openstax College (2012) Social Change. Openstax College, June 4. Available online at http://cnx.org/content/m42948/1.2 (accessed February 5, 2014).

Riley, C. (2006) *Disability and Business*. Lebanon, NH: New England University Press.

Salutin, R. (2013) Universities are not job-training factories. *Toronto Star*, November 1. Available online at www.thestar.com/opinion/editorialopinion/2012/11/01/universities_are_not_jobtraining_factories_salutin.html (accessed February 5, 2014).

Simon, H. (1957) *A Behavioral Model of Rational Choice*. New York: Wiley.

Smith, P., and Routel, C. (2010) Transition Failure: The Cultural Bias of Self-Determination and the Journey to Adulthood for People with Disabilities. *Disability Studies Quarterly*, 30 (1). Available online at http://dsq-sds.org/article/view/1012/1224 (accessed February 5, 2014).

Sparknotes (2013) Public Policy. SparkNotes. Available online at www.sparknotes.com/us-government-and-politics/american-government/public-policy/section1.rhtml (accessed February 5, 2014).

Spiller, L., and Bergner, J. (2011) *Branding the Candidate*. Santa Barbara, CA: Praeger.

Stone, D. (2011) *Policy Paradox: The Art of Political Decision Making* (2nd ed.) New York: W. W. Norton.

Sullivan, W. (2005) *Work and Integrity: The Crisis and Promise of Professionalism in America* (2 ed.). San Francisco, CA: Josey Bass.

Teles, S., and Schmitt, M. (2011) The Elusive Craft of Evaluating Advocacy. *Stanford Social Innovation Review*, 4 (Summer). Available online at www.ssireview.org/articles/entry/the_elusive_craft_of_evaluating_advocacy (accessed February 5, 2014).

The Arc (n.d.) Public Policy: Policy Issues Affecting People with Disabilities. Available online at www.thearc.org/what-we-do/public-policy/policy-issues (accessed February 5, 2014).

Turkewitz, J., and Linderman, J. (2013) The Trap of Supplemental Security Income. *New York Times*, October 20. Available online at www.nytimes.com/2012/10/21/sunday-review/the-trap-of-supplemental-security-income.html?_r=0 (accessed February 5, 2014).

US Department of Justice Civil Rights Division (2011) Statement of the Department of Justice on Enforcement of the Integration Mandate of Title II of the Americans with Disabilities Act and Olmstead v. L.C. Available online at www.ada.gov/olmstead/qanda_olmstead.htm (accessed February 5, 2014).

Urbina, I. (2013) As OSHA Emphasizes Safety, Long-Term Health Risks Fester. *New York Times*, March 30. Available online at www.nytimes.com/2013/03/31/us/osha-emphasizes-safety-health-risks-fester.html (accessed February 5, 2014).

Weinstein, J. (2010) *Social Change* (3rd ed.). Lanham, MD: Rowman and Littlefield.

Winter, J. A. (2003) The Development of the Disability Rights Movement as a Social Problem Solver. *Disability Studies Quarterly*, 23 (1), 33–61. Available online at http://dsq-sds.org/article/view/399/545 (accessed February 5, 2014).

11 Designing disability through structures and products

In Chapter 6, we entered and navigated the scope of the disability park. Now, we meet the park crafters to analyze product and spatial design as a means to maintain the park and to distinguish regular visitors from occasional guests and from park employees. The analytic work in this chapter relies on "reading" visual and material culture" (Candlin and Guins, 2009) as craft for imbuing meaning through object, space, and imagery. To organize the discussion, we move from distal architectural and place to proximal object design and branding.

Architecture

Historically, spatial design was owned by architecture. A cousin to but not a direct descendant from art, which is not regulated by professional standards, architecture has been defined as a field of professional training in which buildings as art, form, and function are planned. Koolhaas (1997) and Rampley (2005) suggest that a major function of architecture is the containment or enclosure of space through building boundaries. And while Venturi and Brown (2004) agree that part of architecture involves the erection of structures, they focus on architecture as meanings and messages to the public through visual signs.

More recently, architecture has extended its reputation and reach, now defined as process, result, profession, inherent structure, art, symbol, and meanings. Moreover, architecture has recently been exposed as a control agent.

We are fascinated by the way in which architectural structures embrace, contain, shelter, frame, and even control the individuals who inhabit them (Buster, 2010). However, architecture no longer sits alone in crafting space and place. Adding design to architectural process and substance seems to best capture this intentionality.

Spatial design as craft

Subsuming architecture, spatial design is a contemporary interdisciplinary craft which brings together full villages of concern to conceptualize and create spaces, their meanings and their functions. Vaikla-Poldma (2013) paints space within a wide circumference of:

- theoretical spaces of knowledge and understanding;
- social and cultural spaces;
- management spaces where decision making takes place;
- physical and virtual spaces that act both as places and as environments;
- dynamic spaces that interact with both mind and body.

This expansive spatial landscape along with Buster's insights remind us that spaces are not simply "concretuals" but rather interact, take on character, and craft who does, feels, and experiences what is within or outside of them.

The crafters, architects, interior designers, product designers, builders, landscapers, computer scientists, engineers, researchers, and even traffic planners, create miniscule to sweeping spatial complexes comprised of material, interactive social, aesthetic, functional, and climate elements (Casakin, Romice, and Porta, 2011). Given the "stuff" of space (Miller, 2010), geography and place communicate their intent, meaning, and welcome, inviting a careful reading of their identity and behavior. Applied to design, undesign and redesign of disability, this fluidity acts as the basis for understanding what spaces are saying and not saying, who is beckoned to them, who is not, what those who occupy spaces are expected to do, where, and how behavior and status (what we refer to as pedigree) are shaped by place.

According to Jencks and Kropf (2007), the first architectural manifesto containing rules for spatial decorum was the Old Testament Ten Commandments. Plato, as reflected even in contemporary literature on the spirit of space (Casakin, Romice, and Porta, 2011), called God the architect of all things (Casakin *et al.*, 2011: 2). As depicted in their words, Jencks' and Kropf's reference to architecture as manifesto reveals its complexity and multidimensionality over chronology, expanding the visual and palpable into the realm of theory, meaning, and rules governing the desirable, the allowable to the prohibited, and setting the analytic stage for architecture as social-cultural gatekeeper (Cuthbert, 2006).

Further supporting architecture as historical and entrenched sentry, Eisenman (2007) focused his retrospective attention on it as far back as the 15th century, labeling architecture "the metaphysics of presence" (p. 376). This term foregrounds the built environment as controller of who can occupy a space, who cannot, and what is expected of occupants.

Providing the segue for return to the present, we visit with a seminal idea advanced by Koolhaas (1997). He coined the term "junkspace" to name those individuals and objects expelled from place by the structures that delimit membership. This concept is particularly relevant to Titchovsky's

(2007) work, betraying the exclusionary properties of inclusion and inclusive design despite assertions to the contrary (Nussbaumer, 2011). Building on Koolhaus's lexicon, we expand the term to "interior junkspace," thereby removing the semantic concealer of inclusion rhetoric which surreptitiously segments spaces into those for us and those for them (Jencks and Kropf, 2007; Sherry, 2000). Despite its claim to the contrary, inclusive design creates co-existing and even deceptively unified environments, at the same time cleaving them as welcoming or denying. So, even adjacent to one another in the same location, bodies may never acquire equivalent access. As example, look at Figure 11.1. This seating pattern, despite being "included" in a public airport, is a billboard advertising deficit and need, crafting a full array of appearance and behavioral expectations for those seats and scolding others who dare to sit in them. These interior junkspaces contain and illuminate those who do not belong to the typical airport crowd.

Figure 11.2 provides another omnipresent example of transportation and navigational junkspace. The logofied and designed recognition of this van invites gazes, perhaps pity, but not integration of diverse bodies into the transportation and passageway fabric of the campus.

Considering the critical importance of space and place to human movement, interaction, performance (Howarth, 2006), membership, and cultural identity, the design of spaces and places is therefore a major factor not only in the creation of an aesthetic but also in erecting and reflecting systems of meaning, value, worth, and privilege. Because, space is not inactive or

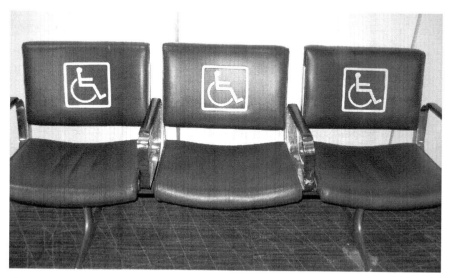

Figure 11.1 Airport junkspace

Figure 11.2 Access van – campus junkspace

apolitical (Lefebvre, 1991), analysis of its design reveals value meanings, cultural priorities, purpose, and use necessary to inform future social action. As both Cuthbert (2006) and Imrie (2005) suggest, spatial designers and the cultural policies that empower them have great influence in creating conditions of invitation, hostility, impermeability, but never neutrality.

Within standard spatial designs, bodies that stray too far from mythic Vitruvian standards of human size, locomotion, sensorium, and behavior are relegated to the metaphorical airport seats or access van maintaining interior junkspace and thus serving to excuse fundamental spatial redesign. Soja might suggest that interior junk space is purposive as it is constructed to obscure political and economic power; "it may be space more than time that hides consequences from us" (Soja, 1989: 1).

Ferreting out who benefits from junkspace is an important but insufficient quest in informing redesign. Once again, we do not indict well-meaning providers as crafters of exclusion. The myths of excess expense in a world branded with scarcity and "that is the way it has always been done" are operative in crafting junk spaces as a constant. Thoughtful criticism is urgently needed to expel these myths as principles underpinning contemporary design craft. As we discuss in Part 2, rather than seeing built space as void of agency, evocative objects (Turkle, 2011), and activated spaces (Buster, 2010) entreat us to engage with them, learn from them and think with them. Rodriguez reminds us,

> Within this panorama, the explanations from artefacts that respond to issues of identity, community, gender, class and other social phenomena, appear to have overlooked the inclusion of architecture as an artifact, as an everyday object and finally as a constitutive element of material culture.
>
> (Rodriguez, 2011)

Architects and spatial designers not only practice their craft to create an area in which "stuff" (Miller, 2010) exists, but do so through the erection of the "stuff" of large material "things" such as buildings, roads etc.

Thinking back to the discussion of policy as craft, and thus illuminating the role of cultural policy in spatial design, listen to what Monica Ponce de Leon had to say in an interview with Seigel:

> SIEGEL: In architecture courses, say when people do projects and learn how to design buildings, do you find that the needs for access have been internalized, that it's part of the way people approach the original task, or is it the overlay? Is it the thing that, oops, let's go back and check to make sure that we also met the law in these regards?
> PONCE DE LEON: It's unfortunately the overlay. In academia, design for the disabled has been thought of as the requirement that we need to fulfill in order to get accreditation as a school.
>
> (Seigel, 2010)

If disability is designed and branded conceptually as compliance, it is not surprising that campus spatial design reflects this curricular appendage. Visualize compliance policy crafted in the campus spaces in Figures 11.3 and 11.4.

Contrasted with the staired entrance on the front of the building (Figure 11.4), wheeled access (Figure 11.3) is in the rear parking lot, in the entrance directing traffic into the bowels of this academic building.

Now peruse the map of our own campus (Figure 11.5), delimiting the story of access to disability parking and entrance spaces only.

> Every map is at once a synthesis of signs and a sign in itself: an instrument of depiction – of objects, events, places – and an instrument of persuasion – about these, its makers and itself. Like any other sign, it is the product of codes: conventions that prescribe relations of content and expression in a given semiotic circumstance. The codes that underwrite the map are as numerous as its motives, and as thoroughly naturalized within the culture that generates and exploits them.
>
> (Wood and Fels, 1986: 54)

Figure 11.3 Wheeled access

Figure 11.4 Front entrance

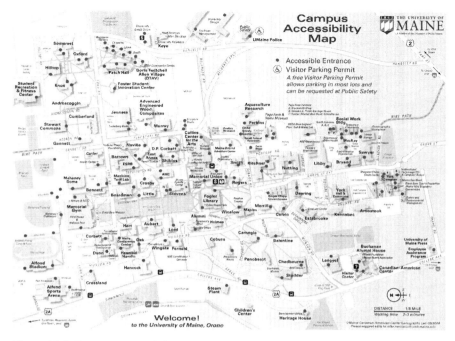

Figure 11.5 Campus accessibility map (reproduced with permission)

As the saying goes, "location, location, location" situates comparative value of space and place. Looking once again at the campus map, Disability Support Services (Figures 11.6 and 11.7) are located adjacent to Peace Studies in an annexed building. While in a location on campus not too far off the center-piece mall, the building remains tucked in between engineering and business schools. Moreover, its exterior design betrays the disability park that lies inside, sporting dilapidated retrofitted ramps as its only entrance choices.

The contrast of the spaces above in Figures 11.6 and 11.7 with Figures 11.8 and 11.9 (the building housing the chemistry department) proclaims the heavyweight champion, not only by its central mall location, but by its design craft. Note the integration of multiple forms of entrance and egress in the front of the building, equalizing the entry view and use for all types of mobility.

This short foray around the campus environment and exemplary images of the disability park in post-secondary institutions aptly demands innovative design education as one indispensable change agent, not only focused on campus ornamentation and sustainability, but expansively on equality of learning and modeling opportunity within the knowledge generation, dissemination and application enterprises (Simons, Decuypere, Vlieghe, and Masschelein, 2011). We pick up this stitch in Part 2, and now move to the design craft of the disability service park.

Figure 11.6 Disability Support Services front entrance

Figure 11.7 Disability Support Services parking lot entrance

Figure 11.8 Entrance for all

Figure 11.9 The asylum?

Design craft in the park

Even more intensified than campus design but often obscured in action is the craft of designing disability as contained and recognizable in institutional services and charity entities. Beginning with park institutions, Figure 11.9 depicts the design of a relatively new building (1992 construction date) housing counseling services primarily for individuals with mental health diagnostic labels of long-term duration. We find that the dark "asylumesque" exterior design of the building only amplifies its visibility and message of peril.

In contrast, Nendo designed a mental health clinic in Akasaka, Tokyo, Japan (Figure 11.10). The interior space presents a *trompe d'oeil*, in that the doors are paintings and entryways into offices and consultation rooms are hidden behind sliding bookcases.

Figure 11.10 a,b Nendo Clinic, Akasaka, Tokyo, Japan

Several rationales for the design craft of this clinic have been offered. First and most stereotypical in design is privacy for clients as they enter and exit services, sustaining the expectation that clients seek secrecy to hide their deficiency (Swide, 2010). Of course, this premise continues to craft park stigma attached to mental health services.

But consider alternative interpretations that refurbish the park through innovative spatial redesign. According to the crafters, this new perspective inscribed in the unique design:

> is an attempt to express this philosophy in space. The doors that line the walls of the clinic do not open, and "ordinary" parts of the walls open up into new spaces. The consultation rooms are entered by sliding the bookshelves sideways. The door at the end of the hallway opens onto a window; the amount of light in the hallway is controlled by opening and closing the door. By providing alternate perspectives for viewing the world, and avoiding being trapped by pre-existing perceptions, the interior allows visitors and staff members to experience opening new doors in their hearts, one after the other.
>
> Whether interior design can go that far we are a little unsure but we wonder whether, just like two wrongs make a right... do two mads make a sane?
>
> (Swide, 2010)

Figures 11.11 to 11.13 depict a curious institution in costume, a center for independent living. As discussed previously:

> The independent living movement has been an important part of a broader movement for disability rights. It is based on the premise that people with even the most severe disabilities should have the choice of living in the community. This can be accomplished through the creation of personal assistance services allowing an individual to manage his or her personal care, to keep a home, to have a job, go to school, worship, and otherwise participate in the life of the community. The independent living movement also advocates for the removal of architectural and transportation barriers that prevent people with disabilities from sharing fully in all aspects of our society.
>
> (University of California, 2004)

Once a counter-culture human rights effort, the independent living movement, has kept its branding but betrays its parkesque nature through its language, spatial design, and the contents displayed within.

Of course, spatial design involves much more than edifice and its contents.

Disability is one of the many narratives, like ethnicity, gender, sexual orientation, national origin, and national identity that advertising helps to construct (Haller and Ralph, 2006). The Shriners have become master

Figure 11.11 Exterior invitation

Figure 11.12 Contents for youth

Figure 11.13 Contents for adults

crafters in designing disability as both tragedy and the object of charity through the advertising imagery captured in the murals and park sculptures in its spatial design.

The penultimate park, often coveted by those who are not park frequenters is disability parking real estate. While privilege is conferred by the iconic placard, segregation as well as public scrutiny are invited by the hues of blue and white.

The images displayed in Figures 11.15 and 11.16 reveal the spotlight in which disability placard holders are staged. But an even more insidious message is crafted by the satirical redesign of the parking placard in Figure 11.17, which, although intended to be humorous, invites and thus crafts only specific atypical bodies as worthy of such segregation. With privilege brings gatekeeping and performativity, such that only the authentic park members are sanctioned as occupants of the "blue."

Now, move indoors to the special education park. Below are verbatim guidelines for the spatial design of these places. With the exception of the international symbol of access logo, we were unsure of how the design guidance would be different for "good" classroom design other than taking its place adjacent to the term resource room" branding segregation by narrative.

Figure 11.14 Sculpted advertising

Figure 11.15 Crafted tragedy

Figure 11.16 The blue parking spaces

Figure 11.17 Junk brothers placard (Junk Brothers News, n.d.)

Source: Junk Brothers News. © Holiday Shopping Disabled Parking Permit. Retrieved from http://www.junkbrosnews.com/2006/11/disabled-parking-permit.htm

1. Design a classroom with work stations or mini-stations. These are designed for hands-on learning, in which students are able to learn at their own pace and the teacher can move among the children to give help and individual attention. The classroom design that allows students to move from one area of learning to another at a pace that suits him is similar to how he learns at home, which makes it easier for special needs children to succeed.

2. Add technology to the classroom. Like other students, special needs children need to learn how to use current technology. Not only is it important to giving them a high level education, it can also help engage the special needs children. This is especially helpful with children that have autism or similar disorders.

3. Design a classroom that is easy for the children to move around. Even children that are in wheelchairs should be able to get around the classroom, interact with other children and make it to different work stations. Both physical and mental needs should be considered and met in the classroom design.

4. Cater the classroom to the students attending the school. Though there are designs that are meant to be used in the special education classrooms, some changes will need to be met for the individual students in those classes. The needs of the students should always be considered and changes should be made to best suit those needs.

(Jain, n.d.)

Just to briefly summarize, the craft of spatial design may go to great lengths in designing recognizable disability geographies, or may simply involve the use of branding to segregate and thus designate the disability park. Campus architecture and design revealed distinctions in the appearance and location of park services, while the exemplars of special education craft spatial segregation through branding rather than design strategies. Occupancy of enviable parking real estate, while close to one's destination, carries with it segregation, embodied expectation and prescription, beyond which one is considered counterfeit and lazy. In all cases, the spaces and places crafted for disability occupancy are potent designers, rendering them ripe targets for new vocations of undesign and redesign.

We now move more proximally to the park products, revealing craft techniques similar to spatial design approaches. Yet, because they are movable and often travel with the user, analysis of product design craft has more factors to "read" (Berger, 2009).

The craft of object and product design

Objects, often referred to as artifacts, are simply defined as concrete tangibles, "showing human workmanship" (Berger, 2009: 16). Although studied as archeology over several centuries, the recent emergence of the field of material culture has brought life interactivity, and intentional scholarly reading interpretation to objects (Berger, 2009; Candlin and Guins, 2009).

Before going further in this discussion, the distinctions among object, thing, and artifact are addressed. There is significant literature arguing about the differences among the three concretuals. As an example, Weibel and Latour (2005) suggest that object is mass-produced while the origin and fabrication of a thing is more proximal and thus discoverable. Yet, the lexical definition of object broadens it from a concrete, ascertainable by senses, through one that is both perceptible and within the realm of ideas. "The category object does not convincingly divide the natural from the artificial world, the material from the immaterial, the animate from the inanimate, or the human from the non-human" (Candlin and Guins, 2009: 2).

For that reason, we interchange and created the neology, concretual, previously introduced (a cousin of conceptuals) for object, thing, and synonyms, implying both materiality and meaning. Specific to disability design craft, the focus in this work is on reading products, items, and adornments that contain, reflect, signify, and interpret.

Similar to the classic work of Fussell (1992), who interrogated how objects can be read as social class locators, Miller (2010) suggests object design and possession as artistic, planful, and rich for analysis. From our perspective, the element of human workmanship along with the stories that can be read about object meaning are potent crafts for analysis and change. An increasingly complex overlay is the branding of object, since the craft of artifact creation does not stand apart from its intentional or inferred name and category. So, in this section, we engage both the substance and concept of concretual reading to reveal the craft of product in designing the park and the identity of its members.

Reading the materiality

According to Berger (2009), object reading should be grounded within a theoretical framework. He calls on Freud, Saussure, Weber, Marx, and others in those traditions, and postmodern and cultural studies to weigh-in on object reading. For us, the work of Candlin and Guins (2009) introduced in earlier chapters, is both illustrious and performative in guiding object reading, in that it relies on pluralism of theory as suggested by Berger, but goes further in employing post-postmodern integrative thinking rather than parsing each theory as a single comparative container.

In their edited volume, Candlin and Guins (2009) included a compelling narrative by Sobchack (2009: 206), in which she contrasts the meaning of her prosthetic legs with those of Mullins (see Chapter 5). For Sobchack, a host of meanings can be read in prosthetics, ranging from functionality through embodied sculpture and the creation of the cyborg.

Thus, for me, there is a certain scandal in the recent rush by cultural theorists to embrace "the prosthetic" as metaphor – and not because I find such metaphorical usage offensive in some facile sense that privileges "authentic" over "discursive" experience. Rather, the prosthetic as metaphor is scandalous because it is too often less imaginatively expansive than it is reductive and less complex and productive in use than is the prosthetic in its mundane context. Perhaps, however, the prosthetic metaphor is most scandalous because it far too quickly mobilizes attention to (and fascination with) artificial and "post-human" body parts in the service of a discourse always located elsewhere – displacing the prosthetic rather than living it first on its own quite extraordinary premises. As a consequence, "the prosthetic" has become a fetishized but "unfleshed out" catchword – a vague and "floating signifier" – for contemporary critical discourse on technoculture.

For Sobchack, the prosthetic is a functional object and, unlike Mullins, Sobchack does not read limb replacement as potential body art. Whereas prosthetic takes on aesthetically inventive and even cyborg propositions for others, for Sobchack limb replacement fits within a functional humanistic paradigm, in which it crafts the ordinary. The contrast between the object readings generated by Mullins and Sobchack reminds us of the importance of choice in solidifying identity, as discussed in Chapter 5. For Mullins, prosthetics synthesize form, function, and frolic, while for Sobchack, her legs design close to normative ambulation where it previously did not exist.

Figure 11.18 illustrates the material "stuff" that is read differently by each user and interpreted even more diffusely by the observing object reader.

For us, choice as the operative right brings us to the craft of object prescription, in which choice is not an option.

Through the ideas of Candlin and Guins (2009), and their invited guests, the framework for object reading, dissecting, and translation necessary for the outcome of progressive redesign includes the following considerations:

- Individual and comparative design appearance and aesthetics.
- Intended uses and for whom? unintended uses and for whom?
- Meanings that the object holds for intended and actual users, viewers of individuals who use it?
- Cultural and social metaphors and stories invoked by the object.
- Identities created by the object for the intended user? Typical user? Atypical user, observer, giver, creator.

To this series, we add two crafts to be surveilled: 1) object branding, implicit or explicit, imaged or inferred, intentional or unintentional; and 2) perception of choice.

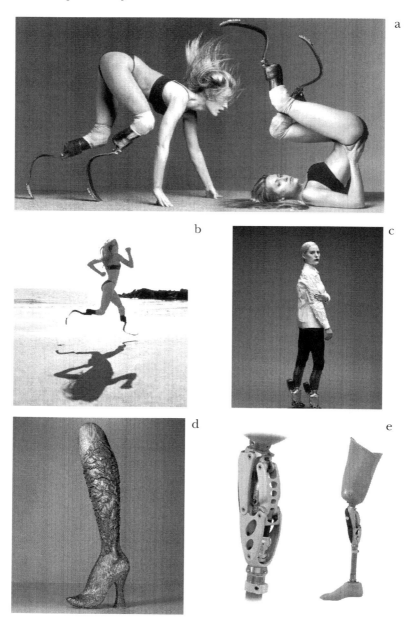

Figure 11.18 Legs: a–b) Aimee Mullins with Cheetah Legs (reproduced with
permission of Beverly Ornstein and Howard Schatz); c) courtesy of
Tetsuraru Kubota; d) Alexander McQueen (British, 1969–2010),
prosthetic leg of carved elm wood, No. 13, Spring/Summer 1999
(© Sølve Sundsbø/Art + Commerce, reproduced with permission);
e) Conventional prosthetic leg

Concretual crafting

We enter the universe of concretual craft reading through technology in general and the "assistive technology" brand name specific to disability design. Assistive technology, in particular, has been a seminal design craft within the park as we discussed in Chapter 6. While the technology artifacts augment and facilitate human function in so many domains, the crafts of brand assignment, object appearance and pricing are the foci of the ensuing discussion. Below, we provide two definitions, one of technology and one of assistive technology to begin an examination of the lexical branding craft.

Assistive technology is defined as:

> any item, piece of equipment, or system, whether acquired commercially, modified, or customized, that is commonly used to increase, maintain, or improve functional capabilities of individuals with disabilities.
>
> (Electronic and Information Technology Accessibility Standards, Section 508, 2000)

The *Concise Encyclopedia* proposes the following definition of technology:

> Application of knowledge to the practical aims of human life or to changing and manipulating the human environment. Technology includes the use of materials, tools, techniques, and sources of power to make life easier or more pleasant and work more productive. Whereas science is concerned with how and why things happen, technology focuses on making things happen. Technology began to influence human endeavour as soon as people began using tools.
>
> (Merriam-Webster, 2013)

Both definitions seem equivalent with the exception of the target user. In both narratives, technology is assistive, but only in the assistive technology definition is technology crafted for disability.

A more detailed and meticulous exploration of assistive technology exposes its branding, distribution outlets, and payment sources as the mechanisms for crafting and branding technology for the park as assistive. Moreover, the craft creates pejorative stereotypes for item users (Lorenzo, 2009). Look at Jancie Grant's analysis:

> No technology is created in a cultural and philosophical void. Like any product, contemporary technology is imbued with a multitude of subtle social meanings based on its assumed user which add (or subtract) value from both the technology and the user.
>
> Technology designed for mainstream consumers is most often associated with freedom, choice, competence, and independence, as evidenced in Apple's iPad descriptions: "With more 300,000 apps made

just for the iPad, there's almost no end to what you can do [...]" Assistive Technology (AT) devices, however, are almost universally associated with limitations and dependency (Foley and Ferri, 2012: 197). Even its description – "Assistive Technology" – implies dependence and a lack of autonomy (Moser, 2006: 384). For example, AT Developer Dynavox describes its AT products as "portable, discreet, and easy-to-use [...]," which "lets [users] feel proud about owning and using them." Clearly, the use of this type of language, within the advertisement for AT, exposes its close and awkward relationship with the medicalized model of disability. Through this narrative, disability is understood and treated as a condition that should be tactfully identified and rendered inconspicuous, and these beliefs are embedded into the design and implementation of AT and its assumption that users "seek to reproduce 'normalcy'" (Foley and Ferri, 2012: 197). It should also be noted that Dynavox's 'Assistive Communication Device' is an $8,000 investment, including device and "accessories." Contrast this pricing to the most expensive iPad. Loaded with hundreds of dollars worth of apps to address communication, academics, social skills, scheduling, and entertainment, iPad would still average less than $2,000. In contrast to Dynavox devices and advertising, Apple brands itself with both aesthetic and functional beauty.

Now consider the nearly-obsolete portable CD player. Due to the inevitable advancement of technology, portable CD players are sold in a variety of colors and styles for roughly $15.00 in commercial venues. Yet, the online AT site 'Enabling Devices' offers a portable CD player for $95.95, with no ability to choose features, styles, or even colors. This same seller offers a simplified MP3 player for 'people with disabilities' with oversized and basic controls for $119.95, while a similar product, the iPod Shuffle, with the same type of simplified controls, can be purchased for $46.00.

This trend of developing and offering products that are aesthetically stigmatizing and financially predatory isn't exclusive to technology design and branding. For example, book holders sold through a disability-specific retailer offer this institutional, unattractive product for $128.49.

(Grant, personal communication, 2013)

Now, consider the term "cognitive prosthesis" for example. Gentry (2011) identified the following devices as assistive technology to be used for individuals with specific pathologies: reminder alarms, schedules, calendars, lists/memos, to do lists, money management, addresses/maps, vocal prompts.

Parente (2011) added electronic tools such as cell phones and global positioning system units to the list, crafting these strategies as prosthetic medical devices. Interestingly, he branded spell-checkers as orthotics.

Given that orthotics is defined as "science that deals with the use of specialized mechanical devices to support or supplement weakened or abnormal joints or limbs" (Farlex, 2013), Parente implies that the need to use a spell-checker stems from weakness, once again denuding the assistive technology brand name as attributing subnormalcy and deficit to users.

A general perusal of rehabilitation and assistive technology catalogs further informs the observer about the power of branding craft in sustaining and growing the disability park. Just consider gardening tools. Items that are sold in typical neighborhood stores can be read as medical necessities if they are advertised in the right location, prescribed as a result of professional assessment and then labeled as assistive for the user branded as disabled. The typical broom and dustpan set advertised for home and office use is medicalized for a targeted population on a website for arthritis supplies: "Sweep up dust and dirt without having to bend over with the Ergo Long-Handled Dust Pan and Broom" (Wright Stuff, 2013a).

Crafting the logo and brand is the following narrative:

> Weeding Out Pain: Gardening doesn't have to hurt for arthritis sufferers. One of the many activities some people give up at the onset of arthritis is gardening. The constant stooping, kneeling and gripping oftentimes becomes difficult for different parts of the body, from hands to knees to backs. Difficult, yes. Impossible? No. According to physical therapists and other experts, all passionate gardeners can still pursue their favorite hobby.
>
> (Wright Stuff, 2013b)

Not only is the product branded, but the narrative answers the seminal questions about object reading, crafting the supplies on this website for pain reduction and functional augmentation under the guidance of expert medical providers (id4 theweb, 2010).

Now read object readings of hearing aids. This short story betrays the craft of designing hearing loss as tragedy to the hearing world, reading the object and its user as deficient, embarrassed, vain, and thus in need of disguise despite the claim made by sign language speakers that they are members of a rich linguistic minority culture.

> Hearing aids were an outgrowth of the invention of vacuum tubes in the early part of the 20th century. The use of large devices resembling rubber ear muffs connected to radio-like boxes were virtually immobile, but still allowed hearing augmentation in limited spaces. While mobility improved with miniaturization of the technological apparati, hearing aids on the go in the mid 20th century were visible, cyborgizing the observed user with embodied wires and batteries. Design trends over the years aimed at camouflaging the hearing aid.
>
> (Washington University School of Medicine, 2005–2009)

Five million Americans need hearing aids. Yet only 1,250,000 wear them! Why is this? A recent survey revealed nine different reasons; the principal one is vanity.

(Davis, 1955, quoted in Bernard Becker Medical Library)

Transistors, and then digital technology, in part mastered the costume craft, winning the hide and seek game to some extent. Adroitness such as crayoning devices in flesh tones, concealing them behind the ear, or embedding them deep within the eustachian tube with only a fine transparent tube visible to the onlooker are pictured in Figure 11.19.

Even in the present, hearing-aid design for most remains masked, reading such objects as betraying undesirable hearing of their users. Recall the audiogram graphic which functions to use graphic design to convince the viewer that chronological hearing patterns are abnormal and thus may be shameful. But as we discuss in Part 2, undesigning hearing acuity as deficit and then redesigning and rebranding it as opportunity for crafting technology and art innovation for public use (and choice) is nascent and just out of the commercial development starting gate.

Above, we introduced the iPad through the thoughts and words of Jancie Grant. Because the iPad has been medicalized and thus apps have been colonized as park property, almost since the iPad release, the device has not only served as a product but has fattened the coffers of park trainers. As example consider the narrative below from ID4 the Web:

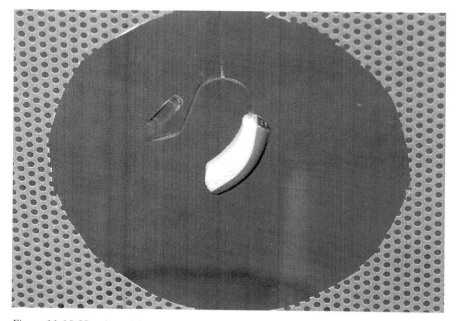

Figure 11.19 Hearing aid

We use the PDA/smartphone training, applied in particular to memory compensation techniques, as a relevant, real-life activity. Not only do we teach how to use the device, but we also provide structured exercises to help make cognitive connections between what you are learning to do with the PDA and your life. So we are simultaneously providing general cognitive stimulation, attempting to build specific new neural pathways, preparing you to apply what you are learning to real life, and teaching you a highly effective memory compensation strategy.

(id4 theweb, 2010)

It is curious that Janger refers to the iPad as a disruptive force in the AT park. We are not sure if the meaning in Janger's words below is laudatory or bemoaning.

It is fair to say that the iPad has become a disruptive force in the assistive technology industry. Where assistive technology solutions had long existed that enhanced the quality of life for PwDs, applications could be downloaded from Apple's App Store that delivered nearly similar benefits at a far cheaper price.

(Janger, 2011)

A perusal of the *iTunes* site is revelatory. To capture and craft disability park users, *iTunes* devotes and brands a significant part of its own web real estate to the park (Apple Inc., 2013). Applications (apps) are marketed to providers as well as consumers. Just a few examples include: iDream, an app for interpreting and journaling dreams, Romatic Ideas 500, an app to guide partner interactions, Phobias, a guide to fear, and uHear, an app to test the age normalcy of hearing.

Crafting appearance and choice

Branding and narrative are only two of a crowd of methods used by park crafters to imbue meaning and capture a target market. Aesthetics, a third craft, is contentious in disability studies literature and praxis. It is not unusual for students in our disability studies and engineering classes to oppose the need for attention to form in products designed to enhance function within the scope of disability. Several factors seem potent in understanding this tension. First, the absence of aesthetics from the seven principles of universal design and its descendants (Nussbaumer, 2011) is very noticeable. Reading this guidance, subsequent universal, inclusive, and accessible designers call for simplicity, intuition, and largess to enwrap the limited universe of bodies that are addressed in traditional and euphemistic notions of inclusion (DePoy and Gilson, 2011), with only perfunctory mention of aesthetics. Second, the assumption that "function should be enough for those people" reads park members as objects who should exude gratitude for functional things regardless of appearance or the identity that such "stuff" confers (Mullins, personal communication, 2013). Third, is the park payment mechanism, medical insurance. As we have already discussed, medical insurance posing as welfare does not compute for us when this troubled source is applied for payment of non-medical expenses, as it artificially and unnecessarily engorges prices along with numerous other undesirable outcomes. Fourth, the medicalization process through which objects are determined to be necessary, prescribed, and acquired is one which does not make room for individuality and choice. All of these factors stirred into the pot of social devaluation brand the park member who is concerned with appearance as a vain and ungrateful taker looking the charity gift horse in the mouth.

We would suggest that lack of attention to materiality as both form and function is one of the most potent park crafters. Omitting choice and aesthetic design imposes park identity and brands the user through simple, surface object reading.

Consider the objects in the following figures. Figure 11.20 depicts head protection design, clearly broadcasting the message of medical diagnosis, while Figure 11.21 offers equivalent protection with choice and contemporary design.

The final object in evidence of park craft shown in Figure 11.22 provides both closure to this chapter and navigates to the next section of the book, undesign and redesign. The walker in Figure 11.22 shouts tragedy, loss, immobility and crafts pity. In the words of Laughlin (2011):

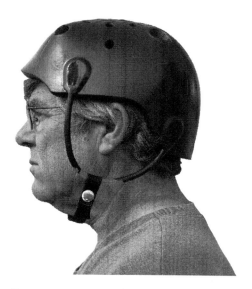

Figure 11.20 Medicalized helmet

Figure 11.21 Smarty

Figure 11.22 Laughlin's tennis ball walker style

Here's what I think about tennis balls on walkers. I really, really don't like them.

Number One, they are garish. I mean neon green or fluorescent yellow or whatever you call it? And tennis balls? Tennis, sadly, is a dim memory for folks who need walkers. Even walking unassisted is a dim memory for me.

Having sporty balls that practically glow in the dark seems just plain silly and insulting.

My husband once found some pale pink tennis balls that he bought and put on my walker for a change of pace. The idea, I believe, was fashion fun. Instead I found them creepy and mildly obscene.

It's not just my imagination. People do notice my balls and often comment on them. Children, toddlers in particular, are hypnotized by them. They will stop dead in their tracks, eyes glued to my tennis balls. They will try to get the attention of their parents and try to form the words to ask the question: Why does that woman have tennis balls attached to her...thing? One mother headed her kid off at the pass, interjecting, "She has trouble walking and the balls help her walk."

One little boy's eyes were huge as he pointed and exclaimed to his mother, "Look, she's got basketballs on her..."

Dogs want to chase them. My cat is afraid of them.

Able-bodied grown-ups don't understand them.

(Laughlin, 2011)

In summary, we have traversed breadth and depth of disability design and branding guided by diverse theory, voices, and silences. Conceptuals, concretuals, and their synthesis within global contexts have prodded new thinking about undesign and redesign awaiting us in the next chapters.

References

Apple Inc. (2013) App Store-medical. *iTunes*. Available online at https://itunes.apple.com/us/genre/ios-medical/id6020?mt=8 (accessed February 5, 2014).

Berger, A. (2009) *What Objects Mean*. Walnut Creek, CA: Left Coast Publishers.

Buster, K. (2010) Resonance. *Metanexus*. Available online at www.metanexus.net/visual-exploration/resonance (accessed February 5, 2014).

Candlin, F., and Guins, R. (2009) *The Object Reader*. London: Routledge.

Casakin, H., Romice, O., and Porta, S. (2011) *The Role of Place Identity in the Perception, Understanding, and Design of the Built Environment*. London: Betham Science.

Cuthbert, A. R. (2006) *The Form of Cities: Political Economy and Urban Design*. Malden, ME: Blackwell.

Davis, L. (1955) American Hearing Aid Association [Quote]. Bernard Becker Medical Library, *Deafness in Disguise*. St Louis, MO: Washington University School of Medicane. Available at http://beckerexhibits.wustl.edu/did/20thcent/part3.htm (accessed February 5, 2014).

DePoy, E., and Gilson, S. (2011) *Studying Disability.* Los Angeles, CA: Sage.

Eisenman, P. (2007) *Written into the Void: Selected Writings, 1990–2004.* New Haven, CT: Yale University Press.

Farlex (2013) Orthotics. *Free Dictionary.* Available online at www.thefreedictionary.com/orthotic (accessed February 5, 2014).

Foley, A., and Ferri, B. (2012) Technology for people, not disabilities: ensuring access and inclusion. *Journal of Research in Special Education Needs*, 12 (4), 192–200.

Fussell, P. (1992) *Class: A Guide Through the American Status System.* New York: Touchstone.

Gentry, T. (2011) Cognitive Prosthetics: Practical Applications. Virginia Commonwealth University. Available online at www.docstoc.com/docs/83088952/PowerPoint-Presentation—-Cognitive-Prosthetics-Practical (accessed February 5, 2014).

Haller, B., and Ralph, S. (2006) Are Disability Images in Advertising Becoming Bold And Daring? An Analysis of Prominent Themes in US and UK Campaigns. *Disability Studies Quarterly*, 26 (3). Available online at http://dsq-sds.org/article/view/716/893 (accessed February 5, 2014).

Howarth, D. (2006) Space Subjectivity and Politics. *Alternatives*, 31, 105–34.

ID4 the Web (2010) Making Cognitive Connections® for Individuals Living With Brain Injury and Other Cognitive Challenges. Making Cognitive Connections. Available online at http://id4theweb.com (accessed February 5, 2014).

Imrie, R. (2005) *Accessible Housing: Quality, Disability and Design.* New York: Routledge.

Jain, H. (n.d.) How to Design a High-Level Learning Special Education Classroom. eHow Mom. Available online at www.ehow.com/how_6551954_design-learning-special-education-classroom.html (accessed February 5, 2014).

Janger, M. (2011) The iPad as a Disruptive Force in Assistive Technology. *Drumbeat Blog*, July 27. Available online at http://drumbeatconsulting.com/blog/2011/07/27/the-ipad-as-a-disruptive-force-in-assistive-technology (accessed February 5, 2014).

Jencks, C. and Kropf, K. (eds) (2007) *Theories and Manifestoes of Contemporary Architecture.* Chichester: Wiley-Academy.

Koolhaas, R. (1997) Bigness: Or the Problem of Large. In *Manifestoes of Contemporary Architecture*, ed. C. Jencks and K. Kropf. Chichester: Wiley-Academy, 307–11.

Laughlin, L. (2011) Tennis Balls for Walkers: A Sorry Way to Help Disabled People Get Around Easier. *View from the Handicapped Space*, December 4. Available online at http://viewfromthehandicappedspace.blogspot.com/2011/12/tennis-balls-for-walkers-sorry-way-to.html (accessed February 5, 2014).

Lefebvre, H. (1991) *The Production of Space.* Oxford: Blackwell.

Lorenzo, R. D. (2009) Cell Phones in Education Part 2: Assistive Technology. Mobile Learner, February 21. Available online at http://themobilelearner.wordpress.com/2009/02/21/cell-phones-in-education-part-2-assistive-technology (accessed February 5, 2014).

Merrium-Webster (2013) Technology. *Concise Encyclopedia.* www.merriam-webster.com/dictionary/technology

Miller, D. (2010) *Stuff.* Malden, MA: Polity.

Moser, I. (2006) Disability and the Promises of Technology: Technology, Subjectivity, and Embodiment Within an Order of the Normal. *Information, Communication, and Society*, 9 (3), 373–95.

Nussbaumer, L. (2011) *Inclusive Design: A Universal Need*. New York: Fairchild Books.

Parente, R. (2011) Cognitive Technology and Cognitive Rehabilitation. Available online at www.docstoc.com/docs/47523493/Cognitive-Technology-and-Cognitive-Rehabilitation (accessed February 5, 2014).

Rampley, M. (ed.) (2005) *Exploring Visual Culture: Definitions, Concepts, Contexts*. Edinburgh: Edinburgh University Press.

Rodriguez, D. (2011) Architectural Artefacts as Material Form of Culture. DESIGN/HISTORY/CULTURE. Available online at http://thedesignaction.blogspot.com/2011/07/architectural-artefacts-as-material.html (accessed February 5, 2014).

Seigel, R., and Ponce de Leon, M. (2010) How The Disabilities Act Has Influenced Architecture. *NPR*, July 26. Available online at www.npr.org/templates/story/story.php?storyId=128778558 (accessed February 5, 2014).

Sherry, J. (2000) Place, Technology and Representation. *Journal of Consumer Research*, 27 (4), 273–8.

Simons, M., Decuypere, M., Vlieghe, J., and Masschelein, J. (2011) *Curating the European University: Exposition and Public Debate*. Leuven, Belgium: Leuven University Press.

Sobchack, V. (2009) A Leg To Stand On. In F. Candlin, and R. Guins, *The Object Reader*. London, UK: Routledge.

Soja, E. (1989) *Postmodern Geographies*. London: Verso.

Swide (2010) A Mental Health Clinic Fit for a Mad Hatter. Retrieved from *Swide*, April 8. Available online at www.swide.com/style-fashion/super-luxury/A-mental-health-clinic-fit-for-the-Mad-Hatter/2010/4/8 (accessed February 5, 2014).

Titchkosky, T. (2007) *Reading and Writing Disability Differently*. Toronto, ON: University of Toronto Press.

Turkle, S. (2011) *Evokative Objects*. Boston, MA: MIT Press.

University of California (2004) The Disability Rights and Independent Living Movement: Introduction. Available online at http://bancroft.berkeley.edu/collections/drilm/introduction.html (accessed February 5, 2014).

Vaikla-Poldma, T. (2013) *The Meaning of Designed Spaces*. New York: Bloomsbury.

Ventury, R., and Brown, D. S. (2004) *Architecture as Signs and Systems: For a Mannerist Time*. Cambridge, MA: Belknap Press.

Wright Stuff (2013a) Ergo Long Handled Dust Pan and Broom. ArthritisSupplies.com. Available online at www.arthritissupplies.com/ergo-long-handled-dust-pan-broom.html (accessed February 5, 2014).

Wright Stuff (2013b) Ergonomic Garden Tools for People with Arthritis. ArthritisSupplies.com. Available online at www.arthritissupplies.com/arthritis-gardening-tools.html (accessed February 5, 2014).

Washington University School of Medicine (2005–09) Concealed Hearing Devices of the 20th Century. Deafness in Disguise. Washington University School of Medicine. Available online at http://beckerexhibits.wustl.edu/did/20thcent/part3.htm (accessed February 5, 2014).

Weibel, P., and Latour, B. (2005) *Making Things Public*. Cambridge, MA: MIT Press.

Wood, D., and Fels, J. (1986) Designs On Signs/Myth And Meaning In Maps. *Cartographica: The International Journal for Geographic Information and Geovisualization*, 23 (3), 54–103.

Part 2

Undesigning and redesigning

12 Using design and branding to dismantle the park

In the current context of fiscal austerity, dismantling the park might sound ominous. However, dismantling the park does not propose that formal responses to human need be decreased or decimated. Rather, what is to be dismantled or undesigned are segregation, stigma, diminished opportunity, non-equivalent rights, exclusion from humanness, and myths about methods for cost and cost containment. Thus, undesign is a prerequisite for the improvement of environments, products, policies, and services and thus the broader scope of human dignity.

The term 'undesign' has become increasingly popular over the past decade. It is curious, however, that undesign as a movement has sprouted in multiple art, design, and virtual arenas, but has yet to substantively migrate to human rights and equal opportunity efforts.

> "Undesigning" practices aim to undo the complex designed world by revealing how human designing implicitly structures our world.
>
> (Sade, Coombes, and McNamara, 2013)

> There are a lot of factors involved in undesigning that are not obvious on the surface. In all actuality, that is the point – to create something that's so intuitive to use that it does not look overly designed. Every element is looked at from both a visual as well as functional viewpoint. Each design element has a purpose: to assist the user in accomplishing their objectives.
>
> (Mann, 2012)

Thus, undesign does not call for the absence of intentional design, but rather is a school of thought and praxis that re-visions aesthetics and function as equal partners, without the near-sighted focus on prescribed style, fad, and sameness. To stimulate and provide further substance for this chapter, we therefore turn to "undesigners" and those with sympathetic ideas who converse with us through direct interaction and reading (Mann, 2012; Pullin, 2013; Young, 2013).

Undesign is defined as "having no ulterior or fraudulent purpose" (Merriam-Webster, 2013). Movements and theory in this tradition seek to create environments, products, and spaces which respect, represent, and respond to humans as unpredictable, organic beings, thereby removing rigid corsets from what is fashioned. Countering hyperdesigned chic, airbrushed imagery, and orchestrated constraint, undesigners romance and see beauty in the messiness of humanity. Although it may seem as if undesign calls for the elimination of discipline or intention, to the contrary, undesign thinking guides designers from any knowledge base or perspective to enact their crafts for the full diversity of product users, art viewers, space occupants, and so forth, rather than for creating and thus manipulating homogenous target groups. Undesign therefore summons the dissolution of essentialism by reintroducing the individual and the proximal into the universes of conceptuals and concretuals.

We see undesign as the critical next phase of rethinking humanity and equality and so preceding redesigning and rebranding. Removing coercive and controlling intellectual and praxis debris is necessary to create a fertile platform for redesign uncluttered by the unintentional negative consequences of the disability park.

Undesigning normal

Two experiences inform the undesign of normal. First, a few months ago, we were conversing with Graham Pullin, author of *Disability Meets Design* (2009). He suggested that his intellectual contribution to undesign and redesign would capitalize on a contemporary design trend, supernormal (Fukasawa and Morrison, 2007). At that point in the discussion, since a major theme throughout the book is the normal–abnormal binary as one of one of several park design power tools, we bristled. The popular and medicalized vernacular and for us pejorative usage of the concept of normal as a statistical phenomenon was first in line. However, before acquiescing to our auto-reflex response, we proceeded to explore Pullin's suggestion.

According to Fukasawa and Morrison (2007), supernormal design is paradoxical, comprising both absence and presence of remarkability. Everyday objects such as stools and trash cans with unique but minuscule creativity are offered as exemplars of the supernormal, revamping the term normal and its superior as imperceptible and attainable exceptionality fitting within daily use and lives. While this design trend is not our sole aim in undesign or redesign, after conversations with Graham Pullin and with Fukasawa and Morrison's inscriptions percolating and smoldered, an epiphany occurred to us. Although not necessarily the goal of supernormal designers, we realized that relocating the concept of normal into the design and object worlds undesigns it as a statistical butcher. Rather than the object of theoretical and empirical counting, normal as the apple of the medicalized eye is undesigned as the grand narrative of desirability, leaving redesigners to the lovely task of attributing new meaning to normal. Thank you, Graham Pullin, and Fukasawa and Morrison.

A second epiphany in undesigning normal came from the Hollywood screen. To attain the educational goal of examining bodies, cyborg manifestations, and the limits of humanness in film, we have assigned *Star Wars* to students in disability studies classes with an accompanying reading from Decker and Eberl (2005). But, as we were watching the film, it occurred to us that normal was clearly undesigned by George Lucas' imagery portraying the diversity of organic bodies on the screen. Figure 12.1 is worth a thousand words, as the atypical becomes the typical when difference trumps sameness as the "norm."

Although part of cinematic creativity and criticized by some film scholars for limiting the powerpacking roles of diverse bodies, Lucas projected a visual message undesigning the normal body. Without normal, its opposite, not normal, has no referent, leaving a void where alternative and human-friendly concepts of predicting the typical can move in and coexist without the axiological baggage carried by the statistical concept of normal. Normal can thus be tucked into place, such that its discriminatory power is jettisoned without eviscerating its progressive utility. Undesigning normal therefore does not mean eliminating its positive epistemic

Figure 12.1 StarWars: The atypical becomes the typical
Source: With permission by Lucas Film

functions but rather containing it within a useful perimeter. Undesigning normal has significant consequences for undesigning other arenas of the disability park.

Undesigning the knowledge craft

Above, we alluded to epistemology. Recall the theme on knowledge discussing nomothetic inquiry as park craft. Through research methods that rely on numbers to both congeal a group and tease it apart from others, humans are sifted into categories that share an essential predefined characteristic.

While measurement has significant merits, undesign of segregating knowledge lies in judicious and internally consistent use of counting. Revisiting the discussion of the International Classification of Functioning (ICF) clarifies this point. Recall that the World Health Organization Disability Assessment Schedule (WHODAS) claims disability as social interactive but fails to include environmental variables in its operationalization. Bickenbach (2009) holds counting responsible for injustice leading to policies which create arbitrary binary groupings, disadvantaging both those considered to have impairments as well as those whose lives are characterized by lack of "talent." "The scientific approach, in a word, does not solve the problem the policy analyst needs to solve" (p. 120).

Thus, according to Bickenbach, designing need through diagnosing and ascribing specialized policy only to the extreme atypical begs for epistemic undesign craft, not only for the medically labeled but ironically for citizens who are considered ordinary, those who fit within the norm, those who have no discernible talents or attributes for which they stand out. Nomothetic knowledge building is in need of disciplinary action as it seems to be rampant and expansive rather than informative and thoughtful for the undesign of segregation and inequity. Perhaps by its very nature in crafting groups, the reign of nomothetic methods as "truth tellers" needs to be democratized, relocated to its most useful purposes, and joined in stature with pluralistic inquiry strategies.

Undesigning stereotype

While on the subject of group recognition, stereotyping as branding comes to the forefront. Stereotype is defined as "something conforming to a fixed or general pattern; especially: a standardized mental picture that is held in common by members of a group and that represents an oversimplified opinion, prejudiced attitude, or uncritical judgment" (Merriam-Webster, 2013).

In other words, a stereotype attributes both design and brand to a group member. Not all stereotype branding is negative (ChangingMinds.org, 2013) as stereotypes follow their deductive logical structure, allowing for prediction. It is curious then that given the aim of nomothetic inquiry to identify group similarities and differences, proponents of evidence-based practice and policy which seek to construct common characteristics of groups, regularly find stereotypes guilty as the lead villains perpetuating disability discrimination. Moreover, in efforts to counter negative stereotype and its identity contingencies, "the things you have to deal with in a given situation because you have a given identity" (Steele, 2010: 2), identity politics, another thematic hallmark of the academy, serves the stereotype brand master by designing affinity groups that can be studied and painted with essentialist logos, all through preferred logico-deductive epistemology.

For disability park members, stereotype branding ranges from extremely pejorative to inspirational and courageous for the unremarkable feats of daily life (Block, 2001–2013; Mullins, 2013), all which promote sunken expectations, devaluation, and dismissal.

> With only the rarest exceptions, disabled people are not counted among the quality people who grace our society. We don't expect them to be great artists, scientists, or politicians, and if they are, their disabilities are well concealed or, perhaps, we just don't see their disabilities. It is too incongruent to think of great achievement and disability in the same breath. Our culture does not expect very much of disabled people in general.
>
> (Levin, 2010)

Yet, listen to how Marcus, through the words of Seibers, undesigns such a lowly reputation:

> Neil Marcus, the disabled dancer, observes that "Disability is not a brave struggle or courage in the face of adversity. Disability is an art. It's an ingenious way to live." I agree that disabled people have to be ingenious to live in societies that are by their design inaccessible and by their inclination prejudiced against disability. It requires a great deal of artfulness and creativity to figure out how to make it through the day when you are disabled, given the condition of our society.
>
> (Levin, 2010)

For the most part, however, with the exception of some who experience embodied impairment or fetishize it, (Abasiophilia Information, n.d.), clamoring to be designed and branded as disabled is unlikely.

Several formal, theory-based approaches to demolishing stereotypes have been suggested for marginalized groups. As we briefly discuss them, it becomes noticeable that all are planned and canned programs that fall prey to the very exclusion by inclusion that Titchovsky (2007) described. As example, van der Meij's (2004) review revealed that education and contact were most potent in making change, but caution is indicated given the limited systematic assessment of positive outcomes. Strategies target specific groups and bring them in as conceptual or actual "show and tell" or inspirational events, demoting the negative aspects of perceived impairment by highlighting the positive contributions made and typical lives lived by people with embodied diagnoses.

A classic approach still used today is Allport's (1954) contact hypothesis, which proposes the seminal role that direct interaction can play in stereotype and conflict undesign. On initial inspection, this approach seems sensible. Getting to know individuals from a group held in low esteem ostensibly should enrich interaction beyond disdain for the essential grouping feature. However, contact theory has been criticized for several obvious reasons. First, formal programs that design coming to know an individual prop open the door for "exception to the rule" to enter and be ascribed to the contrived intimate. Second, the nature of interaction is a critical part of undesign, in that not all interaction elicits respectful outcomes (Amichai-Hamburger and McKenna, 2006). Unintended consequences such as etching stereotype even deeper than prior to the interaction are not uncommon when staged exchange goes awry (Bramel, 2004).

The extent to which screen-mediated interaction is context relevant and productive has been raised by several scholars (Amichai-Hamburger and McKenna, 2006; Haller, 2006). Disability studies literature spans the approval to disapproval continuum of using the embodied atypical as a marketing tool. In opposition to this practice is the telethon argument, suggesting that bodies and their viewers are exploited for charitable or profitable currency (Garland-Thomson, 2009; Haller, 2006; Janger, 2012; Lyle, 2003; Palotta, 2008). Yet, excluding the visual atypical from viewing is met with equally vehement criticism, read as disapproval, fear, and devaluation of bodies that deviate too far from perfection, symmetry, youth and so forth.

> If we're not in the media how do people know we exist? Media in whatever form – movies, TV shows, online series and advertising can open your eyes to disability, but a lot of people don't think about including disability and it is left out of discussions of diversity and minorities. Shows may be ethnically diverse but I think a lot of time disability gets left out. Media affects society more than anything else. It is our gateway to other people and situations and circumstances and disability needs to be a part of it.
>
> People may think that it will be a hassle to accommodate us on set or have other fears that we are sick, in pain – often disability has negative associations. In fact, disability often doesn't complicate life – it is just one way of how we are different. Interactions with a person with disability doesn't require someone to say "I'm sorry" or "I hope you get better." You can have a fabulous, whole life, travel all around the world and play sports and do more than some able-bodied people – disability is not a bad thing.
>
> (Sherer, 2011)

Given the ubiquitous screen of the twenty-first century, we agree with Janger's undesign approach, although we do not espouse his implication of the reality or constancy of disability apart from its design and branding.

> By changing the advertising narrative to one where people in the advertisements are seen for who they are, not what they have (or don't have), this can have a powerful impact on attitudinal perceptions of people with disabilities, and help rewrite the cultural meme for this demographic.
>
> (Janger, 2012)

Undesign calls for thoughtful, innovative, regularity of portrayal of diverse body imagery. As example, consider the the appearance of Ryan Langston, a youth with a diagnosis of Down syndrome, in a Target advertisement.

> All Target was doing was selling kid's apparel, and using cute kids to send the message. They did not even announce the kid in any of its press releases.
>
> Thrilled about the non-announcement of Ryan and his disability, Rick Smith wrote about Target's advertisement on his blog, Noah's Dad. Disability advocates and others saw his post, and in a matter of hours it went viral. Rick told me, two days after his post, of his amazement at finding over 8,000 likes on his blog post (it is now over 21,000 as of this writing).
>
> The reaction was huge, and almost uniformly positive. It was inclusive advertising, done in a powerful and unobtrusive way that delivered plenty of positive brand equity to Target.
>
> (Janger, 2012)

Target seems to illustrate the contemporary design thinking of Fukasawa and Morrison (2007), and Pullin (2013). Invoking the tradition of supernormal design seems to make more sense than contrivance in undesigning stigma. As introduced above, despite the seemingly oxomoronic quality of the term supernormal, its underlying tenets guide design as goodness-of-fit and natural occurrence with polish rather than concocted manipulation. Replacing hyperdesigned stigma reduction schemes with more authentically appearing efforts synthesized with relevance to context would seem to dim rather than intensify the spotlight on targeted groups such that comfort and fit into the continuum of humanness can occur.

In agreement, Bramel (2004) along with Kymlica (2007) and Michielson (2008) suggests moving to fundamental skepticism about the existence of categories. "So, is there such as thing as 'disability?' Or is it something that we, as a society, have created because of binary thinking" (Michielsen, 2008).

Given the nature of categories as human constructions, this question is not answerable. Existence of disability as with gender, race, ethnicity, or any other category is an artifact of its definition and then its tautological numeric reification. We would see the more cogent question as why the conceptual category exists and under what circumstances if any, it remains purposive. Such a question undesigns the category as parkesque without exterminating it and any utilitarian features of it that could be translated to human flourishing.

As posited by Bickenbach (2009), policy targeted to individual groups, rather than creating fit and rights, requires that groups be kept intact at least conceptually, be recognizable, and continue to offer distinctive figure ground such that they do not cease to stand out and invite scrutiny. Undesigning policy may very well start with dismantling the myth that disability as a category is useful, comfortable, that its members, however they are recruited, should even be identified for branding. The herd of diverse federal definitions of disability substantiate the profaner's doubt.

Before leaving conceptuals, we would be remiss not to discuss physical appearance in the park as it is the mothership of judgment in a visual culture. In a recent introductory disability studies class, a student new to disability studies highlights the violation of visual acceptability often superseding atypical function as a ticket to park membership.

> I think that a disability doesn't just have to be physical; it can be visual as well. People who are considered ugly can be discriminated against more than people with a physical disability. Also, I think that people with physical disabilities can have a stigma not because of the disability itself, but for how they look because of it. For example if someone is in a wheelchair, he might be stared at because he appears to look odd. People are not staring because of a spinal cord injury.
>
> (Speech given by Amanda Thurlow, January 2012)

The visual materiality of the body itself provides a bridge that crosses from idea to the tangible. As reflected by Thurlow's insight (Orrell, 2012), beauty is most often conceptualized as a static quality observable or ascertainable by a viewer and disabling in its absence (Steiner and Mulder, 2012). Undesigning this conception, Steiner proposes that beauty be rethought as interaction. Removing beauty from the position of fixed-observable deconstructs it as a predefined cultural standard to be achieved.

> I think we must stop seeing beauty as a thing or quality and see it instead as a kind of communication. Beauty is an unstable property because it is not a property at all. It is the name of a particular interaction between two beings, a self and an other. The experience of beauty involves an exchange of power and as such it is often disorienting, a mix of humility and exhalation, subjugation and liberation. Finding someone or something beautiful entails becoming worthy of it.
>
> (Steiner and Mulder, 2012: 65)

Undesigning beauty as a property of materiality thus removes it from objective scrutiny relocating it as moveable and changeable. If beauty becomes fluid, then so does its opposite, dissolving the binary into a dynamic complexity of continua.

In an interview with Levin (2010), Seibers proposes the atypical body as a foil so to speak capable of undesigning commercial conceptualizations of beauty. According to Seibers, contemporary art is considered beautiful despite the frequent discolorations and distortions of body in these images.

> Aesthetic culture views human variation increasingly as the motor that drives the appearance of the beautiful. Here discussions of imperfection do not make a great deal of sense because the idea of aesthetic beauty does not mirror ideals of physical perfection. On the other hand, we live in a commercial culture that markets human beauty. This idea of beauty is linked specifically to the human body, and it seems to be growing more narrow even as it grows more influential. This last culture is the one that seems intolerant of imperfections. It is the culture of the beauty pageant and plastic surgery.
>
> (Levin, 2010)

Although we would look at contemporary depictions of body in art as more complex than an interpretation of beauty and the body themselves, Seibers raises the potential for undesigning beauty as symmetry, prescribed proportions, and smooth texture, crafting a space for redesign of beauty as relational aesthetic pluralism. The beautiful body as object is animated and put into dialogue for negotiated undesign of commercial attributes.

Undesigning by object reading

Introduced earlier in the book, object reading in essence is a process similar to the undesign of beauty as discussed by Levin (2010). The process of reading concretuals instills movement and interaction in what were at one time considered to be static materials. On its surface, the built environment as object can be read as a major offender of access, a container for the disability park, and the creator of human junkspace (Koolhaus, 2007). As discussed in Chapter 7, architectural access guidelines, when they do exist, prescribe tweaking such that meaningful undesign and redesign, seen as costly for an already devalued group, are never approached. The placement of a ramp or braille opens a steam valve to expel pressure such that the angry exclusion pot fails to boil over and demand profound attention. Moving beyond mediating architectural barrier through a minimal curtsey only to politically correct groups with advocates or political voice requires a much more substantive object reading of space as agentic, interactive, malleable, and aesthetically pluralistic. It is unlikely that prescriptive proportions, heights, efforts and other legislated standards will foster creativity and harness the human capacity necessary for space that serves the human as more than simply its corpus.

Contrary to the principles of universal design, the first step of spatial and environmental undesign of the park is the recognition that humans are not universal (Caan, 2011). Unseating Vitruvian man as the model for architectural and spatial proportionality is a requisite if space and built environments are to cease defining humanness by who can fit through entrances and act within. In her remarks at a graduation recognition ceremony, Ayer expressed undesign succinctly: "What I learned in my disability studies courses is that one design for everyone fits no one (Ayer, 2012).

This insight from a student who is just beginning her scholarly career resonates with contemporary theory and design praxis. As expansively articulated by Caan (2011), space and the built environment must serve physiology, emotion, and psychology or what she refers to as the un-universal man. Chapman and Rosenfeld (2011) refer to unassisted living, once again accenting the "unpark." The homes in their volume disassemble institutional incarceration euphemistically disguised as assisted living and nursing home facilities, illustrating that alternatives to such arrangements are not only possible but diversely elegant without wresting people who need or desire care away from communities, families, and generations in order to reduce burden in the economic climate of the twenty-first century.

The architectural undesign of the park means relinquishing segregation, control, rigid standards, hyper-planning, and devaluation (Klausner, n.d.), re-reading the environment as diverse, changeable, beautiful in its noncommercial sense (Steiner and Mulder, 2012), and above all, humane.

> If an inhumane habitat diminishes us, a *"Humane Habitat"* must make us feel, enlivened, enriched. A humane habitat meets our needs, tempers our environment, supports our day to day activities and in the best examples enables us to engage with the highest parts of ourselves. A humane environment therefore complements us as a species by putting us in balance with our world and thus completes us. If we allow ourselves to think at our highest levels for a moment, an environment that completes us, in every sense of the word must be beautiful.
>
> (Lyons, 2011)

Before moving from spatial design to its contents, we take on the undesign of park signage. As discussed in previous chapters on space and imagery, the international symbol of access (ISA), rather than identifying access features of an environment simply denotes a wheelchair user at rest or more recently in motion (Basken, 2013), of anonymous gender, age and other embodied characteristics. Figure 12.2 presents disability park signage adjacent to its undesign. Note that the symbols to the left in the figure identify features for the euphemistic sliver of the atypical body, or the view of disability as both embodied and restricted to mobility, sight, and hearing

Park signage design	Undesign
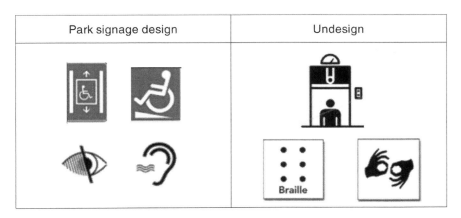	

Figure 12.2 Design and undesign by sign

impairment. Undesigning identity signage is not simply activating the wheelchair in motion but rather shifts the accent to the environmental resource for anyone to use. The undesign strategy is clear; remove the ISA simulacra in any form so that signage redesign can occur.

The images on the right of Figure 12.2 begin the undesign process, but are still linked to the particular euphemistic embodied conditions that comprise the impairment apex of the park hierarchy. Chapters 13 and 14 advance the symbolic undesign trend, uncoupling implied impairment from access symbolism.

Re-reading things

Inherent in the discussion of object reading is undesign guidance. First, the awareness that design is both culprit and solution to stigma precedes any other action or thinking process.

Artifact undesign is not owned exclusively by and the sole province of professional designers. Listen to Thurlow again.

> I think that the most stigmatizing thing about this design [of the wheelchair] is that it is a big huge heap of metal that is common among people who can't walk. Most of the time that same black metal wheelchair is given to everyone. It is big and noticeable and not very attractive. There is a young girl who comes into my workplace who has a pink wheelchair. And each week she has different color ribbon wrapped around it. I believe it is things like color and ribbon that make a design 100 times less stigmatizing. Why can't producers design wheelchairs like they do cars? All kinds of different makes and models.
>
> (Thurlow, 2013)

Second, parkesque object branding words are too well fertilized, over-ripened, and in need of culling. As example removing designations such as "assistive" and "adaptive" from the larger category of things "unpositions" park artifacts. To illustrate, two examples, one of assistive technology and one of adaptive tools, are presented below. Look at the two iPad training advertisements presented in Table 12.1.

Despite identical content, the New England Assistive Technology site segregates its training while Apple does not, perhaps for profit reasons rather than moral imperative, but nonetheless an important lesson to illustrate the power of the market climate in provoking undesign.

Profit from adaptive branding, however, is not as clever as Apple strategies nor does it aim its market strategies at expansion of its consumer segment in order to keep prices reasonable. We compared costs for identical shovels, one branded as a farm shovel and the other an adaptive shovel listed on an adaptive gardening website. Not unexpectedly, but fodder for informing undesign thinking, the farm shovel was priced over US$50 less than the US$87 adaptive tool. Simply using the term adaptive as a brand limits the market such that engorged prices become a poorly considered method for corporate profit in the park.

Table 12.1 iPad training example

Park training	Undesigned training
iPad training for youth with disAbilities FREE TABLET TRAINING for youth with disAbilities	The Apple Store is much more than a store. It's also the best place to learn about your new Apple product.
Come learn new skills using our Kindle Fire, iPad, Nook, Microsoft Surface (Alliance of People with disAbilities, 2013)	**Come back for free workshops.** Come join us for free iPad workshops at your favorite Apple Retail Store. You'll learn about iOS 6, built-in apps, iCloud, and the App Store. You can also find out about iMovie, GarageBand, and more. (Apple, 2013)
The New England Assistive Technology (NEAT) Resource and Education Center at Oak Hill in Hartford is hosting a series of professional development workshops to train educators on assistive technology tools that reach students with special needs and disabilities as well as all learners. Training focuses on iDevices, such as Apple's iPad, that break down barriers to accessing information technology for students with vision, hearing, motor skills and other disability challenges.	
	(Karam, 2012)

The shovel exemplar unearths the next undesign principle, access. Dissimilar to the park vernacular usage of the term, in the context of our discussion of things, access in this context refers not only to spatial entry but also to the who, where, and how of object attainment. As illustrated in venues such as Herrington, a retail online and print catalog, non-medicalized unbranding can be followed by undesigning park domination of products, such that they are available to anyone who wants or needs them without assessment, prescription, or medical insurance approval.

A quick perusal of this ubiquitous catalog reveals that its contents include orthotics, portable spinal traction units, joint support braces, and even heat therapy equipment, all items which had been the property of the disability park, but in expanded commercial entities can be accessed and used for many who read comfort meanings in these items. Branding such as Weekend Warrior Compression Wrap further undesigns artifacts as park products, rereading stigma as relief.

In an interesting twist, the word, therapy, is applied by an innovative company to interior apartment design, undesigning both the concept and its translation into object reading akin to the supernormal design trend proposed by Pullin (2013) and Fukasawa and Morrison (2007).

> We opened the store to offer an antidote to over-design. We consider the objects we stock to be humble, straightforward and beautiful for their simplicity and directness. Often they are traditional goods that have developed over generations or anonymous design found in general stores, DIYs and kiosks, products created by not one personality but things that are the result of local aesthetics and needs.
>
> (Apartment Therapy, 2013)

The Smarty protective head gear pictured in Chapter 11 illustrates the place in undesign of the park and advancing access that can occur from simplicity, and avoidance of medicalized or hyperdesigned products.

Undesigning myths: Cost and cost containment

The how question of "thing and service cost and access" is a difficult discussion as it doubts the current "insurance" logic for supporting the purchase of items and services to augment human function at all and specifically through both public and private medical insurance or what we have referred to as medical welfare. Before proceeding further with this undesign principle, recall that preferred outcomes are often reached through disparate thinking and diverse moral pathways and thus arguments that call for revision of the "how" are often dismissed because they are not teased apart from their rationales. But persevere and stay with us, please.

First, we would suggest that the assumption of the disproportionately high cost of function engendered by atypical bodies is not an artifact of impairment but rather artificially constructed and living in capitalist myth. Look back to the shovel and the Herrington Catalog for tiny examples and then expand this thinking to more profound needs. The myth is accepted as meme and thus institutionalized into the cultural consciousness without question. But what happens when we challenge this lore? Once exposed as fable, passion can be rerouted to undesign of a system that maintains park poverty and dependence.

For many reasons including but more expansive than inflated costs of park objects and services, it is not only ill advised but not possible to actuarialize the average cost of functioning in the world, and thus the myth of excessive cost of living with an atypical body implores undesign. Diversity of bodies in context requires differential costs of living unrelated to the fictitious construction of normal and its obverse, not normal. Thus, the undesign of the fairytale of high cost of the needs of an atypical body is in order and fundamental to equivalence of opportunity and choice.

Consider this example. The myth maintains that using wheeled mobility is more costly than ambulating and thus wheelchairs are designed for fiscal subsidy. But compare the cost of heating one's house, getting to and from destinations, and even participating in community related to geographic residence. Dissimilar to the disability park, none of these conditions is justified for relief. Just for a moment look at what happens when we substitute the word geography for the disability park term (mobility impairments) in the identical sentence.

> People with mobility impairments have disproportionately high costs of navigation compared to their non-impaired counterparts because they must purchase, operate, insure, and maintain a mobility device.
> People in rural settings have disproportionately high costs of navigation compared to their urban counterparts because they must purchase, operate, insure, and maintain a mobility device.

While the disproportionately low income and underemployment of people with embodied limitations looms in our thinking, uncritical acceptance of assuming that the atypical embodied creates higher costs than other factors of being human in a global market contradicts our fundamental premise that disability is a function of design and branding. Accepting the fable of excessive cost of atypical bodies as causal of poverty allows tolerance for inequality and derails profound change, as it provides the rationale for inertia, continuing the medicalization model of disability and all of its trappings.

Second, using pubic or private medical insurance to support daily activity is not our preferred undesign approach, as it does just the opposite. Perpetuating dependence on any medical insurance for what others can choose to purchase from their earnings keeps the park intact and maintains poverty by never taking it on directly. Medical welfare in the form of public or private insurance also engenders insidious outcomes, such as segregation, truncation of individual choice, control of lives and identities by well meaning but unaware park employees, and artificially englutted prices for things that are needed but once ensconced as medical device can only be afforded with help by too many park members and the insurance industry. Moreover, maintaining medical welfare as a source of support provides a major disincentive for independent earning even in the presence of legislation in the United States that ostensibly was passed to undesign reluctance for competitive employment, should it even be available. And finally, the causes and thus targets for undesign of poverty itself are eclipsed by providing subsistence and fear of its loss.

In our classes, students often articulate the belief, that given the high cost of medical insurance, choice and design are frivolous and unnecessary considerations for people who are diagnosed as impaired and thus need things to augment their function. As we noted previously, we often hear students articulating the well oiled belief that mere functionality of an object should elicit gratitude. Take the wheelchair as the classic example. Mobility devices with highbrow designs are often more costly than standardized chairs. Careful reading of the visual has already been discussed, but what about the payment mechanism? If disability things are financed by medical insurance, undesigning disability as medical deficit is not a logical demand. But a quagmire exists on several intersecting axes.

A cogent argument for public support for park objects is the excessive expense of functioning in a non-standardized manner. Wheeled mobility is not typical as an individual matures beyond infancy and thus for those who need it, it is costly.

Look at the tautological reasoning in Figure 12.3, which is so clever in maintaining cost myths and the dependence engendered.

Once the tautology is exposed it can be easily undesigned by asking two simple questions:

- Is the cost an inherent property of a park artifact?
- Is the cost an artifact of the inflated market?

Look at the work of Winter (2012) who designed wheeled mobility for under US$200 for developing nations. Why this design has not been relevant for all geographies is an important and revealing "how" question to ask. Similar objects for retail distribution, such as bicycles, are sold at diverse price points, in multiple designs and are obtained through varied payment options. We would therefore query why and where the distinction is made between park and non-park things and their payment sources. We revisit Winter in the next chapters, as his thinking unfolds to further inform redesign as choice with affordability.

Superimposed on the "how" of park objects is the high cost of objects branded for park distribution and use, as illustrated above in the example of the adaptive vs the farm shovel, despite the equivalent production costs.

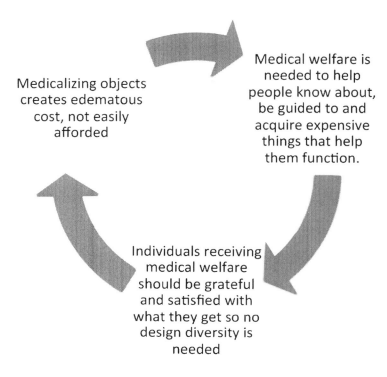

Figure 12.3 Tautology

Undesigning the "how" of access is not a simple discussion, but rather requires depth of object reading that uncouples disability brand designation from its tautological medicalization through the venues of appearance, fabrication, cost, and payment.

Magnification eyeglasses for the bolus of aging baby boomers provides a model for such "things" to be separated from the park. The choice of reading glasses, once extracted from the medical market, is explosive and transparent. Once read as vision impairment paraphernalia, eyeglasses have been undesigned and transformed into a fashion statement for typical aging or just for those who want them.

> Fake glasses, also known as clear lens glasses or non prescription glasses, are gaining an increasing popularity among glasses-wearers. They are fake in the sense that they are non prescription and all people are free to wear eyeglasses with non prescription lenses even if they have good eyesight. You can show different look and your distinct individuality by wearing stylish clear lens eyewear.

Here, we stock a GREAT collection of fake glasses and frames featuring varying trendy styles, materials and colors like aviator glasses, oversized glasses, cat eye glasses and more. Come on, go ahead and take on a pair of cool fake spectacles and you will have great fun.

(Firmoo, 2014)

But even more profound in this model, accompanied by other methods of "seeing," is the potential for all to afford to see. With innovative tweaking, the visual model undesigns inequality and poverty of vision.

Summary

Much conceptual and praxis ground has been engaged in this chapter, some of it broaching difficult threats to current economic concerns of individuals who are park members. Directions for undesign call for pluralism, dialog stripped of politically correct debris, and avoidance of continuing and thus enlarging myth, stigma, separation, and inequality. Responsible undesign forgoes rapidity in favor of careful study and anticipation of its many consequences. Common to all strategies is relevance, equivalence of choice, creativity, affordability, and a view of humanness that moves beyond the myth of business as usual. The next chapters look ahead to redesign, rebranding and thus reading the embodied object through different spectacles.

References

Abasiophilia Information (n.d.) The Disability Fetish. Retrieved from Abasiophilia Information: Available online at https://sites.google.com/site/abasioinfo/Home/disfet (accessed February 14, 2014).

Alliance of People with disAbilities (2013) IPad training for youth with disAbilities. Alliance of People with disAbilities, April 24. Available online at http://disabilitypride.org/wordpress/?p=1639 (accessed February 14, 2014).

Allport, G. W. (1954) *The Nature of Prejudice*. Cambridge, MA: Addison-Wesley.

Amichai-Hamburger, Y., and McKenna, K. Y. (2006) The Contact Hypothesis Reconsidered: Interacting via the Internet. *Journal of Computer-Mediated Communication*, 11 (3), 825–43.

Apartment Therapy (2013) Kiosk: The Un-design Shop. Retrieved from Kiosk: Available online at www.apartmenttherapy.com/shopping/store_profiles/kiosk-1-74348

Apple (2013) The Best Place to learn About Apple Products. Apple Retail Store, Apple Inc. Available online at www.apple.com/retail/learn (accessed February 14, 2014).

Ayer, M. (2012) *Remarks: Thoughts on Disability*. Orono, ME: Center for Community Inclusion and Disability Studies, University of Maine.

Basken, P. (2013) A Team of Academics Redesigns an Icon. *Chronicle of Higher Education*, May 20. Available online at http://chronicle.com/article/New-York-City-Embraces-a/139355/?key=ST4lcFRoNHYSMCtlNjxJYD9UbXxqNkt0anVIYn0iblBQEA== (accessed February 14, 2014).

Bickenbach, J. E. (2009) Disability, Non-talent, and Distributive Justice. In K. Kristianesen, S. Velmas, and T. Shakesphere (eds.), *Arguing About Disability: Philosophical Perspectives.* London: Routledge, 105–23.

Block, L. (2001–2014) Stereotypes About People With Disabilities: On The Image of Disability. Disability History Museum. Available online at www.disabilitymuseum.org/dhm/edu/essay.html?id=24 (accessed February 14, 2014).

Bramel, D. (2004) The Strange Career of the Contact Hypothesis. In Y.-T. Lee, C. McCauley, F. M. Moghaddam, and S. Worchel, *The Psychology of Ethnic and Cultural Conflict: Psychological Dimensions to War and Peace.* Westport, CN: Praeger, pp. 48–67.

Caan, S. (2011) *Rethinking Design and Interiors.* London: Lawrence King.

ChangingMinds.org (2013) Stereotypes. *Changingminds.org.* Available online at http://changingminds.org/explanations/theories/stereotypes.htm (accessed February 14, 2014).

Chapman, W., and Rosenfeld, J. (2011) *Unassisted Living.* New York: Monacelli Press.

Decker, K. S., and Eberl, J. T. (2005) *Star Wars and Philosophy: More Powerful Than You Can Possibly Imagine.* Popular Culture and Philosophy Series, Vol. 12. Chicago, IL: Open Court.

Firmoo (2014) Fake Glasses. Firmoo.com. Available online at www.firmoo.com/fake-eyeglasses.html (accessed February 14, 2014).

Fukasawa, N., and Morrison, J. (2007) *Super Normal: Sensations of the Ordinary.* Lars Muller Publisher.

Garland-Thomson, R. (2009) *Staring: How We Look.* New York: Oxford University Press.

Haller, B. (2006) Are Disability Images in Advertising Becoming Bold And Daring? An Analysis of Prominent Themes in US and UK Campaigns. *Disability Studies Quarterly,* 26 (3). Available online at http://dsq-sds.org/article/view/716/893 (accessed February 14, 2014).

Janger, M. (2012) Hey, That Limb Is Missing! Debunking Disability Stereotypes In Advertising. Retrieved from *Drumbeat Blog,* January 13. Available online at http://drumbeatconsulting.com/blog/2012/01/19/hey-that-limb-is-missing-debunking-disability-stereotypes-in-advertising (accessed February 14, 2014).

Karam, A. (2012) Assistive Technology Training Series For Educators Of Students With Special Needs And Disabilities. *Hartford Courant,* October 9. Available online at http://articles.courant.com/2012-10-09/community/hcrs-66304hc-statewide-20121004_1_workshop-oak-hill-ipad (accessed February 14, 2014).

Klausner, A. (2004) Undesigning America. *Core 77.* Available online at www.core77.com/reactor/undesigningamerica.asp (accessed February 14, 2014).

Koolhaus, R. (2007) Junkspace. In C. Jencks and K. Kropf (eds.), *Theories and Manifestoes of Contemporary Architecture* (2nd ed.), Chichester: Wiley, pp. 370–1.

Kymlica, W. (2007) *Multicultural Odyssey.* Oxford: Oxford University Press.

Levin, M. (2010) The Art of Disability: An Interview with Tobin Siebers. *Disability Studies Quarterly,* 30 (2). Available online at http://dsq-sds.org/article/view/1263/1272 (accessed February 14, 2014).

Lyle, D. (2003) Disability and the Media – the Role for Advertising. Speech by Dominic Lyle, Director-General, EACA, Media and Disability Conference organised for the EU by the European Disability Forum, Athens, 13–14 June 2003. Available online at www.media-disability.org/documents/Dominic%20 Lyle%20Presentation.pdf (accessed February 14, 2014).

Lyons, F. (2011) Geoff Baker Celebrates the Work of Jim Stirling. *Humanearchitecture.com,* July 30. Available online at www.humanearchitecture.com/architecture-blog (accessed February 14, 2014).

Mann, A. (2012) Understanding Undesigning. Simply Adam Mann Blog. Available online at http://simplyadammann.com/blog/2013/1/16/understanding-undesigning (accessed February 14, 2014).

Merriam-Webster (2013) Undesigning. *Merriam Webster Dictionary.* Available online at www.merriam-webster.com/dictionary/undesigning (accessed February 14, 2014).

Michielsen, A. (2008) Breaking the Binary: Does Disability Exist? *Grand Bend Strip,* 2 (2). Available online at www.grandbendstrip.com/2008/05/breaking-the-binary-does-disability-exist.html (accessed February 14, 2014).

Mullins, A. (2013) A Work in Progress. *The Moth: True Stories Told Live,* August 6. Available online at http://themoth.org/posts/storytellers/aimee-mullins (accessed February 25, 2014).

Orrell, D. (2012) *Truth or Beauty.* New Haven, CN: Yale University Press.

Palotta, D. (2008) *Uncharitable.* Medford, MA: Tufts University Press.

Pullin, G. (2009) *Disability Meets Design.* Cambridge, MA: MIT Press.

Sade, G., Coombes, G., and McNamara, A. (2013) Call for Proposals: Undesign. *Design Journal and Conference Calls,* June. Available online at http://designcalls.wordpress.com/2013/04/25/call-for-proposals-undesign (accessed February 14, 2014).

Sherer, T. (2011) Teal Sherer Actress and Advocate. *Advertising and Disability,* October 20. Available online at http://advertisinganddisability.com/2011/10/20/teal-sherer-actress-advocate (accessed February 14, 2014).

Steele, C. (2010) *Whistling Vivaldi: How Stereotypes Affect Us and What We Can Do.* New York: Norton.

Steiner, W., and Mulder, A. (2012) Beauty as Interaction. In J. Brouwer, A. Mulder, and L. Spuybroek, *Vital Beauty.* Rotterdam: Colophon.

Thurlow, A. (2013) Remarks on Uglo-Americans. Speech Orono, ME.

Titchkosky, T. (2007) *Reading and Writing Disability Differently.* Toronto, ON: University of Toronto Press.

van der Meij, S. and Heijnders, M. (2004) *The Fight Against Stigma: Stigma Reduction Strategies and Interventions.* Paper Prepared for the International Stigma Workshop held at Soesterberg, From 28–11 to 2–12, 2004.

Winter, A. (2012) Amos Winter: The Cheap All-Terrain Wheelchair. TED Ideas Worth Spreading, November. Available online at www.ted.com/talks/amos_winter_the_cheap_all_terrain_wheelchair.html (accessed February 14, 2014).

Young, C. (2013) Undesigned. Available online at http://undesigned.bigcartel.com/about (accessed February 14, 2014).

13 Redesign

Redesigning and rebranding through innovative knowledge and skill, visuals, conceptuals, and "concretuals"

Guest authors: James Ferguson, Engineering Design and Commercialization, Janice Grant, Technology, Communications, and Disability Studies, and Kelly Sadlon, Interdisciplinary Industrial Designer

The principles, histories, and narratives of undesign imply guidance for redesign. Yet, redesign efforts must not fall prey to refilling the undesigned void with "what has been." Reliance on history and non-example to advance rather than recreate is therefore in order. In the last twelve chapters, we have analyzed disability design as less than desirable within context, albeit often created by well meaning crafters. Yet, unintended consequences of current design and branding tend to result in unsatisfactory outcomes, maintaining a world in which theoretical, built, and virtual standards may tolerate small bulges, but rip and scar over to eliminate more significant offenders. In such a universe, the disability park, despite its walled containment outside of the standard world, looks like an inviting option for out-group comfort even while segregating and branding its members as needy and inadequate.

Redesign and its sidekick, rebranding, must be extensive and complex (Norman, 2011) if the park is to be dismantled and the universe revised for profound diversity comfort in the twenty-first-century global context. By profound diversity comfort, we refer to a context in which people of all shapes, sizes, functionality, and persuasions who fit within democratically negotiated civility can find a place to be named as full members and comfortably fit without being remanded to a segregating conceptual or concrete park. As we develop and illustrate in this chapter, the principles of seamlessness, elegance, skepticism, proximity, and polyphony guide redesign and rebranding practices that seek to meet and craft profound diversity comfort.

Seamlessness

Seamlessness is defined as continuity. Synonyms explicating its relevance to redesign include smoothness, congruence, fluidity, and coherence (Synonym.com, 2001–2013). Seamlessness therefore escorts designers away from strategies, ideas, and creations that carve humans into segments, leaving the landscape clear of fencing and thus fertile for symmetry.

To provide concrete examples of seamless redesign, return once again to navigation and movement through diverse methods. In the current park design, wheelchairs, crutches, canes, and prosthetics are contained and thus not woven into the fabric of a "movement world for everyone." As discussed previously, not only is the wheelchair branded as undesirable, but its cartoonesque representation even when activating its stick figure inhabitants (Basken, 2013), is the iconic brand for the disability park. Yet, throughout the globe, wheeled mobility reminiscent of wheelchair design, and perhaps not even as efficient in moving users through interior and exterior spaces, is integrated into environments such that all forms of transport seem natural and the choice of the user. In a seamless scheme, even if a transport "thing" is the object of staring, object reading does not elicit pity, anxiety, or aversion, but rather curiosity and even admiration. Each of the photographs in Figure 13.1 depicts an image of wheeled mobility, none of which is branded as a current and explicit disability park people-mover. All fit "seamlessly" into their indoor and/or outdoor environments as they assist the user to navigate. The objects range in cost from cobbled together at home through high-cost, high-tech devices.

While walking through Amsterdam, we noticed two minuscule cars, both branded with the Canta logo and almost identical in design. On closer inspection, we observed that one of the models (Figure 13.2a) was built for an individual driving while seated in a wheelchair while the other (Figure 13.2b) was for ambulatory drivers. The wheelchair user opens the rear door and rolls into the car, anchoring the wheelchair as the car seat. This design illustrates the essence of seamlessness, eliminating not only the functional division between "us and them" mobility styles but also aesthetic constancy.

Placing an exemplar next to its non-examples sharpens the focus. So, refer back to Chapter 11 to view the Access Van in comparison, read the medicalized text below, and then breath new fresh air deeply knowing that innovations such as the Canta have ventured over the proverbial horizon as they become integrated into contemporary redesign.

The mission of Mobility Sales is to create a friendly sales atmosphere when you are looking for a new or used wheelchair accessible vehicle through The Select Dealer Network. It is a big decision to purchase an accessible vehicle conversion and we want our disabled customers to feel comfortable throughout the entire process. We offer the best

Figure 13.1 Wheeled mobility

Figure 13.2 Kanta seamlessness

selection of quality handicap vans, wheelchair accessible vehicles, wheelchair lifts, and scooter lifts in America!

(www.mobilitysales.com)

Elegance

While the term "elegance" conjures images of red-carpeted entryways into opulence, in its contemporary usage, elegance has been applied to describe theories, equations, and science that do extensive work without obfuscation or ostentation. For us, redesign elegance refers to precision, quality, efficacious labor, and enduring communicative beauty as discussed by Steiner and Mulder (2012), without fanfare or opulence. Pilloton (2009) captures the essence of elegance in her claim, "I believe that design is problem solving with grace and foresight" (Pilloton, 2009: 10). Similar in intention to supernormal design (Fukasawa and Morrison, 2010), elegance as a characteristic of design is a seminal element for seamless, pluralistic, and thoughtful redesign. Look at what Ferguson has to say about the role of elegance in designing function and emotion.

> An example of elegant design is the Karman Ghia . . . little more than a Volkswagen wrapped in a Porsche body. The performance was just like the Volkswagen Beetle, but the sleek presentation and design earned it the designation "one of the most beautiful things in the world." It did not perform like a Porsche or look like a Volkswagen, but is a good example of form follows function that was brought to a very high

standard. I own a 1970 version that I am very slowly restoring! I feel good when driving it and get positive input from people. I do not feel like I am driving a Bug.

(Ferguson, personal communication)

Elegance has been used, albeit sparingly, to jailbreak medicalized park design. In the early 1990s, Ron Williams (2009) designed the Elegant Wheelchair, which made its way into the Design Museum in London as an exhibition from 1991 to 1993, but has been missing in action in the public ever since. Note the aesthetic congruence of this device with its surrounding furniture, illustrating seamlessness in context as well as elegance.

Applied to redesign, elegance is not simply about grace but rather a principle that imbues refinement, replacing the conspicuous with goodness of fit, comfort and positive identity. Williams' chair accomplished this aim with one exception, its lexical branding, which for us once again activates exclusion by inclusion (Titchkosky, 2007). We might have preferred the brand name "Williams Chair" to augment the visual and complete seamlessness, rather than scream for attention by name.

Cohen uses photography of unexpected subjects, elder women and men, not only to pulverize disparaging views of aging, but to rebrand elders as elegant. "I have never considered old to be a bad word. The ladies I photograph challenge stereotypical views on age and aging" (Cohen, 2012).

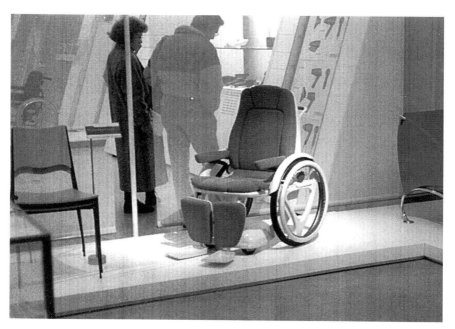

Figure 13.3 Elegant Wheelchair (Williams) (reproduced with permission)

In the foreword to Cohen's artful rebranding, Kalman (2012) clarifies that a particular style does not prescribe elegance. Rather, elegance is diverse as it counters crude distaste too frequently attached to bodies, products, and ideas that frequent the disability park, and as foregrounded by Cohen (2012), the aged real estate within the park.

> My piano teacher, Mrs. Danzinger, well into her 80s, always wore an elegant dress, sheer stockings and high heels. She had a braid wrapped around her head with a powder blue ribbon running through it. Albert Einstein sailed his boat wearing a ratty sweatshirt. Frumpy pants. His hair disheveled. He looked incredible.
>
> (Kalman, 2012)

The Gitlows, in Figure 13.4, both in their late 80s, display elegant lives, rebranding a feared time of life as vital and admirable. Now look at the images in Figure 13.5 of two women who, despite embodied conditions and the telltale accouterments that would invite them into the park, walk among others in the city of Budapest seamlessly sporting simple elegance.

Stephen's back brace provides alternative fodder as elegance. Object reading of the back brace in Figure 13.6 brings humor and a "cool" factor to what otherwise might be considered a tragic even, a fractured spine.

Figure 13.4 Raya and Bernard Gitlow

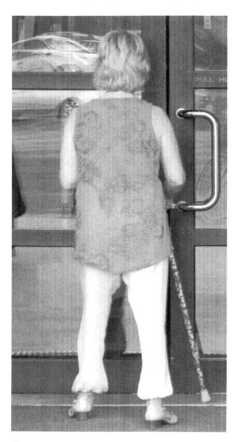

Figure 13.5 Budapest women

As we have noted throughout this work, profit incentive is a powerful incubator of twenty-first century creative redesign, without which design stalls and wilts. Nevertheless, lessons abound from the market economy inciting redesign. We are pleased to see an increasing number of elegant products make an appearance outside the disability park. Consider canes, for example:

> For the perfect, distinguished accent to your wardrobe, or simply for a fashionable touch to your look, browse our extensive selection of designer canes. We are happy to offer you a wide range of options, so you can be sure that you will find exactly what you are looking for. Whether you prefer the interesting look of clear amber, the flair and sparkle of rhinestones, or the classic shine of nickel, brass or chrome, there is something here to suit your tastes. Each of these beautiful

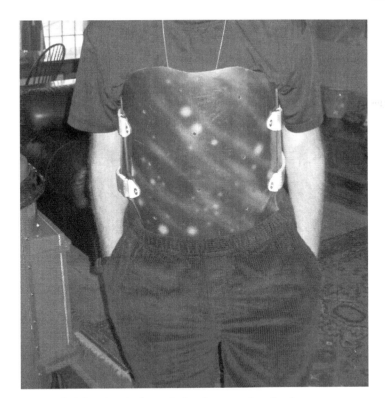

Figure 13.6 Stephen's thoracic lumbar sacral orthosis

pieces features a sturdy construction from durable materials like solid hardwood shafts and more. No matter which design you prefer, you're sure to love your purchase for years to come.

(Fashionablecanes, 1993–2013)

Not only does the text speak to elegance, but note that the narrative does not segregate those who need mobility support from others who might find a walking stick desirable for other reasons, another contemporary sample of seamlessness. The prices range from a mere US$20 to US$590, extending this product line to all consumers without assessment or prescription. Now compare the Merry Therapeutic Cane, priced at US$199: "Merry Therapeutic Cane designed to assist each person with self-rehabilitation by providing a weight adjustable and height adjustable cane to allow them, with each step to restore arm, leg and back muscles" (Sherman Oaks Medical Supplies, 2008).

The proliferation of elegant objects is heartening. However, we have not seen any recent examples of elegant policy within rights legislation or rulings, and perhaps understandably so, given the perceived absence of an immediate profit motivation. Looking further down the chronological road, however, it is not only feasible but likely that elegant policy would be profitable as well as efficient. MacFarlane expresses a similar lament:

> Governments need the word to determine eligibility for social security payments and programs/services. On that score I'd prefer, as recently suggested in the McClure Report on Welfare Reform and elsewhere (ACOSS), the idea of one level of payment (based on adequate living expenses) to everyone in need, with additional payments based on impairment-related, or child/aged care costs…but that's another debate. Though the question of specialist services for "people with disability" is trickier, as in the past when generic services were given that role as well there just wasn't the management will or staff expertise to do a good job servicing the needs of "people with disability" in mainstream agencies catering to everyone. This would be the ideal, though.
>
> (MacFarlane, 2013)

The McClure Report (2000) referenced by MacFarlane argued for orchestrated simplicity and elegance in solving what were considered as severe market, government, and voluntary sector failures to remediate poverty and disparity in early twenty-first-century Australia. The text also suggested what we refer to as polyphony below, the convergence of multiple melodies or voices in a single solution to much needed welfare reform.

In sectors distal from rights and resources for populations considered as vulnerable, and thus the object of need and charity, there are some budding exemplars of elegant policy. Consider this example from renewable energy.

> The state of Connecticut has found an innovative solution to adoption paralysis. Recognizing the desirability of removing food waste from the municipal waste stream, the state passed SB1116, which mandates that organic waste generators meeting a certain annual threshold must separate their waste and arrange for it to be brought to a compost facility or anaerobic digester. However, the law is only triggered once there are at least two permitted facilities that can accept food waste. Furthermore, a generator must be within a reasonable distance to one of the facilities, or else they remain exempt.
>
> Voilá. Elegant in its simplicity, the entire legislation could almost fit on Twitter and makes the Gettysburg Address seem long-winded. Developers can go ahead and plan projects knowing that if they are built, feedstock will be available. Waste generators have the clarity of understanding what they will be required to do and when. Investors have peace of mind that the pieces will align.
>
> (Pierotti, 2012)

This policy text illustrates MacFarlane's (2013) vision and provides a lesson yet to be learned by human rights and resources policy makers. Anticipation, brevity, cooperation, and advanced planning joined hands to create an elegant solution to head off diverse barrier configurations that could have prevented efficiency of cost and progress.

Skepticism

The term skepticism is often conflated with ordinary doubt that can be healed with one dose of convincing evidence. Yet in order to accomplish redesign and rebranding the skeptic must not stop questioning after a single convalescence, nor must he/she adopt cynicism. Rather, redesign skepticism, following the model of philosophical skepticism (Klein, 2010), is ongoing and exhaustive, eliminating the potential for complacency or acceptance of a single monistic truth. Such dynamic thinking for us is a requisite for innovative redesign capable of meeting the rapid shifts of the twenty-first century global universe. Craig illustrates skepticism in his plea for rebranding of disability:

> When you believe everyone has something to offer, the mission becomes one of helping them reach their maximum potential. Not taking care of them. Not ignoring them. It just so happens everyone does have something to offer – history tells the tale of marginalized people ranging from women to left-handed people to the hearing impaired fighting for the right to be full participants in society. They add value every time they win, meaning the rest of us win, too. Look at Stephen Hawking – in a different time, he would have been seen as a lost cause. Look at Lisa Raitt – she turned a battle with post-partum depression into an opportunity to help others. Do you wear glasses? Then look in the mirror. There was a time when you would've been a lost cause, too.
>
> (Craig, 2013)

Consider universal design as example. As discussed previously, universal design originated as a set of seven guiding principles to achieve social justice. Yet, the term and its essence, without critical skepticism, have been colonized and distorted resulting in differential design guidance and thus segregation of expansive designer disability domains including but not limited to product, space, policy, and education. Look at the screen capture in Figure 13.7 as example, with Americans with Disabilities Act (ADA) standards highlighted front and center.

Without skepticism, universal design has gone unchecked albeit unintentional by its adopters, perpetuating the segregation, stigma and exclusion that it was intended to eradicate (Bringhoff, 2008). Recall the sage words of Marissa Ayer in her 2012 graduation speech, "one design for everyone fits no one."

Figure 13.7 UniversalDesign.com

Ferguson's thinking about protective head-gear resonates with Ayer's insight and illustrates the potential of skepticism to guide redesign. Because Ferguson questioned how a product could possibly protect those who refuse to use it, he eschewed the utility of current medicalized helmet design. Rather than simply tweaking existing headgear with a color palette, Ferguson engineered a unique, thin moldable protective material to be used in numerous styles of typical head-wear. To inform his redesign, Ferguson engaged in ongoing skepticism, challenging the wisdom of turning to medical providers for guidance. He reasoned that health provider expertise is about the corpus, health and illness, rather than in the aesthetic that would encourage regular usage of protective head-gear. Instead of proceeding down the usual medicalization route to design a health promotion device, Ferguson recruited the product user, positioning him/her not as the disability park recipient of prescribed equipment, but as the purchaser, chooser, end user and consumer expert. Through skepticism, Ferguson reached out to seamlessness and elegance as well, designing protection choice, and fashion within an affordable price point.

Policy provides fertile ground for skeptical redesign. Business as usual, such as the expansion of the ADA in 2008 to even more diagnostic categories, beckons the curiosity and questioning of the skeptic. Look at Hensel's (2011) cogent analysis of how the ADA shoots its own claim of antidiscrimination in its foot within the profession that purports to uphold it.

> In order to establish coverage in the protected class, litigants must demonstrate not only the presence of a disability, but also that they are qualified for the position in question, or capable of performing the essential functions of the position with or without reasonable accommodation. Because impairments must now be quite severe in order to satisfy the requisite threshold, the two components are in serious

Figure 13.8 Protective head gear: The Smarty brand

tension with each other… This is reflected in case law involving the bar, which at times reflects skepticism that an attorney can be both sufficiently disabled to qualify for legal protection and still qualified to engage in the exacting practice of law.

(Hensel, 2011: 637–56)

Hensel turned skepticism inward on his own profession. He reasoned that if one is eligible for protection under the ADA and its amendment cousin, the individual must assert severe functional incapacity of long term or permanent duration. The claim of incapacity certainly does not put one's positive attributes ahead of perceived limitations, and thus is not likely to engender enthusiasm from an employer for hiring the protected individual on the basis of a narrative of need, ergo the proverbial bind for both employer and interviewee. Moreover, how many employees do not need equipment (e.g. computer, chair, car etc.) in order to do a job? Not only does the ADA require policy eligibles to infuse a job interview with potential employer dread, but it serves to segregate and distinguish equipment used by eligibles from typical equipment used by any employee, even when identical or equivalent. The skeptic would look askance at the inherent flaws of this legislation such that redesign would move beyond simply expanding it to even more unsuspecting eligibles.

Proximity

Proximity is defined as nearness. Its synonyms however, give it more relevance and clarity as a principle for redesign: "adjacency, appropinquity, closeness, concurrence, contiguity, contiguousness, immediacy, juxtaposition, propinquity, togetherness: (Thesaurus.com, 2013).

Proximity directs redesign closer to the user, beneficiary, typical citizen. We are not suggesting that government and large firm involvement in redesign is not essential in the corporatized twenty-first-century globe. Rather, as originator, partner, or even provocateur, proximal redesign can be conceptualized as human problem solving. A recent full edition of the *New York Times Magazine* was devoted to proximal innovation (Lindgren, 2013).

Lindgren (2013) included the Band-Aid® in this compendium of omnipresent "things." Earle Dickinson, husband of Josephine, created the Band-Aid for his wife, who regularly sliced her fingers while cooking. At the time, skin abrasions were covered with rags or other crudely cobbled cloth. Thus, the Band-Aid, like so many solutions, originating from the proximal marriage of need with elegance of use: "The sheer volume and range of these inventions demonstrate a rapidly growing population of problem solvers with the tools to turn their ideas into tangible things."

Earle Dickenson is a penultimate exemplar of redesign. While a strategy existed to solve the problem of bleeding skin invasions, it was not satisfactory, and thus more of the same did not suffice for him. Just in a simple Band-Aid, the brand now iconic, one can see seamlessness, elegance, skepticism, and proximity. Polyphony is also obvious in his solution as discussed next.

Polyphony

Rather than using equivalent words such as relevance or harmony, we have chosen to name this principle polyphony since it precisely depicts the artful cooperation that this guidance choreographs. Within the music vernacular, polyphony is defined as "a style of musical composition employing two or more simultaneous but relatively independent melodic lines" (Merriam-Webster, 2013).

Similar to relevance but infused with cultivated merger of many voices, polyphony refers to graceful blending of sometimes disparate perspectives. Without calling for full consensus, this principle considers what is pertinent to and fitting in context and well informed by more than a single crafter. Similar to so many commercial products, the participating voices are all or some of the following:

- The individual or group who articulates an unmet need or desire.
- The crafter who realizes an unmet need or desire.
- The end user who has a series of ideas, preferences, and innovations which can shape the conceptual or concretual solution to a problem.

- The distributor.
- The social context in which the solution is realized and read.

Similarly, polyphony within conceptual design embodies consistency and synchronicity without sameness. Thus, universals are eschewed by the principle, as design and branding must be context relevant and emergent from at least the benefactor and the beneficiary in order to heal chasms and eliminate the staring, stigma, and segregation that results without polyphony. Polyphony, although branded with other labels as discussed by Grant (2013) below has been used successfully in the commercial sector. We turn to her work now for illustration.

> Many large corporations have managed to stay on the forefront of innovation by drawing on its consumers' well of skills, experience, and perspectives to reinvigorate new product development (NPD). By interacting with consumers directly, professionals can use common design preferences to visualize, create, and circulate marketable products (Abrahamson, 2011: 622). For example, LEGO maintains an online community where company professionals collaborate with users to develop fresh ideas and designs into products (Boudreau and Lakhani, 2013: 66), and Wikipedia is founded on the knowledge-sharing of countless users to develop, update, and maintain its website (Boudreau and Lakhani, 2013: 66). Most significantly, Apple's success with iTunes, iPads, and iPhones is largely due to the large number of independent users and developers who have created a nearly limitless array apps and podcasts that augment Apple products (Boudreau and Lakhani, 2013: 62).
>
> Whether it's called collective intelligence, crowdsourcing (Poetz and Schreier, 2012: 246), or common design (Schreier, Fuchs, and Dahl, 2012: 19–20), user-generated product design has shown great potential in the broad consumer market (Magnusson, 2009: 591; Poetz and Schreier, 2012: 248; Schreier, Fuchs, and Dahl, 2012: 22). Recent research determined that consumer ideas and designs were significantly more innovative and beneficial to customers than those generated by professionals (though sometimes appearing slightly less feasible to the doubter) (Poetz and Schreier, 2012: 245). Additionally, the use of user-generated design enhances consumer perspective of companies with respect to consumers' intentions to purchase and recommend the product to others, and in willingness to pay for the product, due to beliefs that the number, diversity of people involved in idea generation is a bonus, as well as the added insight brought by actual users who aren't bound (as professionals are) by company constraints in product development (Schreier, Fuchs, and Dahl, 2012: 29).
>
> (J. Grant, unpublished course paper, University of Maine, 2013)

Not only does polyphony bring a village of thinkers together to debate, deliberate and ultimately solve a problem, but as importantly, invests the participants in the process as idea owners and ongoing contributors.

As example, consider the work of Open IDEO (2012) in expanding full access to voting for all people. The following challenge was posted on the Open IDEO website.

> For many citizens in democracies around the world, the ability to cast an election ballot is often a given. But what if you had a disability, difficulties with language or reading, limited mobility or other conditions that excluded you from participating in the election process? In fact many people face a variety of social and technological barriers that impede their ability to cast their ballot privately and independently. In this challenge, Open IDEO and the Information Technology and Innovation Foundation are asking our community to find ways to improve election accessibility for people with disabilities and other limitations. With your help, we're eager to design new solutions that make the entire voting process – from registering to vote to casting a ballot – accessible for everyone.
>
> (Open IDEO, 2012)

Gautam met the challenge with skepticism, illustrating the absence, in the principle of polyphony, of espousing the party line in order to be considered a full participant.

> Dear Ashley and Meana, its indeed a challenge in need. However, I am disappointed to notice that the brief refers to people with mobility or other limitations as "disabled" and not "differently- abled." There has been ongoing debate on how to make the systems inclusive for people with varied 'disabilities'. The biggest challenge has been to remove the stigma associated with being "disabled"... Also,... it is wrong to call a person handicapped, as he/she is handicapped by the design of environment around him, whereas he/she might be differently abled. A lot of products designed and developed for disabled are not adopted/used by them due to social stigma associated with using a product as it designed for someone who is "disabled." In order to arrive at inclusive solutions, it requires a mind-shift, we/society (normal people) need to look at people with so called "disabilities" at the same platform like any one of us.
>
> (Gautam, 2012)

Solutions as simple as voting by telephone through those as complex as messages to communicate to the public that voting is not perfunctory have been posted on the site, expanding the innovations that meet the challenge of equality of voting opportunity.

As we emphasized above, given significant fiscal and competitive incentives, it is not surprising that the commercial sector incubates such a high degree of innovative and diverse redesign. This realization points to the cogency of infusing social change with strategies that have successfully served the profit master. Palotta (2008), whose work we introduced earlier, aimed his critical arrow at the same social change target, albeit with a different bow. He urged the non-profit sector and its legal-institutional bosses to disassemble the partitions between for-profit and not-for-profit establishments to remove barriers preventing successful profit making strategies from being actualized by the "helping businesses."

Crowdfunding is one trend that actualizes polyphony synthesized with Palotta's vision. Look at the text introducing the Pozible initiative:

> Pozible is a crowdfunding platform and community-building tool for creative projects and ideas. It was developed to help people raise funds, realise their aspirations and make great things possible. Crowdfunding with Pozible is a way for motivated makers to access funding beyond "official" channels by talking directly to switched-on consumers, fans, peers and like-minded strangers.
>
> (Pozible PTY, n.d.)

We now turn to two innovative redesigners, one well seasoned and known and the other beginning her design career, inviting market wisdom to playfully join their own creativity for the purpose of enticing redesign propositions that meet human diversity with delight.

Norman (2011), a seasoned thinker and creator, has been an important influence in the field of design in general and accessible design in particular. We often assign his work on emotional design to our students, titillating them with Norman's ideas about daily object design. Norman's insights provoke thinking unseating the medicalization model of disability to make room for an understanding of designed disablement.

In his recent work, Norman takes on designing for complexity. Because embodied diversity fits within his parameters of complexity, typical notions of disability are essentially dismissed by Norman as categorical, illustrating seamlessness. He then further describes the complexity required of some individuals by illustrating how those whose bodies do not comfortably fit standardized environments must convolute themselves and creatively find ways to navigate and attain their goals. Norman's work is particularly relevant for park undesign and access redesign.

> The most important first step is to increase the awareness of designers and companies of the need to accommodate everyone. The disabled are not just some small, disenfranchised group: they represent all of us. So the first step is education, awareness, and empathy.
>
> (Norman, as cited in Steere, 2008)

Norman, while applauding the intent of universal design thinking, debunks the potential to redesign a complex universe as simple: "The challenge for the designer is to provide well-structured, cohesive experiences, where the complexity can reveal its desirable face, not its ill-tempered, mystifying one" (Norman, 2011: 253). Yet, he also does not suggest that complexity is ubiquitous:

> Even though many things are complex out of necessity, not everything needs to be complex. Many otherwise simple things are overdesigned, far too complicated. Why is so much of our modern technology badly designed, disfigured with excessive features? Why does the disease of featuritis strike so often despite the existence of remedies and preventative measures? Why are so many things needlessly complex, needlessly complicated?
>
> (Norman, 2011: 253–4)

Norman concludes his design guidance with polyphony. Designers, according to Norman, must become partners of users as well as friends with conceptual knowledge to inform product design.

Now we visit K. Sadlon (personal communication, 2013), who has graciously shared her process in redesigning an ambulation staple of the park, the crutch. Her work as a nascent designer not only reflects object reading as the basis for innovation, but enlivens it in a 'thing" that most often connotes debility. Sadlon weaves her own experience together with industrial design in her unique understanding of objects as evocative (Turkle, 2011).

Crutches with a Language
Kelly Sadlon
As an athlete I have been on crutches more than a few times in my life, but never for a long-term injury. Even in the short time that I was on crutches, the discomfort I felt was something I could not imagine simply tolerating for the rest of my life, had it been a long-term injury. Maybe I didn't have enough arm strength or maybe I was just doing it wrong, but how does an individual know if she is doing it right? Can I create a crutch design that lends itself to the least amount of user error?

I originally looked at the American design that braces up on the inner portion of the ribs and rests under the shoulders. One of the main concerns with these crutches is that there is a lot of user error. The human underarm is not meant to hold any load, but due to the design of the standard crutch, the user assumes that applying weight to the armpits is the easiest and most comfortable way to crutch around. This effort actually makes it harder to move through the crutching motion and when this motion is continually repeated, damage could be done to the nerves that run through the armpit. This design flaw has been fixed already with the creation of the forearm crutch. Instead of the user bracing crutches against his ribs, he actually brace his own arms close to the body as forearms are supported by the upper-most part of the crutch. This position helps to reduce user error when using the crutches uninitiated and without instruction. This is why, when deciding to modify current crutches I choose to make an attachment to the existing forearm crutch, rather than the underarm crutch.

I researched prosthetics and saw the ways in which people with quadriplegia were using certain crutches and prosthetics to move around. It was interesting to see at what angle the prosthetics were attached as well as where they were in relation to the center of mass of the individual. I also observed the motion and biomechanics of the movement while a person is moving through the crutching position depending on which gait is used. This observation furthered my idea that I needed to combine the concept of prosthetics with crutches to increase ambulation efficiency as well as change the perceptions about users on crutches to something more positive and motivating for the crutch walker. The crutches I ended up designing give the user the notion that "she is moving" and is not limited by the crutches, but rather she is just as capable in ambulation as someone walking without crutches. Since crutches can become part of someone's identity, it is important to consider not only the function, but also the aesthetics through a holistic approach.

Maneuvering on crutches is not a typical way of moving and therefore crutch design requires an innovative way of thinking. Advancement in the study of movement can only progress through a deeper understanding of what motion can be for an individual, versus what it should be. There is no certain way to walk, or crutch, so the key is to develop a set of crutches that allows for an individualized, but fluid, gait while still being user friendly. There is no age limit or physique description for crutches, so how can I design for all those components? My sole focus, from a biomedical standpoint, is to take the energy exerted into the in-step of the crutching motion and then release that same energy to the user on the outstep. This exchange allows for a slight "push" to the user making the motion more fluid and less tiresome than with how current crutch design influences movement and energy. While focusing on these aspects of crutch-aided ambulation, I became even more aware of how weight and the crutching gait altered the efficiency of the crutches. Crutches are sometimes used as a substitution for a limb, while other times they are simply used as an assist and what I would call a "helping mechanism." In each scenario the energy exerted in the in-step and outstep varies. This knowledge led me to choose carbon fiber as my material, seeing as its flex varies based on weight, impact position, and compression/tension.

Design can be looked at from many different angles, but how does a design-concept change when a problem is solved through the use of vocabulary? As humans we describe things around us and place judgments and perceptions on what we find interesting or what we do not understand. So what if there was a way to change everyday perceptions by linking an object with empowering words? Unfortunately many people associate crutches with words such a weak and unable, but the opposite needs to be conveyed to show the actuality of the situation.

Design language is my way of expressing a certain vocabulary, which I hope to then embody through my crutch design. If my crutches can aesthetically define a new perception through movement and form, then my design can communicate language. I can venture to say that when handed an object, many people begin to describe it not by its color, but how it makes them feel or they express words that come to mind as they admire the object. Language defines and shapes our world, so why not create beautifully designed objects that bring about confidence and empowerment not only to the user, but to those encountered on a daily basis? If the form of the crutches, functionally, physically, and aesthetically can communicate movement, agility, and beauty, then the perceptions surrounding the individual using the crutches have now been elevated through the use of language, as portrayed through design.

(K. Sadlon, personal communication, 2013)

Themes redesigned

In Chapter 1, five seminal themes were introduced that guided the work throughout this book. The first was language. While the postmodernists extracted meaningful communication from linguistic signifier, we accept the polyphonous interpretation of meaning in words, but remain steadfast in our belief that language as image, word, expression, while often indeterminately bewildering is a beautiful bond among humans that begs to be exercised, clarified, debated and elegantly used in this work for the purposes of design, undesign and redesign. Using diagnostic language to brand embodied diversity and then subjecting it to political correctness as the euphemistic disguise of medical vernacular, does not seem elegant or purposive to us. It appears as both an odd practice and one which circumvents change by sidestepping any of the redesign principles we have posited. The process cleverly maintains the park by creating an impermeable linguistic perimeter that halts action at the level of semantic banter. As reiterated throughout, our intent in critiquing a diagnostic vernacular is not to diminish its importance in the health and illness universe, but rather to draw the dividing line between illness and disability and to locate medical knowledge and professionals where they belong and do their best work, in the health and illness sector. And while medicalization is captured in the eyes of the beholder, appearing and sounding different to each observer and listener, in the absence of any pathological condition to be treated, we query its linguistic and conceptual relevance to elegantly explaining and seamlessly responding to corporeal variation.

Knowledge production and use constitute the second theme. The foundation for the gold standard of "evidence-based practice" in the medical world as well as in the park is deductive empiricism. The myth of philosophical monism scuffles with axiology (both value and devalue) in designer disability, often obfuscating the relativity and multiplicity of truths within context, theory, and other human constructions. Of the redesign principles advanced in this chapter, polyphony and elegance may be the most useful in guiding knowledge innovation necessary to inform human flourishing in diverse contexts and environments during park demolition. Logico-deductive methods build on existing knowledge and thus their use lies in prediction and incremental theory advancement. Yet, because this inquiry tradition builds on literature already generated, the inquirer must look behind in order to ground research in logic and a substantive cannon of acceptability. One cannot move forward and invent if constrained by what has already been done. Polyphony guides the use of more than one approach to knowledge generation, and thus elegantly and seamlessly braids inductive and abductive systematic approaches with deduction. The well-used term "thinking out of the box" is achieved only if the redesigner is not always gazing backwards and thus incrementally building on previous work, the retrospective directional rules required by deduction. Abduction reminds the knowledge redesigner of the existence of polyphonous theoretical options to be used as explanatory loners or as a village, while induction proceeds to unexplored territory. Each strategy has its place, but in combination, the logic triumvirate is a powerful body builder for ingenuity and new vision.

The normal–not normal parables comprise the third major theme. We first meet normal as a statistical artifact and watched its seamless infusion into medicalization and then into the social, cultural, and mythical fabric of societies which support advanced systems of health intervention as healer as well as human controller. As discussed in depth, carving humans into this binary is both a product of deduction and its foundation in counting. Tautology serves this dualist scheme well, as "most frequent" is translated into normal and then reified as "what should be" by the seductive bell curve. Rather than the object of theoretical and empirical counting, normal as the apple of the medicalized eye can and has been skeptically undesigned as the grand narrative of desirability in increasingly larger social circles, leaving redesigners to the lovely task of attributing elegant, proximal meaning to normal.

Integrating the themes of language and deconstruction of the normal/not normal binary, we have seen the term supernormal (Fukawasa and Morrison, 2007) recraft the meaning and value of "not normal." Supernormal in itself implies something other than normal by the addition of the qualifier "super." Moreover, wresting the term away from frequency counting imbues it with new dimensions and rich texture. Thus, even the lowly trashcan can be elevated to seamless innovation if quiet elegance is part of its design.

The craft of visual culture and materiality in designing and redesigning disability vigorously rears up in many of the chapters throughout the book. We encountered space, place, policy, product, imagery, and even human branding within the context of twenty-first-century visual culture through excavating and skeptically reading what is seen and thus told about disability.

Of particular power for us is Steiner's and Mulder's (2012) reconceptualization of visual beauty as interactive (Austin, 2013), fluid, and communicative. Although we do not fully agree with Siebers' (2010) claim of contemporary art displaying a new aesthetic driven by embodied disability, we do understand his vision. Several initiatives such as images of Guidotti (2012), Lady Gaga (Wade, 2010), Newton (2012) and Cohen (2012) provide a polyphonous sound so to speak on a future in which commercial aesthetics may coexist with diverse notions of allure even in the westernized world in which symmetry, youth, constants, and other unattainables for most people are held as the pinnacle of the appearance enchantment hierarchy. Look at Guidottis' (2012) journey.

> Positive Exposure was founded in 1998 by award winning fashion photographer, Rick Guidotti. Rick worked in NYC, Milan and Paris for a variety of high profile clients including Yves St Laurent, Revlon, L'Oreal, Elle, Harpers Bazaar and GQ. He took photographs of what were considered the world's most beautiful people. But one day, on a break from a photo shoot, a chance encounter on a Manhattan street changed everything. Rick saw a stunning girl at the bus stop – a girl with pale skin and white hair, a girl with albinism. Upon returning home Rick began a process of discovery – about albinism, about people with genetic differences and about himself. What he found was startling and upsetting. The images that he saw were sad and dehumanizing. In medical textbooks children with a difference were seen as a disease, a diagnosis first, not as people.
>
> So Rick turned his world upside down – he stopped working in the fashion industry and created a not-for-profit organization that he named Positive Exposure.
>
> How do you get people to see those with differences not as victims, but kids and people first and foremost? The pity has to disappear. The fear has to disappear. Behavior has to change. These kids need to be seen as their parents see them, as their friends see them, as valuable and positive parts of society, as beautiful.

The photos give people the permission to see beauty and interpret beauty in their own right. Not to see beauty that is dictated by industry's ideas of what is acceptable.

(Guidotti, 2012)

An alternative pathway out of the park is the redesign of symbolic brands. Consider access as example. As reconceptualized in the concluding chapter of this work, images which uncouple specific atypical body parts from access designations in diverse environments serve to seamlessly unrestrict and thus denote expanded accessibility to all bodies. Although simple imagery, this elegant thinking and design, if applied to built, policy and economic domains can decrease and ultimately evaporate the competition for attention among excluded categories.

As illustrated in our concluding chapter, because of their ubiquity in the daily life of all people, rethinking products not simply as functional, but as contemporary contextual objects read polyphonously by the designer, user, fabricator, distributor, and observer is a third redesign method. Eyeglass frames model for us, stripping away the stigma of visual impairment from the need for optical refraction and magnification, and replenishing the lacuna with choice and style. Similar to Cohen (2012), Allinson, the founder of the *Eyebob* website illustrates (2013):

Every 8 seconds, someone turns 40. Eyes over the age of 40 begin to lose their flexibility which makes focusing at close range more difficult (also called presbyopia).

No, you don't need longer arms, more light or a menu written in larger type. Diet, exercise and cryogenics will not stave off this condition. We hate to break it to you, but reading glasses are inevitable.

Now the good news! You are not doomed to wander the racks of drugstore readers in search of the least ugly pair of cheaters. Consider this: reading glasses are an opportunity to express yourself!

(www.eyebobs.com)

Style and choice however, are not the only valuable features of the eyeglass frame exemplar. Reading glasses have been severed from medicalization, detaching typical aging vision from the park in several ways. First, prescription is unnecessary, naming the "seer" as responsible enough to determine his/her visual needs and wants. Secondly, eyeglasses have been removed from the economic stronghold of the park, recrafting specs seamlessly as commercial rather than medical objects. They move into the affordable range as discussed previously, collaborating with other twenty-first-century strategies to eliminate vision poverty. Thus, magnifiers become "reread" as choice of fashion, expenditure, and convenience for any user.

Recently, we observed a similar model in the tourism industry. Regardless of hearing capacity, all participants on an organized tour were outfitted with individual listening systems such that they could hear the guide. Each had the option to use or not use the device or to turn it to the desired volume. No assessment or prescription was needed. We asked the tour guide about the seamless devices and were directed to the Williams Sound company.

> The Williams Sound DWSPCS3 Personal Communication System uses Digi-Wave™ digital technology which makes hearing easier for a vast array of personal-listening applications. By reducing background noises, as well as compensating for distance from the sound source or poor room acoustics, this personal communication system gives you crisp, clean audio, that's perfect for everything from everyday conversations to hearing every word of your favorite TV program! The Digi-Wave is easy to use: The presenter speaks into the included microphone, or the listener simply places the DLT-100 transceiver near the source of the sound he or she wants to hear.
>
> (www.audiolinks.com)

As we have noted, similar hearing devices, some at no cost whatsoever and thus at the discretion, choice, and under the control of the user, are following in the elegant footsteps of the reading glasses model.

Summary

In this chapter, building on the analysis of disability as designed and branded, we have rolled up our theoretical and praxis sleeves to pose five redesign principles. We invited and showcased the words and practices of redesigners from the accomplished to the novitiate to illustrate innovation. Each principle then made its way back to the thematic scaffold introduced in Chapter 1 and woven throughout the book, illustrating its muscle and future potency.

References

Abrahamson, A. (2011) The Iron Cage: Ugly, Uncool, and Unfashionable. *Organization Studies*, 32 (5), 615–29.
Austin, S. (2013) Deep sea diving…in a wheelchair. Retrieved from *Talks/TedX*, January. Available online at www.ted.com/talks/sue_austin_deep_sea_diving_in_a_wheelchair.html (accessed February 25, 2014).
Basken, P. (2013) A Team of Academics Redesigns an Icon. *Chronicle of Higher Education*, May 20. Available online at https://chronicle.com/article/New-York-City-Embraces-a/139355/?key=ST4lcFRoNHYSMCtlNjxJYD9UbXxqNkt0anVIYn0iblBQEA%3D%3D (accessed February 14, 2014).
Boudreau, K., and Lakhani, K. (2013) Using the Crowd as an Innovation Partner. *Harvard Business Review*, 91 (4), 61–9.
Bringhoff, J. (2008) Universal Design: Is it Accessible? *Multi: The RIT Journal of Plurality and Diversity in Design*, 1 (2), 45–52.

Cohen, A. S. (2012) *Advanced Style*. New York: powerHouse Books.

Craig, C.-E. (2013) Rebranding Disability as Opportunity. Wakata, February 21. Available online at http://cce-wakata.blogspot.com/2013/02/rebranding-disability-as-opportunity.html (accessed February 14, 2014).

Fashionablecanes (1993–2013) Designer Handle Walking Canes. Fashionable Canes and Walking Sticks. Available online at www.fashionablecanes.com/Elegant_Handle_Walking_Canes.html (accessed February 14, 2014).

Fukawasa, N., and Morrison, J. (2007) *Super Normal: Sensations of the Ordinary*. Baden: Lars Muller.

Gautam, M. (2012) How Might we Design an Accessible Election Experience for Everyone? Comment on the Brief. *Open IDEO*, February 9. Available online at www.openideo.com/open/voting/brief.html (accessed February 14, 2014).

Guidotti, R. (2012) Positive Exposure. About the Program. Available online at http://positiveexposure.org/about-the-program-2 (accessed February 14, 2014).

Hensel, W. F. (2011) The Disability Dilemma: A Skeptical Bench and Bar. *University of Pittsburgh Law Review*, 69, 637–56.

Kalman, M. (2012) Foreword to A. S. Cohen, *Advanced Style*. New York: powerHouse Books.

Klein, P. (2010) Skepticism. Stanford Encyclopedia of Philosophy, Dec 8, 2001; substantive revision October 28, 2010. Available online at http://plato.stanford.edu/entries/skepticism (accessed February 14, 2014).

Lindgren, H. (2013) Who Made That? *New York Times Magazine*, June 7. Available online at www.nytimes.com/packages/html/magazine/2013/innovations-issue/#/?part=introduction (accessed February 14, 2014).

MacFarlane, R. (2013) What's the Difference Between an Illness and a Disability? *E-Durable Employment Village*, April 11. Available online at http://dee-village.org.au/content/whats-difference-between-illness-and-disability (accessed February 14, 2014).

Magnusson, P. R. (2009) Exploring the Contributions of Involving Ordinary Users in Ideation of Technology-Based Services. *Journal of Product Innovation Management* 26 (5): 578–93.

McClure, P. (2000) *Participation Support for a More Equitable Society: Final Report of the Reference Group on Welfare Reform, July 2000* [the McClure Report]. Canberra: Department of Family and Community Services.

Merriam Webster (2013) Polyphony. *Merriam Webster Dictionary*. Available online at www.merriam-webster.com/dictionary/polyphony (accessed February 14, 2014).

Newton, H. Helmut Newton and his Women. *Vogue*, March 22, 2012. Available online at http://en.vogue.fr/fashion-pictures/celebrity-photos/diaporama/helmut-newton-and-his-women/7733 (accessed February 25, 2014).

Norman, D. (2011) *Living with Complexity*. Cambridge, MA: MIT Press.

Open IDEO (2012) How Might We Design an Accessible Election Experience for Everyone? Available online at www.openideo.com/open/voting/brief.html (accessed February 14, 2014).

Palotta, D. (2008) *Uncharitable*. medford, MA: Tufts University Press.

Pierotti, D. (2012) Adoption De-Paralysis: Examples of Elegant Policy Models for Anaerobic Digestion Development. *RenewableEnergyWorld.com*, October 17. Available online at www.renewableenergyworld.com/rea/news/article/2012/10/adoption-de-paralysis-examples-of-elegant-policy-models-for-anaerobic-digestion-development (accessed February 14, 2014).

Pilloton, E. (2009) *Design Revolution.* New York: Metropolis.

Poetz, M., and Schreier, M. (2012) The Value of Crowdsourcing: Can Users Really Compete with Professionals in Generating New Product Ideas? *Journal of Product Innovation Management,* 29 (2), 245–56.

Pozible PTY (n.d.) What is Pozible Available online at www.pozible.com/help/i/aboutus (accessed February 14, 2014).

Schreier, M. F., and Dahl, D. (2012) The Innovation Effect of User Design: Exploring Consumers' Innovation Perceptions of Firms Selling Products Designed by Users. *Journal of Marketing,* 76, 18–32.

Sherman Oaks Medical Supplies (2008) Merry Walker 511035 Merry Therapeutic Cane. Available online at https://www.shermanoaksmedical.com/511035_p/96-003.htm (accessed February 14, 2014).

Siebers, T. (2010) *Disability Aesthetics.* Ann Arbor, MI: University of Michigan Press.

Steere, M. (2008) *Designers Challenged to Include Disabled.* http://edition.cnn.com/2008/TECH/science/10/30/design.approaches/index.html?eref=edition_technology&utm_source=feedburner&utm_medium=feed&utm_campaign=Feed%3A+rss%2Fedition_technology+%28RSS%3A+Technology%29 (accessed March 27, 2014).

Steiner, W., and Mulder, A. (2012) Beauty as Interaction. In J. Brouwer, A. Mulder, and L. Spuybroek, *Vital Beauty.* Rotterdam: Colophon.

Synonym.com (2001–2013) Seamlessness. Available online at www.synonym.com/synonyms/seamless (accessed February 14, 2014).

Thesaurus.com (2013) proximity. *Roget's 21st Century Thesaurus* (3rd ed.) Available online at http://thesaurus.com/browse/proximity (accessed: February 14, 2014).

Titchkosky, T. (2007) *Reading and Writing Disability Differently.* Toronto, ON: University of Toronto Press.

Turkle, S. (2011) *Alone Together: Why We Expect More from Technology and Less from Each Other.* New York, NY: Basic Books.

Wade, L. (2010) Lady Gaga's Disability Project. *Sociological Images: Inspiring Sociological Imaginations Everywhere,* January 22. Available online at http://thesocietypages.org/socimages/2010/01/22/lady-gagas-disability-project (accessed: February 14, 2014).

Williams, R. (2013) The Elegant Wheelchair. Retrieved from *Coroflot,* March 9. Available online at www.coroflot.com/ronhwms/The-Elegant-Wheelchair (accessed February 14, 2014).

14 Knowledge and skills for creating profound change

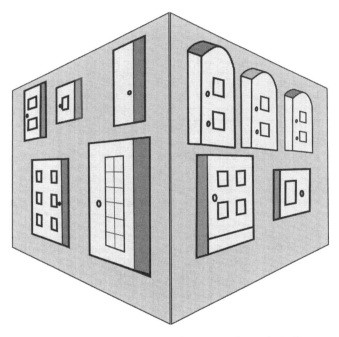

Figure 14.1 Windows and door of opportunity and challenge

The chapters in this work raise many contentious issues and arenas for thought and dialog about categorizing humans in general, and branding people with the disability moniker in particular. It is our hope that the ideas, even the most critical, can be heard and engaged for debate and innovation. We began our work by advancing the major proposition: twenty-first-century disability is an artifact of human ingenuity, design and branding. Proceeding through the book, we analyzed the contexts, crafts, and landscapes that activate design and branding to create what we have referred to as the disability park, a contained, targeted set of products, services, landscapes, images, and even knowledge productions that define and maintain disability as a segregated but permeable and dynamically changing population segment snagged in an often well-intentioned but disadvantageous and visible web of scrutiny, prescription, and medicalization, rendering the fringes of human experience as spectacle, pathological, undesirable and in extremes, located outside the boundaries of humanness. From that stance, we proposed the purposive relocation of medicine, healthcare, and related policy and knowledge production away from these disparaging roles back to their purposive, exquisite expertise in healing the human corpus. Doing so removes the atypical body from the medical spotlight, leaving room for it to fit snugly within communities of human variation. Thus, in this work, disability is defined as an artifact constructed by design and branded by labeling and imagery. So when we call for the elimination of the disability park and of disability altogether, we do not refer to eugenics but rather see a world in which all bodies find comfort, ergo advance the profound diversity comfort agenda.

Following analysis, we presented and exposed the crafts of disability design and branding. Part 2 contains chapters that begin to explore contemporary opportunities, exemplars, and principles for undesign and redesign. This final chapter sets out a pathway for the accomplishment of a profound diversity comfort agenda.

While not a simple task nor one that can be implemented within a short timeframe by prescribed methods, we suggest that disability redesign and rebranding must set their sights on refashioning and expanding the scope of human appearance, activity, and experience as typical, and thus "normal." At first glance, it seems to some extent oxymoronic to return to the concept of normal to achieve an authentic, egalitarian, diversity-respectful agenda. Yet, we take a lesson from Deiter Rams (Lovell, 2011) and supernormal designers already introduced (Fukasawa and Morrison, 2007; Graham Pullin, personal communication, 2013), who have redesigned the lexical brand of normal to mean "every day innovation" or seamlessness, while maintaining elegance and upholding the remaining redesign principles posited in Chapter 13. Purging the bifurcating function from the lexicon of normal redesigns it as usual, severing the spectacle of the feared atypical from the "not normal" grip.

According to Deiter Rams (Lovell, 2011), as little design as possible, while engaging in innovation for maximum utility, aesthetics, and quality accomplishes the seamless integration of products into daily life. We would suggest that the body regardless of its attributes, undesigned as medical contrivance and conceptually redesigned as normative, not in the sense of statistical frequency but rather eliminated from the gaze of curiosity and anomaly, has great potential to heal the cleavage between "them and us" and to create comfort for the full diversity of humanness in community.

Synthesizing history and current context reveals what endures, expunging passing fad from the knowledge base informing timeless profound diversity comfort. We have already summoned history to edify the analysis of disability design and branding as it currently exists today. However, looking back at ideas that continue to withstand and ascend beyond temporary criticism and conquest moves beyond classical cannon to recognize and incite progressive thinking and action necessary for universality of human dignity. Recall that we criticized universal design in previous chapters. While the term, 'universality" seems similar, we make the distinction here. Unlike universal or one size fits all, by universality we mean comprehensive and exhaustive.

Consider universal rights policies that were penned before the era of identity politics. Four classical/historic human rights instruments, the English Bill of Rights of 1688, the American Declaration of Independence of 1776, the European Convention of Human Rights 1953, and the Universal Declaration of Human Rights deserve high awards for universality as they sought to formalize a moral imperative of equivalence of rights for citizens without carving and then serving human segments on platters garnished with inequality. As stated by Santa Cruz, a member of the committee that drafted the original 1948 version of the Universal Declaration of Human Rights:

> I perceived clearly that I was participating in a truly significant historic event in which a consensus had been reached as to the supreme value of the human person, a value that did not originate in the decision of a worldly power, but rather in the fact of existing – which gave rise to the inalienable right to live free from want and oppression and to fully develop one's personality. In the Great Hall... there was an atmosphere of genuine solidarity and brotherhood among men and women from all latitudes, the like of which I have not seen again in any international setting.
>
> (United Nations, 2013)

Although currently fractured by what we have named contemporary "bodies and backgrounds diversity" (DePoy and Gilson, 2011), one can still look back to the pioneering expression of humanness in 1948 rights policy, as well as the other three mentioned to guide the equivalent comprehensive attribution of humanness to all who exist. As we noted in Chapter 8, we are fully cognizant that even following the promulgation of the elegant human rights policy in 1948, abrogation of rights continued to occur, prompting population specific policy as the means to eliminate discrimination. And while these laws served an initial function, their unintended consequences of branding, inequality, and even exclusion now beseech alternative redesign such that seamlessness and universality can be fabricated.

Recall the themes that have been threaded throughout the book; language, knowledge production, normal–not normal binary, material and visual culture, and humanness. Each on its own and then amalgamated is instilled with extensive transformative power. Supported by a foundation of the sustained ideas of time-honored thinkers, superimposing the redesign principles suggested in Chapter 13 (seamlessness, elegance, skepticism, proximity, and polyphony) on the five themes in this work creates a multi-dimensional scaffold robust for advancing profound diversity comfort. To conclude this work we provide exemplars that illustrate the beauty and outcomes of this redesign craft in meeting human need as the disability park is dissolved. The redesigners presented bring their ideas and techno-logical ingenuity to promoting a world in which profound diversity comfort may not be a pipe dream.

Example 1: Literacy translation – Tobacco Access Portal

The proximal problem tackled in this project was limited access to web-based smoking prevention and cessation information ascribed to populations with limited reading skills (Gilson and Depoy, 2009). Upholding the United Nations assertion of web access as a human right (Kravets, 2011) and skeptical of developing specialized solutions specific to diagnostic or non-normal causal attribution, the Tobacco Access Portal was created as a website to automate alternative literacy level translation within the English language. Illustrating polyphony and similar to subsequent initiatives such as Bioaid, the no-cost hearing aid application for the iPhone 5 previously introduced (Coldewey, 2012), a computer engineer, web designer and two faculty developed this beta initiative to promote full access to smoking cessation information on the web. The free server-side translator is available to anyone with an internet connection, seamlessly and elegantly decreasing high levels of literacy to a fourth-grade reading level if chosen by the web user, rendering the text simple to read and amenable to accurate text to speech translation for those who prefer or need voice translation. Full access is extended to any user without park branding or erosion of dignity. And illustrating the broad reach of proxi-mal innovation, similar sites proliferate, complimenting and expanding the network of translation across languages and communication venues.

Example 2: Leveraged Freedom Chair

We have included Amos Winter's (2013) work as a redesign exemplar because each model embodies the five redesign principles posited in Chapter 13. In thinking about seamlessness, just begin with the brand name itself which we love. Not only does the logo omit the parkeseque name "wheelchair" but it connotes liberty, not confinement, for what Winter refers to as riders rather than users. Just by its branding, the Leveraged Freedom Chair (LFC) is positioned seamlessly alongside ergonomic chairs designed for all bodies. A similar logo, Human Freedom Chairs, is used by the corporation that fabricates upscale seating solutions, similar in appearance to the office chair with wheels that we included in the mobility collage in Chapter 13.

> The brainchild of renowned designer Niels Diffrient, Humanscale Freedom Chairs have superb functional design which offers responsive, high-quality ergonomic support without the use of adjustment knobs or levers.
>
> The contoured cushions on the Freedom Chair cradle your body in full to ensure an even distribution of weight, while the counter-balance mechanism instantly adjusts the recline tension to your movements, resulting in a supportive yet organic sit.
>
> (Human Solution, 2003–2013)

Winter's chair illustrates polyphony: "[He] focuses on the marriage of mechanical design theory and user-centered product design to create simple, elegant technological solutions for use in highly constrained environments" (Winter, 2013). And proximity:

> We designed the LFC out of locally available materials. We took advantage of the fact that bicycles, and bicycle shops, are everywhere in the developing world. Every moving part on the chair is a bicycle part, enabling the LFC to be repaired even in remote villages. The LFC frame is made out of mild steel, enabling wheelchair riders to modify the chair to fit their unique needs.
>
> LFC riders around the world have reported that they were able to visit their local bicycle shops to repair punctures, change bearings, and tune-up their chairs.
>
> (GRIT, 2013)

And elegance – see Figure 14.2. The design, although not simple in its mechanical structure, once developed can be artfully and easily crafted to meet rider preference, identity, budget, and context.

Example 3: Access to the built environment

Expanding built and natural environment access signage, example 3 illustrates an elegant initiative severing symbolic imagery from the diagnosed corpus. Dissimilar to the international symbol of access (ISA), that visually prescribes which bodies are or are not invited to use landscapes and their contents, redesigning access branding of the built and natural environment provides information to all bodies about environmental features. Figure 14.3 presents redesigned symbols that expunge parkesque message from mobility access signage. This approach sets the precedent for expanding non-euphemistic, respectful access signage which serves to hold the feet of environmental designers, spatial policy developers, architects to the

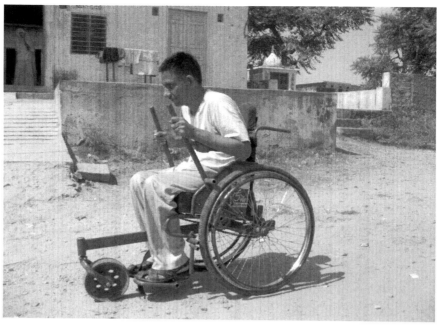

Figure 14.2 Leveraged Freedom Chair styles
Source: With permission of Prof. Amos G. Winter MIT Dept. of Mechanical Engineering

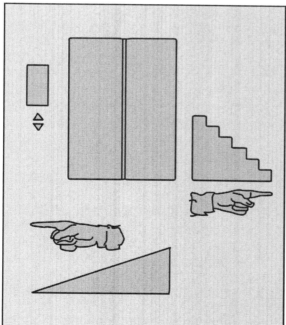

Figure 14.3 Mobility access
                   signage
                   redesigned

proverbial fire through displaying what the environment offers to all humans.

However, these cartographic visuals by themselves are insufficient to advance well-rounded access knowledge. Polyphony among contemporary multi-sensory instruments expands accessibility markers to highlight diverse environmental features for all bodies. Consulting history, once again informed this redesign. DaVinci's attempt to image ideal narrative proportionality of human spatial context resulted in a single visual that continues to drive architectural and product standards, revealing the limitations of a single ideal symbolizing the human body (Gilson and DePoy, 2007). Similarly, our criticism of universal design is that human diversity, need and preference cannot be met by enacting and depicting a single strategy. Gilson reversed this directionality, placing the responsibility for access and its swagger on environmental design attributes rather than on a single cartoon of an anonymous stick figure seated in a wheelchair sketch.

Current strategies awaiting their own symbols to proudly boast about their presence and compliment Gilson's elegant redesign. Rebranding is timely and the climate is ripe for transparency and polyphonic collaboration. As example, accessibility features beyond the ISA euphemism, can now join the pluralistic visual and thus be simply communicated to anyone with diverse signifying formats.

> There are more sophisticated indoor-navigation systems, like the new Indoor Positioning System chips, but this one doesn't require any special hardware (other than standard sensors like an accelerometer) and no beacons or cameras need to be installed in the building. And because it doesn't use wireless signals, it can be used in places like hospitals and museums that frown on such transmissions.
>
> (Coldewey, 2012)

Redesigning and rebranding access imagery as environmental response serves even greater purposes than merely informing the public of wheelchair, hearing, and visual access features. First, by avoiding the oxymoronic phenomenon of the included body as excluded (Titchkosky, 2007), access rebranding eliminates identity politics and warring between groups whose needs are not considered for world entrance.

Second, rebranding access publicly displays environmental design features such that they or their absence cannot be concealed. Third, rebranding access as environmental creates a system of signifiers that has the potential of expanding dignity and profound diversity comfort to all.

Harkening back to Chapter 5, the questions of "why now" and "how does the spark ignite" are raised. Mullins recounted that even ten years ago, she would not have been recruited as the spokesperson for L'Oreal. As reflected in the themes and building on classical and contemporary theories of social chance, we suggest the critical importance of capturing contextual relevance to propel change is operative in answering both questions.

Example 4: The Smarty product line

We introduced the Smarty product line in previous chapters. Explicated in the excerpt below, Ferguson, Castle, and Caccese exhibit polyphonic contemporary redesign, arousing change through exploiting the market economy and material culture.

> Ferguson, a design engineer who said he formerly performed energy management work, first designed a cushioning headband for the youth soccer team he was coaching on Cape Elizabeth.
>
> "The kids were hesitant to head-butt the soccer ball, so I made them a 'Clash' band so they wouldn't sting their heads," he says.
>
> A visit from a friend from California, Dr. Steven Castle, who is the geriatric physician who conducted the consumer preferences clinical trial for Alba-Technic's helmet and also is clinical director of geriatrics at the VA Greater Los Angeles, prompted Ferguson to try to broaden the use of the Clash band.
>
> "He said his sons were using it for soccer, but I said 'I know exactly what that's for.' We don't have a product and there's a need for this in older adults. It could become like a seat belt," says Castle.
>
> Castle also is the friend who wore the current prototype of the helmet, which has a detachable visor, at the Mexican restaurant. "The key we found is that patients are going to wear it," he says. "I think this will make a difference. It could become more of a mainstream product." Of the dozen patients he tested, half wearing the Smarty and half a competitive helmet, 88 percent wore the Smarty for 12 hours a day on average, whereas they wouldn't wear the other helmet in public. "They saw the competition as not for them, saying 'If I am that bad off, I wouldn't be going out.'"
>
> Castle adds that sizing is a key feature in that the helmet must accommodate use of the telephone, as well as hearing aids and glasses.
>
> (Valigra, 2013)

Example 5: Lessons from the Amazon rain forest

Entering the natural environment of the rain forest evokes the ambiguity of trepidation and incredulity. To traverse these ecosystems, one might conjecture that only the surefooted and sensorially strong could be so privileged as to navigate and experience the curious juxtaposition of lurid beauty. Our initial encounter came close to verifying the Amazon Lodge that we chose for a short vacation as a disability park, excluding even the most infinitesimally offending bodies. We both were commanded to keep up with the pace of the hikers or be remanded to a rickshaw to be portaged through only minimal parts of the environment. Enter four redesigners, a French architect, an English barrister, and two Ecuadorian Amazon guides.

The French architect, demonstrating elegance, reading and thus redesigning a parkesque object (the walking stick) through language. He replaced the term mobility impaired with the phrase Tyrolean Hikers, rebranding medicalization vocabulary with literary style.

As the barrister seemed to be imprisoned behind us on narrow walkway which required single file passage, we motioned her on, moving to the side to let her pass. But rather than accepting the offer, she remained behind us as we methodically placed our feet and newly branded Tyrolean hiking sticks with deliberation and great care, to avoid all the barriers the forest offered up. This eloquent barrister redesigned "too slow," a developmental parkesque relativist phrase, by relishing in walking behind. She read and redesigned inconvenience and obstruction with the luxury to capture the grandeur and minute through photography that she would not have accomplished if moving at a faster pace.

Finally and perhaps the most potent lesson is photographed in Figures 14.4 and 14.5.

David Galarza and Wilson Cerda (Figure 14.4) unceremoniously illustrated each of the redesign principles. The seamless, elegant redesign of a canoe seat (Figure 14.5) to allow comfortable and safe passage for all sitting

Figure 14.4 Amazon guides: David Galarza and Wilson Cerda

Figure 14.5 Five redesign principles in a canoe

bodies was accomplished polyphonously by these two guides, by simply altering the standard height of the bench. Proximal materials already in use in the vessel were placed vertically on top of one another until the desired height was reached. In the forest, the beauty and ingenuity of beings in collaboration with one another brought yet another lesson to light.

Final words: Designing a post-disability world

The ideal culmination of profound diversity comfort for us is a post-disability world. But what does this term mean? Looking at the literature on post-racial utopias did not provide a useful model. Theory and research reveal that even in the United States, once Barack Obama was elected as president (originally 2008 and then again 2012) and race was denied as genetic phenomenon, racism and discrimination are still woven into the national tapestry, either through history, institutional racism, individuals who still carry racial prejudice, and/or a constellation of posited factors (Bonilla-Silver, 2006; Higginbotham, 2013). Instead, we turned to hand dominance for guidance. Historically, the small minority of left-handed individuals was the object of discrimination, subjected to all types of "rehabilitation" so to speak, to change upper extremity lateralization:

Left-handedness has sometimes been treated as pathological. Cesare Lombroso, the infamous 19th-century physician who identified various facial (and racial) features with criminal traits, also saw left-handedness as evidence of pathology, primitivism, savagery and criminality. And I was brought up with the story that a generation ago, in the bad old days (and in the old country), foolish unenlightened people tried to force left-handed children to convert and use their right hands. My father said that my uncle, his older brother, had had his left hand tied behind his back as a child.

(Klass, 2011)

The negative associations and connotations of the use of the left hand among cultures are varied. In some areas, in order to preserve cleanliness where sanitation was an issue, the right hand, as the dominant hand of most individuals, was used for eating, handling food, and social interactions. The left hand would then be used for personal hygiene, specifically after urination and defecation. These rules were imposed on all, no matter their dominant hand. Through these practices, the left hand became known as the "unclean" hand. Currently, amongst Muslims and in some societies including Nepal and India it is still customary to use the left hand for cleaning oneself with water after defecating. The right hand is commonly known in contradistinction from the left, as the hand used for eating.

(Wikipedia, 2013)

As reflected in the quotations above, once branded as bodies in violation, left-handedness entered the province of revision, redesign, and even elimination. Similar to other forms of the embodied atypical, left dominance was the brunt of disparaging remarks and symbolic and actual disdain as well. For example, "having two left hands" denotes clumsiness. In common with current issues faced by owners of atypical bodies, left-handed people were met with difficulty when attempting to use tools standardized for right lateralization (Wikipedia, 2013). The cacophony of colloquialisms, slurs, negative attitudes and lack of fit is recognizable as a clear exemplar of disjuncture. Yet, the left-handed disjuncture at least in the United States has been healed, illuminating a model for a post-disability universe.

Rather than revising, reinventing or eliminating left dominance as a human attribute, it is preserved, seamlessly integrated into human diversity, elicits uniquely designed and coveted products, and informs a broader knowledge of human asymmetry through thoughtful neuroscience investigation, all attributes of full juncture.

Looking into the history of left dominance acceptance, it is apparent that showcasing not only the "normalcy" but additionally the endowments accompanying left-handedness were particularly powerful in influencing acceptance, to the point of the last several presidents of the United States being left dominant.

The elements of "post-left handedness" craft the vision, redesign, and rebranding for post-disability:

- acceptance rather than revision, reinvention or elimination of human diversity;
- elimination of essentialism;
- recognition that owners of the diverse characteristic have much to offer to knowledge, humanness, and community;
- seamless integration;
- choice;
- rights;
- dignity;
- full juncture;
- profound diversity comfort.

Design and branding as contemporary relevant strategies can orchestrate innovation to imagine and achieve a post-disability universe.

References

Bonilla-Silver, E. (2006) *Racism Without Racists*. Oxford: Roman Littlefield.

Coldewey, D. (2012) Smartphone app could help blind navigate indoors. *NBC*, May 18. Available online at www.nbcnews.com/technology/smartphone-app-could-help-blind-navigate-indoors-780588 (accessed February 14, 2014).

DePoy, E., and Gilson, S. (2011) *Studying Disability*. Los Angeles, CA: Sage.

Fukasawa, N., and Morrison, J. (2007) *Super Normal: Sensations of the Ordinary*. Baden: Lars Muller.

Gilson, S., and DePoy, E. (2007) Da Vinci's Ill-Fated Design Legacy: Homogenization and Standardization. *International Journal of the Humanities*, 5 (7), 145–54.

Gilson, S., and Depoy, E. (2009) Completed Projects – Tobacco Access Portal Project. University of Maine, Center for Community Inclusion and Disability Studies, September 14. Available online at http://ccids.umaine.edu/research-projects/completed/tap (accessed February 14, 2014).

GRIT (2013) Leveraged Freedom Chair. GRIT: Global Research Innovation and Technology. Available online at http://gogrit.org/lfc.html (accessed February 14, 2014).

Higginbotham, F. M. (2013) *Ghosts of Jim Crow*. New York: NYU Press.

Human Solution (2003–2013) Humanscale Freedom Chairs. The Human Solution. Available online at www.thehumansolution.com/humanscale-freedom-chairs.html?gclid=CPXtysLlzbgCFa1FMgodqhsAvg (accessed February 14, 2014).

Klass, P. (2011) On the Left Hand, There Are No Easy Answers. *New York Times*, March 6. Available online at www.nytimes.com/2011/03/08/health/views/08klass.html?_r=0 (accessed February 14, 2014).

Kravets, D. (2011) U.N. Report Declares Internet Access a Human Right. *Wired*, June 6. Available online at www.wired.com/threatlevel/2011/06/internet-a-human-right (accessed February 14, 2014).

Lovell, S. (2011) Deiter Rams: As Little Design as Possible. New York, NY: Phaedon.

MacFarlane, R. (2011) What's the Difference Between an Illness and a Disability? *E-Durable Employment Village*, April 11. Available online at http://dee-village.org.au/content/whats-difference-between-illness-and-disability (accessed February 14, 2014).

Titchkosky, T. (2007) *Reading and Writing Disability Differently*. Toronto, ON: University of Toronto Press.

United Nations (2013) The Universal Declaration of Human Rights: History of the Document. Available online at www.un.org/en/documents/udhr/history.shtml (accessed February 14, 2014).

Valigra, L. (2013) Winthrop Company Aims to Prevent Brain Injury, in Style. *Mainebiz*, June 10. Available online at www.mainebiz.biz/article/20130610/CURRENTEDITION/306069999/winthrop-company-aims-to-prevent-brain-injury-in-style (accessed February 14, 2014).

Wikipedia (2013) Bias Against left-Handed People. *Wikipedia*, June 10. Available online at http://en.wikipedia.org/wiki/Bias_against_left-handed_people (accessed February 14, 2014).

Winter, A. (2014) Amos G. Winter. MIT. Available online at http://web.mit.edu/awinter/www (accessed February 14, 2014).

Index

DATE DUE	RETURNED